D1607562

Turkey since 1970

Turkey since 1970

Politics, Economics and Society

Edited by

Debbie Lovatt
Lecturer in International Relations
Dokuz Eylül University
Izmir
Turkey

WITHDRAWN

palgrave

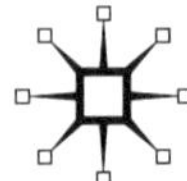

Editorial matter and selection © Debbie Lovatt 2001
Chapters 1–8 © Palgrave Publishers Ltd 2001

All rights reserved. No reproduction, copy or transmission of this publication may be made without written permission.

No paragraph of this publication may be reproduced, copied or transmitted save with written permission or in accordance with the provisions of the Copyright, Designs and Patents Act 1988, or under the terms of any licence permitting limited copying issued by the Copyright Licensing Agency, 90 Tottenham Court Road, London W1P 0LP.

Any person who does any unauthorised act in relation to this publication may be liable to criminal prosecution and civil claims for damages.

The authors have asserted their rights to be identified as the authors of this work in accordance with the Copyright, Designs and Patents Act 1988.

First published 2001 by
PALGRAVE
Houndmills, Basingstoke, Hampshire RG21 6XS and
175 Fifth Avenue, New York, N. Y. 10010
Companies and representatives throughout the world

PALGRAVE is the new global academic imprint of
St. Martin's Press LLC Scholarly and Reference Division and
Palgrave Publishers Ltd (formerly Macmillan Press Ltd).

ISBN 0–333–75378–X

This book is printed on paper suitable for recycling and made from fully managed and sustained forest sources.

A catalogue record for this book is available from the British Library.

Library of Congress Cataloging-in-Publication Data
Turkey since 1970 : politics, economics and society / edited by Debbie Lovatt.
p. cm.
Includes bibliographical references (p.) and index.
ISBN 0–333–75378–X
1. Turkey—Politics and government—1960–1980. 2. Turkey–
–Politics and government—1980– 3. Turkey—Economic conditions—1960– 4. Turkey—Social conditions—1960–
I. Lovatt, Debbie, 1968–

DR593 .T86 2000
956.103—dc21

00–052455

10 9 8 7 6 5 4 3 2 1
10 09 08 07 06 05 04 03 02 01

Printed and bound in Great Britain by
Antony Rowe Ltd, Chippenham, Wiltshire

To Taryn

Contents

List of Tables and Figures

Tables

Figure

Acknowledgements

My thanks for this idea finding its way to becoming a book are due firstly to my husband for his constant support and encouragement. Also I am extremely grateful to my department for all their assistance. I would also like to thank my friends at the *Turkish Daily News* Izmir office for their support and help, in particular Hüseyin Kandemir, whose insights have been most valuable.

List of Abbreviations

ANAP	Motherland Party
AP	Justice Party
BSEC	Black Sea Economic Cooperation
CAP	Common Agricultural Policy
CCT	Common Customs Tariff
CHP	Republican Peoples' Party
CSCE	Conference on Security and Cooperation in Europe
CU	Customs Union
DEP	Democracy Party
DP	Democrat Party
DSP	Democratic Left Party
DYP	True Path Party
EC	European Community
ECO	Economic Cooperation Organization
ECSC	European Coal and Steel Community
ECU	European Currency Unit
EEC	European Economic Community
ELG	Export-led growth
EP	European Parliament
EU	European Union
FP	Virtue Party
GAP	Southeastern Anatolian Project
GDP	Gross Domestic Product
GNP	Gross National Product
HADEP	Peoples' Democratic Party
HEP	Peoples' Labour Party
HIC	High-income country
HP	Peoples' Party
IMF	International Monetary Fund
ISI	Import-substitution industrialization
ISIC	International Standard Industrial Classification
KOBİ	Kuçuk ve Orta Büyüklükte İşletmeler
LDC	Developing country/Less Developed Country
LIC	Low-income country

MDB	Media Information Unit
METU	Middle East Technical University
MHP	Nationalist Action Party
MIC	Middle-income countries
MP	Member of Parliament, also referred to as Deputy or State Deputy
NAFTA	North American Free Trade Area
NATO	North Atlantic Treaty Organization
NICA	non-interest current account
OECD	Organization for Economic Cooperation and Development
OEEC	Organization for European Economic Cooperation
OIC	Organization of the Islamic Conference
OPEC	Organization of Petroleum Exporting Countries
PKK	Kurdistan Workers' Party
PSBR	public sector borrowing requirement
RCD	Regional Cooperation for Development
RP	Welfare Party
RTÜK	Radio and Television Supreme Board
SEE	State Economic Enterprise (Kamu İktisadi Teşebbüsleri, KİT)
SHP	Social Democratic Peoples' Party
SIS	State Institute of Statistics
SME	Small- and Medium-Sized Enterprises
SPO	State Planning Organization
TBMM	Parliament, Grand National Assembly
TL	Turkish lira
TOSAM	Centre for the Research of Societal Problems
TOSAV	Foundation for the Research of Societal Problems
TRT	Turkish Radio and Television Corporation
TİKA	Turkish Cooperation and Development Agency
UN	United Nations
WEU	Western European Union

Notes on the Contributors

Sencer Ayata has a BS in Sociology from the Middle East Technical University (METU) in Ankara, and a PhD in Sociology and Social Anthropology from the University of Kent in Canterbury. He is currently Professor in the Sociology Department at METU. He has carried out research on various social processes in rural and urban areas, and has written books and articles on the social and cultural problems of urbanization, the role of religion in Turkish culture and politics, and on the informal sector.

Canan Balkır is Professor of Economics at Dokuz Eylül University, Izmir. She works closely with local business groups and organizations, particularly with regard to Turkey–European Union issues, a subject on which she has published widely; she received a European Commission grant in 1981. She has been a Fulbright scholar in the USA and a British Council scholar in the UK. Her academic career has taken her to the Institute of Development Studies, University of Sussex, UK, as a research fellow; University of Exeter, UK, as Honorary Visiting Professor (1991) and to Colorado College, Colorado Springs, USA, as a lecturer (1997). She is on the Editorial Board of Longman Publishers, London, for European Urban and Regional Studies, and on the Editorial Board and a columnist for *Gözlem*, a weekly economic journal in Turkey. She is widely published in Turkey, Europe and the United States.

Doğu Ergil is Professor of Political Sociology and Chair of the Department of Political Behaviour at Ankara University. He is President of the Centre for the Research of Societal Problems (TOSAM, Ankara). He has written 20 books and numerous scholarly articles. He has been a columnist for the *Turkish Daily News* and is a frequent contributor to several international publications.

Ayşe Güneş Ayata received her BS in Sociology from the Middle East Technical University in Ankara, and a PhD in Sociology and Social Anthropology from the University of Kent in Canterbury. She is Professor of Sociology in the Department of Political Science and Public Administration, METU. She has carried out research on the Turkish political structure and culture, including ethnic and religious movements, and has published articles on urban ethnicity, religious revivalism, the internal structures of political parties and voting behaviour.

D. Beybin Kejanlıoğlu has master's degrees both in government (Middle East Technical University) and mass communication (Leicester University). She is a PhD graduate of Ankara University. She worked at the Department of Radio, Television and Film, Eastern Mediterranean University, Northern Cyprus, as a lecturer in the first half of 1999. She is currently a lecturer in the Faculty of Communication, Ankara University. She has published on Turkish media, especially on radio and television, focusing on broadcasting policy, 'public sphere' and the media, thus drawing widely on political theory and sociology of culture. She has also contributed to national and international media research projects. She is currently working on a range of problematic communications policy issues in Turkey, such as allocation of frequencies, ownership, obscenity, and so on.

Mehmet Haluk Köksal received his MBA from Dokuz Eylül University in Izmir, and his PhD in Management Studies from the University of Exeter, UK. He is an Assistant Professor in the Department of Business Administration at Dokuz Eylül University and guest lectures at other universities. He has carried out research and consultancy on new product development and marketing, and has published related articles.

Debbie Lovatt is a Lecturer in the International Relations Department of Dokuz Eylül University, Izmir and a researcher and writer contributing to academic, specialist and local publications. At Exeter University she studied Arabic followed by a Master's in Middle East Politics. She also works as a journalist.

Naci Sevkal is a Research Assistant in the Department of Public Administration at Dokuz Eylül University, Izmir. His research interests are housing markets, housing policies, and urbanization.

Osman Taştan is an Associate Professor in the Department of Islamic Law at Ankara University's Faculty of Divinity. He is a PhD graduate of Exeter University, UK. He has published articles on the theory and history of Islamic Law and researched population policy in Islamic law and politics. His current areas of research include war and peace in Islamic law.

Utku Utkulu is a PhD graduate of Leicester University. He is now an Assistant Professor in the Economics Department, Dokuz Eylül University, Izmir. He has published widely on the Turkish economy, focusing on international economic aspects such as trade liberalization, trade and growth, and the external debt issue. He has contributed articles to leading international economic journals including *Applied Economics* and *Economics of Planning*. He is currently working on the issue of sustainability of Turkey's external debts.

Introduction

On the whole, Turkey in the 1920s was an agrarian society and economy; today the country is generally urbanized and rapidly industrializing. The social upheavals and economic and political changes such a transformation engenders have placed tremendous strain on the Turkey of its founder's, Atatürk's, vision and the military has intervened four times (1960, 1971, 1980 and 1997). They see themselves and are viewed as the guardians of Atatürk's principles and, therefore, the state.

Today's Turkey often appears to be juggling a mixed bag of agenda issues: radical Islam, terror, separatism, enemies without, enemies within, corruption, inflation, mafia–government links, natural disasters, and so on, with other consistent factors in the country's recent history being military interventions of varying degrees and short-lived wobbly coalition governments.

Turkey since 1970 covers roughly the last thirty years and is designed as a kind of 'starter kit' for anyone interested in Turkey. It was the 1970s that witnessed lawful social expression through workers' unions, syndicates, and professional chambers for example giving way to mass social discontent and violence. This was the decade which also saw rural–urban migration gather pace and the private sector start to take its place in the national make-up.

The 1970s in particular were the years during which the state was particularly anxious about the threat of communism as the Cold War was still very much part of the world order. Political Islam at that time was seen as less of a threat than communism although the Islamic Revolution in neighbouring Iran in 1978 cast doubts on that.

The 1980 coup (known simply as '12 September') is pointed to as the biggest life-changer with people looking back to the previous couple of decades as the years of freedom. It is also the most memorable coup for the loss of life incurred, particularly among intellectuals and those of a left-wing persuasion, and for its effect on the country until now. Meanwhile, the 1982 constitution is still in place; it is accused of being over-restrictive and some say it halted the democratization process.

At the end of the 1990s a previously undemanding populace gradually started to develop its own expectations and stir at the grassroots level. Money is power, the state is very much the policy- and decision-maker, and while the politician may not fulfil his/her role as constituency representative, there are organizations (and some political parties) bringing the demands of the little guy to the attention of the centre. Television plays a key role in this, particularly through phone-ins and discussion programmes, and increasingly too the internet, not least because they bring new terminology, and, therefore, new concepts, into the language. (One such example is 'non-governmental organizations', NGOs, which are sometimes translated as 'lobi' (lobby) groups.) The internet also allows access to a wider array of information, viewpoints, and ideas than before, with many users being active on discussion sites and chat programmes.

The impact of the fundamental social, economic and political changes the nation is continuing to experience can be hard to determine. Perhaps Turkey can represent the evolution of an urban society, a social re-engineering away from dependence on the immediate and wider family and local community network towards attachment to or membership of organizations such as trade unions, football teams, professional associations. The country can also be seen as typical of a developing (industrializing) country: it is pockmarked with grandiose projects either underway or left unfinished; there is an immensely complicated bureaucratic system; intense poverty sits opposite phenomenal wealth with a gradually expanding middle-income-earning bracket starting to emerge somewhere in between without closing the income divide; expectations are low, disappointments high; and the majority of the population is under 21.

In the period this book covers, the social and economic changes have outstripped the political. Television arrived in the 1970s, but it was the economic liberalization of the 1980s (the 1983–89 Özal period) that really ushered in new trends – in particular, buying patterns and materialistic expectations. As the eighties became the nineties these changes had become the norm and the centre was once again strained as demands grew for political liberalization to match that on the economic front. Civil organizations stepped into the frame tentatively at first, but with greater confidence as the new millennium approached. Although their emergence has perhaps been overshadowed by the presumed threat to democracy represented by the success of political Islam in the form of the now-banned Welfare Party (RP) and its successor, the Virtue Party (FP), they indicate a grassroots dynamism and are recognized as a vital part of any thriving democracy. When they are critical they are criticized, and when they are supportive they are supported. Turkey's democratic tradition is still very immature.

While the pace of economic change is sometimes seen as an underlying cause of much of the social and political tension and unrest, it is worth noting that mass marginalization from the decision-making process should also shoulder some of the responsibility for this. Cultural dislocation resulting from rapid urbanization has also not been without its consequences. This rural–urban migration has separated hundreds of thousands of people from their geographical, cultural and family bases and thrust them into a new environment with different traditions and lifestyle. The difficulties and confusions are only just being 'spoken' about – for example, a 1998 pop music video shows a village man going to the city to find work. He leaves his family and his wife and small baby behind to head for the city; we see him counting his earnings; at first he sends frequent letters home full of hope and promises, but when the letters stop coming his wife goes to the city and after a long search finds her husband. He is in a mental health institute. Artistic expression often comes before expression of the same issue in society as a whole, and maybe this one pop song is the beginning of a trend towards a kind of collective soul-searching or yearning for whatever is perceived to have been lost.

The book

The chapters that make up *Turkey since 1970* cover a wide spectrum and are based on areas frequently asked about or discussed. At the end of most chapters there is a section giving suggestions for further reading.

The writers have given as clear and broad a picture as possible of the last thirty or so years so that readers can get a feel for and insight into this fascinating and rapidly changing country. It is important to stress that we have purposely avoided giving conclusions; our aim is to give a picture of the country in as unfettered a way as possible. Students in particular will be pleased to know that individual chapters can be read separately.

Suggestions for further reading

For anyone wishing to experience many aspects of life in Turkey a great favourite among foreigners resident in Turkey and visitors – including the armchair traveller – is Jeremy Seal's *A Fez of the Heart* (London and Basingstoke: Picador, 1996). It is an entertaining and fact-packed insight into the country past and present.

As for general histories, first on the list is Bernard Lewis's *The Emergence of Modern Turkey*, 2nd edition (Oxford University Press, 1968, reprinted 1979) with Erik J. Zürcher's, *Turkey: a Modern History* (I.B. Tauris, 1993) providing a great follow-on. Two other key works are *Modern Turkey* by Geoffrey Lewis (Praeger, 1974), and *The Making of Modern Turkey* by Feroz Ahmad (Routledge, 1993).

A note on pronunciation

Turkish is easy to pronounce and read. While most letters are pronounced as they appear, the exceptions are listed below:

c like 'j' as in 'jam'
ç like the 'ch' in 'church'
e like the 'e' in 'get'
ğ this letter lengthens the preceding vowel and is best ignored
i like 'ee' in 'see'
ı like the 'in' at the end of 'cousin'
j as in French
ö just as in German, like 'Köln' (Cologne)
ş like the 'sh' in 'ship'
ü like the 'oo' sound in 'blue'
v is soft and almost sounds like a 'w'

Throughout the book, Turkish spellings have been retained in all but two cases: the dot has been removed from the initial 'İ' of both Istanbul and Izmir.

1
The Turkish Economy: Past and Present

Utku Utkulu

Chapter outline

Turkey is typical of a developing country (LDC) in many respects. While generally supporting other LDCs on international economic issues, she has remained an active member of the North Atlantic Treaty Organization (NATO) and the Organization for Economic Cooperation and Development (OECD). She joined the European Community (EC) as an associate member in 1963 on the signing of the Ankara Agreement, and in 1987 applied for full membership, a decision on which was postponed following a discouraging preliminary assessment by the EC Commission. Although a customs union agreement between the European Union (EU) and Turkey was signed in 1995 (valid from 1996), the prospects for full membership still look gloomy. Turkey's political background has witnessed considerable instability during the last thirty years: a number of changes in the ruling coalitions, three constitutions, and three military interventions (the last one in 1980).

This chapter presents an overview of the Turkish economy, from 1950 to date. The methodology is mostly descriptive. The focus is based on an interpretative evaluation of the economic policies implemented. The section on economic background summarizes the general characteristics of the Turkish economy and provides an economic background including some comparisons with other middle-income countries. There follows a section on the early foundations of economic development during the period 1923–29, state-led industrialization (étatism) in the 1930s, economic aspects of the development strategies adopted during the Second World War and postwar years (1939–50), and the experience of liberalism under the Democrats (1950–61). The inward-oriented phase of development is then examined and the performance of the economy is covered in the 1962–79 period of national planning under the influence of étatism. The next section introduces the 1980 reform package and evaluates the performance of the 1980s policy of market orientation and export-led growth (ELG). The economic performance of the 1990s and the prospects for the new millennium are discussed in the final section.

Economic background

For half a century, from the 1930s to the beginning of the 1980s, except for a short period of liberalization between 1950 and 1953, Turkey followed a strategy of growth through inward-oriented import-substitution industrialization (ISI) coupled with intensive government intervention. The government played a leading role in the economy by creating public enterprises while imposing barriers to trade and financial flows.[1] Turkey's changing development strategies and their periodization are illustrated in Table 1.1.

From the early 1930s to the early 1980s Turkey's economic policies are characterized as interventionist and protectionist.[2] Accordingly, policies were mainly designed to protect domestic industry from foreign competition and increase government controls over the allocation of resources and production of goods. These included.[3]

a) encouragement of the domestic industrial sector with minimal foreign competition (infant industry argument) through the introduction of quotas, high tariffs and licensing requirements;
b) a high level of monetary expansion to finance large fiscal deficits;
c) support to the industrialization process and the avoidance of bottlenecks by the creation of state economic enterprises (SEEs, Kamu İktisadi Teşebbüsleri, KİTs) in sectors such as steel production and mining;
d) control over the quantity and price of credit to influence the sectoral composition of investment within the private sector;
e) the maintenance of fixed exchange rates and exchange controls resulting in an overvalued domestic currency.

Table 1.1 Turkey's Development Strategy, by Period

Period	*Institutional setting*	*Development strategy*
1923–29	Private enterprise, free trade with low tariffs (Lausanne Treaty)	Westernization, recovery, infrastructure, industrialization, tax reform
1929–39	Étatism, mixed economy with large public enterprise sector, balance of payments controls, primitive 5-year planning	Inward-looking import substitution, infrastructure, industrialization
1939–46	Étatism, mixed economy, war economy for neutrality	Military considerations
1946–50	Relaxed étatism, mixed economy, controls	Recovery, increased emphasis on agriculture
1950–53	Democracy, trade liberalization, mixed economy	Agricultural expansion and mechanization
1953–59	Democracy, mixed economy, balance of payments controls	Agricultural expansion, import substitution
1959–62	Democracy replaced by military regime, étatism, mixed economy	Stabilization
1962–78	Democracy, mixed economy, comprehensive planning, labour market liberalization	Import substitution
1978–80	Same as 1962–78	Stabilization
1980–85	Military regime followed by limited democracy, mixed economy, trade and financial liberalization, labour market repression	Stabilization, export-oriented growth
1985–to date	Democracy, mixed economy, trade and financial liberalization, accelerating inflation	Export-oriented growth

Source: Hansen (1991), p. 264.

Turkey's political instability has carried over into her economic policy-making. All the Turkish governments have been interventionist, by which we mean that the state has tried to direct the pattern of investment while limiting foreign ownership and management, yet there have been changes in emphasis over the years. For example, rightist governments have been more willing to rely on the private sector and reduce trade restrictions, while the left has placed more emphasis on social welfare programmes and economic autarky. In this respect, governments have used their economic power (in terms of both price intervention and the operation of SEEs) to implement a consistent set of economic policies. Although the reforms of 1980 were significant, Turkey remains an economy in which the public sector accounts for about 60 per cent of national investment, owns and operates about 40 per cent of all manufacturing enterprises, and controls the minerals sector. This pattern is no exception among developing countries (LDCs).

Although it may be inappropriate to call any country 'typical', Turkey is, in many respects, a typical middle-income country. Table 1.2 provides a comparison of middle-income countries (MICs), low-income countries (LICs), and high-income countries (HICs) with Turkey. Turkey lies near the average of MICs in terms of the development indicators presented, but is more 'dualistic'. The World Bank classifies Turkey as an upper middle-income country.[4]

Table 1.3 presents a comparison of Turkey with the norms calculated in Chenery and Syrquin[5] for a 'typical' LDC with approximately the same per capita GNP and population as Turkey. The comparisons are reported for three years (1977, 1984 and 1997) to point out the similarities and differences in economic structure for the years of inward and outward orientation followed by those of economic liberalization. In 1977 Turkey differs from the typical LDC in a number of respects:

a) Both exports and imports are quite small as a percentage of GDP. Exports, especially, are extremely low and grew much less rapidly than in comparable LDCs.
b) Gross domestic savings are relatively low compared to the typical LDC. Gross domestic investment is above the norm;

Table 1.2 Some Development Indicators for Turkey: a Comparison

	GNP per capita ($US) 1997	*GDP growth rate (%) 1990–97 average*	*Public expenditure on health 1990–95 (%) of GDP*	*Life expectancy birth (years) 1996*	*Adult illiteracy (%) 1995*	*Average population growth (%) 1990–97*	*Electrical power consumption (kilowatt-hours) 1995*
Turkey	3 130	3.6	2.7	69	18	1.8	1 057
MICs	1 890	2.5	3.0	69	19	1.3	1 183
LICs	350	4.2	0.9	59	47	2.1	269
HICs	25 700	2.1	6.9	78	0–5	0.7	7 748

Source: World Development Report (1998/99), World Bank.

Table 1.3 Turkey: Comparison of Performance with Development Norms (per cent of GNP unless otherwise stated)

	Chenery norm of a typical DC	*Turkey 1977*	*Deviation from norm*	*Turkey 1984*	*Deviation from norm*	*Turkey 1997*	*Deviation from norm*
Agricultural output	24	28	+4	19	–5	17	–7
National savings (gross)	22	17	–5	11	–11	18	–4
National invest. (gross)	23	26	+3	20	–3	24	+1
Exports (goods)	11	5	–6	12	+1	14	+3
Imports (goods)	13	12	–1	22	+9	25	+12

Note: Chenery norm of a 'typical' DC is derived for a large country with GNP per capita of $US570 in 1964, population of 42 million and average capital inflow of 2 per cent of GNP. The methodology used is discussed in Chenery and Syrquin (1975). The 1977 and 1984 figures are from Conway (1987). The 1997 figures are taken from the State Institute of Statistics and World Development Report, 1998/99.
Source: Conway (1987); *World Development Report, 1998/99*.

foreign borrowing and workers' remittances financed the gap between investment and savings.

c) A large proportion of the economy remains in the agricultural sector.

The comparison of the norm to performance in 1984 and 1997 explains both the increased outward orientation of the recent period and the remaining structural imbalances within the economy:

a) The share of agricultural output in GNP has decreased consistently, suggesting a transformation in the economy.
b) From an economy with below-norm shares of GNP for exports and imports, the economy has evolved to one with well-above-norm shares of imports and exports proving the sustainability of Turkish trade liberalization. The gap between import and export shares, however, widened, raising questions about the sustainability of external deficits.
c) This structural problem is also evident in the investment-savings imbalance. Investments exceed savings by 9 per cent of GNP both in 1977 and 1984. The investment–savings gap narrowed to 6 per cent in 1994. The main difference between 1977 and 1984 is that both investments and savings have fallen suddenly. In 1997, however, compared to the 1984 figures, there was an increase in both investment and savings. National savings were still below 'normal' by 4 per cent in 1997, and national investment rose above-norm in 1997 from below-norm in 1984.

An important change is the steady decline in agriculture's share from about 45 per cent in 1950 to 17 per cent in 1997. Meanwhile, industry's share came from about 12 per cent in 1950 to about 30 per cent in 1997. The services sector also increased its share of GDP to well above 50 per cent in 1997. These developments underline the extent of the transition process that Turkey has realized during the postwar years. Despite its diminishing share of GDP, agriculture still remains a very important sector. It accounts for about half of all employment, and its raw products are important components of most of the country's exports. During this period, government policies of subsidized credit, price and quantity protection, and a considerable amount of public investment were used to assist the manufacturing sector.

The manufacturing sector mainly consists of three sub-sectors: public, large-scale private, and small-scale private. The public sector (SEEs) dominates heavy industry and receives the largest share of investment. Large-scale private industry was supported by the government through the allocation of credit and a high level of protection from foreign competition until the 1980s. Although the country became more trade-oriented (or less anti-export biased) during the 1980s, some industries, such as the automotive industry, are still protected from foreign competition to a considerable extent by high tariff rates. Private small-scale manufacturing appears to be the closest to being an internally competitive sector. Naturally, wages and capital-to-labour ratios are lower, and market entry is relatively easier. High growth rates have been avoided, however, by the sector's difficulty in draining funds from credit markets. Recently, the main objectives of the government have been to support the manufacturing sector by:

a) encouraging exports;
b) promoting private investment;
c) lowering capital-to-output and capital-to-labour ratios;
d) improving the efficiency of the SEEs.

The economy's average real annual GNP growth rate for the period 1950–97 is above 5 per cent, although this varies significantly within sub-periods. The periods of most rapid growth were 1950–58, 1970–76 and 1981–90 while the period of slowest growth was from 1977 to 1980. If we term the 1980s the 'lost years' in terms of investment and output growth for many heavily indebted LDCs, Turkey's average real annual GNP growth rate of 5.2 per cent during that time of world-wide recession deserves much appreciation. It is also worth noting that the rapid growth in the mid-1970s was misleading since it was paid for by rapidly rising trade deficits and additional foreign debt. The slow growth of the late 1970s was the result of a foreign debt crisis, structural adjustments associated with changing global factor prices, and macro-economic stabilization policies.

Turkey comprises about 780 000 km^2 of which 97–98 per cent lies in the Asia Minor land mass (that is, Anatolia) and the rest on the

European side of the Dardanelles and the Bosphorus. For a country of its size, Turkey is only moderately endowed with mineral resources – coal, lignite, oil, iron ore, chrome, boron and so on. Although oil is Turkey's most (economically) valuable mineral, domestic production accounts for only about 12 per cent of total petroleum consumption. The mining sector accounts for less than 2 per cent of GDP and less than 1 per cent of total employment. It is important to note that these proportions have not changed considerably since 1960.

Turkey is starting to take greater advantage of its favourable location. During the 1980s, particularly since the beginning of the war between Iran and Iraq, Turkey's exports to the Middle East (although OECD countries have been Turkey's traditional trading partners) have increased substantially to about 30–40 per cent of export earnings. Service exports to the Middle East have also risen.[6] Turkey is also a major competitor for medium-sized construction projects in Middle East and Gulf countries.

As regards demographic developments, the population has grown rapidly during the postwar period and is now above 65 million. The main reason appears to be efficient public health measures which have led to reduced infant and adult mortality. The annual average total population increase went from 3.2 per cent during the 1950–60 period to about 2.3 per cent during the 1985–90 period, and to about 2 per cent during the 1990s. Apparently, there has been a sharp fall in total population growth since the 1970s. This development may well be due to improved female literacy, which correlates negatively with birth rates. However, it is important to note that even if the number of children per mother declines sharply, the population is expected to continue to increase rapidly since half of it is under 20 years old.

Rapid and unbalanced urbanization is another important demographic factor. During the 1950–95 period, the annual average urban population increase has always been higher than the total population increase, mainly due to migration from rural areas to cities, including the major cities such as Istanbul, Ankara and Izmir.

The labour force has grown more slowly than the total population. One reason for this may be that female participation is much higher in agriculture than in other sectors of the economy. It is also worth pointing out that Turkey has been a net exporter of labour, mainly to Germany and other European countries, since the early 1960s. This has resulted in some important effects on the whole economy. Workers' remittances form a significant fraction of Turkey's foreign exchange earnings, labour migration has eased the domestic unemployment problem, and the domestic labour force has been more qualified due to returning workers.

Early foundations and the postwar era

The Ottoman legacy and the early years, 1923–29

The young Turkish Republic inherited a seriously handicapped economy without a modern manufacturing base. Manufacturing in the Ottoman era was overwhelmingly composed of small workshops which processed primary products for the domestic market. Boratav[7] refers to the 1920s as 'an extension of the late Ottoman economy'. Hershlag[8] tends to see it as a 'transitional period of trial and error' due to the postwar reconstruction of the economy.

Although terms such as 'liberal' and 'market economy' are used to describe the 1923–29 era (as far as economic policy is concerned), these phrases are generally used to refer to the contrast between the 1920s and the étatist 1930s. The leaders of the new Turkish Republic decided to let industrialization be based on private entrepreneurship and to support the emerging industry. They also aimed at accelerating private capital accumulation in the industrial sector with government intervention whenever necessary. Therefore, the economic policy of the 1920s cannot appropriately be termed 'liberal'.[9]

During the early 1920s political issues relating to the formation of the Republic undoubtedly played an important role in shaping the economic policies adopted as a whole. Some of the provisions of the 1923 Lausanne Peace Treaty acted as constraints on the new republican government[10] because, in addition to the peace settlement, it also covered some important economic matters. While the government's industrialization policies during the 1920s were ambiguous, they became more explicit and much more protective after 1929 when the provisions of the Lausanne Treaty expired and the Great Depression began.

Table 1.4 suggests that the 1923–29 period is characterized by the high growth rates typical of postwar periods. Domestic demand was the main source of the expansion in national production in these

Table 1.4 GDP Growth, by Source of Demand, 1923–38, as a percentage

		Source of expansion			
Period	*Average annual growth rate*	*Domestic demand*	*Exports*	*Import substitution*	*Total*
1923–25 to 1927–29	7.5	72.7	8.8	18.5	100
1927–29 to 1931–33	5.6	32.0	10.8	57.2	100
1931–33 to 1936–38	7.0	94.9	2.1	3.0	100

Note: Annual growth rates are measured on GDP at 1938 prices. Import-substitution figures are calculated on the basis of initial import propensities of each period.
Source: Hansen (1991), chap. 9.

years. In a compromise between ideology and realpolitik, the leaders of the new republican government adopted a relatively free trade and finance policy during the years of reconstruction (1923–29).[11] The government, to the extent possible given the external constraints, subsidized an inward-looking infant-industry strategy and an export-oriented agricultural-development strategy, shifting taxation from the rural to the urban population.

The étatist experiment, 1929–50

The year 1929 – the beginning of the Great Depression – marked a turning point for the economic development of Turkey. It was the year Capitulations were abolished and, among other things, the country eventually obtained tax and tariff autonomy. Because Turkey was an exporter of primary commodities, the Great Depression caused a sharp deterioration in her external terms of trade. Also in 1929 the first instalment of the old Ottoman foreign debts was paid (repayments continued until 1953).

With the 1929 developments the government had to search for a new strategy for economic development. The policies and measures associated with this new strategy are referred to as 'étatism' and are recognized as the official economic ideology of the republican government. According to 'étatism', the government would continue to acknowledge the importance of private enterprise, but would have to participate in economic affairs in order to raise the level of welfare. In practice, this meant a situation in which the state took an active role in economic affairs, emerging as a major producer and investor. During the 1930s the government started a heavy investment drive in key manufacturing industries through the creation of the publicly owned SEEs which became a key factor in the development process during the period 1930–50.

The foundations of Turkish industrialization, which created a remarkable change in the economy, were laid during the early 1930s. Average annual industrial growth during the 1930s was about 10 per cent. Moreover, industry's contribution to the national product increased from 14 per cent in 1929 to 19 per cent in 1939.[12] Despite the remarkable increase in the number of SEEs, private enterprises have had a reasonably high share in the manufacturing industry. Between 1933 and 1939, total gross investment was around 9–10 per cent of GNP, and the private sector's share about 50–65 per cent of the total.[13]

The first five-year industrial plan (1934–38) was a detailed list of investment projects that the public sector aimed to pursue in industry, mining, and energy, and was not a comprehensive exercise in planning in the technical sense of the term.[14] Despite a small number of deviations, the targets were achieved within the plan period.[15] The second five-year industrial plan was interrupted by the Second World War.

Although Turkey maintained her neutrality during the war, full-scale mobilization together with shortages of raw materials caused a severe recession and a substantial reduction in output. Between 1940 and 1945, the average annual decrease in GNP was 6.3 per cent, and production levels fell by an average of 5.6 per cent and 7.2 per cent in industry and agriculture respectively. Nevertheless, there was a foreign trade surplus of $US250 million due to the low level of imports.[16] During the war the state increased its control over the economy through SEEs, and with military considerations taking priority, civilian economic development efforts reduced dramatically.

Experience of liberalism and failure, 1950–61

The late 1940s marked the beginning of a multi-party system in Turkey, and the general elections of 1950 transferred political power from the (étatist) Republican Party to the newly formed Democratic Party. The Democrats placed more emphasis on issues such as infrastructural investment, support for agriculture and the private sector, and the liberalization of domestic and foreign trade. Although these policies led to an economic boom period in the first half of the 1950s, the second half saw severe economic difficulties stemming from the lack of any sort of planning, the crop failure of 1954, and the foreign trade deficit of the late 1950s.

As the economic situation deteriorated the new government's economic policies changed accordingly. Until the dramatic crop failure of 1954, the favourable terms of trade of primary products created an optimistic environment for the government to follow more liberal economic policies towards trade, and to implement a growth strategy financed by agricultural exports. Thus, the government encouraged agricultural production via high price supports on major agricultural products using, mainly, the substantial financial support of the Marshall Plan. Hershlag[17] notes that this American aid financed about half the increase in imports in the late 1940s and the early 1950s, as well as about 40 per cent of the increase in investment spending. Since land productivity was virtually constant in the 1950s,[18] once the force of agricultural expansion had been exploited, with the further constraints of a crop failure in 1954,[19] the rate of increase of real GNP slowed down. In addition, starting in 1953, the trade and payments regime became increasingly restrictive in response to growing balance of payments difficulties. The government reacted to this development by increasing its foreign borrowing and restricting imports through licences with the aim of rationing scarce foreign exchange. The trade deficit increased rapidly, and by 1958 total foreign debts amounted to more than 25 per cent of the country's GNP. Thus, on the eve of the 1960 military coup, Turkey was on the edge of a debt crisis.[20]

In response, in 1958, the country embarked on a stabilization programme coupled with a devaluation of the Turkish Lira (TL). The difficulties were mainly due to an exceedingly ambitious investment programme that required funds much more than the domestic sources could afford.[21] In addition to the devaluation and unification of the TL, the stabilization programme consisted of not only changes in the foreign trade regime and in the domestic economy but also the consolidation and rescheduling of the outstanding foreign debt. A substantial amount of additional credit came from international lenders, including the International Monetary Fund (IMF) and the United States. The programme also included import liberalization, removal of price controls and increases in SEE prices. For almost four years, the Turkish economy experienced a recession as a consequence of the 1958 stabilization programme. The trade deficit also increased during the programme years.

The foreign trade regime of the 1950s was characterized by constantly changing controls, regulations, and multiple exchange rates. Thus, the trade policy did not reflect any long-term aim or strategy. On the contrary, it became increasingly restrictionist as a result of ad hoc measures introduced in response to the growing trade deficit. The initial experiment with a liberal trade policy (1950–53) was not an attempt to pursue a lasting course towards free trade. The 1958 measures were essentially corrective and were not aimed at permanently creating a more liberal trade regime. The devaluation package had some distortion-reducing elements, but the anti-export bias was maintained. The overall economic policy during the 1950s was essentially inward-looking, but it was based neither on an explicit economic theory nor on formal planning. Economic policy was made mostly on an ad hoc basis, and there was a general lack of interest in coordinating economic policies. By the late 1950s the economy was pushed to the point of international bankruptcy. Overall, the most criticized aspect of the Democrat government in the 1950s was its unplanned and uncoordinated economic decisions which originated from its perception of 'liberal' economic policies. Towards the end of the 1950s, economic crisis resulted in political crisis, and the Democratic era was ended by a military take-over in 1960.

National planning years with étatist orientation, 1962–79

In the aftermath of the 1960 coup, Turkey entered an era of planned economic development. The new constitution imposed comprehensive development planning and preserved the mixed economy with planners deliberately going for inward-looking ISI strategies but also liberalizing the labour market.[22] Five-year plans were established by a new institution, the State Planning Organization (SPO), which was in charge of proposing and implementing plans for socio-economic development under a High Planning Council. The first three five-year plans under the new constitution included the years 1963–67, 1968–72, and 1973–77; the fourth plan was delayed due to the foreign debt crisis (a severe liquidity crisis) of 1977–79. The development plans of the 1960s and 1970s had the following main objectives in common.[23]

a) economic growth;
b) structural change by setting higher growth targets for manufacturing industries;
c) the development of import-competing industries and diversification of exports.

According to the planners, the role of trade policy would be to provide protection to domestic industries ('infant industry' argument) and to allow the import of capital goods and raw materials considered essential to achieve these three objectives. The planning of the 1960s and the 1970s was far more comprehensive than that of the 1930s and covered most aspects of socio-economic development. During the period, the main features of industrialization were priority, protection, and incentives for private industry. A protected domestic market and incentives for private industry were the most explicit forms of priority given to industrialization. The share of industry in total fixed capital investment was targeted to increase in the first three five-year plans (1963–77), and it exceeded targets except in the third five-year plan (1973–77) (see Table 1.5). During the same period, value added in industry increased remarkably,[24] and the composition of manufacturing industry's output changed in favour of intermediate and capital goods.[25] The consensus was that the state must play a leading role in promoting development and that the country must industrialize as fast as possible.

Planning methodology in Turkey was strongly influenced by Professor Jan Tinbergen who served as Chairman of the United Nations Development Committee in the early 1960s and became chief consultant to the SPO. In accordance with UN recommendations, a growth target of 7 per cent was adopted, expanding to 8 per cent with the 1973–77 plan. Inflationary financing of public expenditure was banned by the new constitution and fiscal policy was regarded as the major economic policy instrument. Investment, to a

Table 1.5 Sectoral Distribution of Fixed Capital Investments, 1963–77 (percentages)

Sectors	*1st plan period (1963–67)*		*2nd plan period (1968–72)*		*3rd plan period (1973–77)*	
	Target	*Actual*	*Target*	*Actual*	*Target*	*Actual*
Agriculture	17.7	13.9	15.2	11.1	11.7	11.8
Mining	5.4	5.6	3.7	3.3	5.8	3.7
Industry	16.9	20.4	22.4	26.8	31.1	28.2
Energy	8.6	6.5	8.0	9.0	8.5	7.4
Transport	13.7	15.6	16.1	16.0	14.5	20.6
Tourism	1.4	1.3	2.3	2.1	1.6	1.0
Housing	20.3	22.4	17.9	20.1	15.7	16.9
Education	7.1	6.6	6.7	4.7	5.0	3.3
Health	2.3	1.8	1.8	1.5	1.4	1.1
Other	n.a.	6.6	5.9	5.4	4.7	6.0
Total	100.0	100.0	100.0	100.0	100.0	100.0

n.a.: Not available
Source: Kepenek (1990, Table VI.8)

large extent, oriented towards import-substitution, and exchange rate policy was not on the agenda after the strong de facto devaluation in 1958 (formalized in 1961). All sorts of foreign exchange controls including import and export licensing, quotas, tariffs, premiums, tax rebates and subsidies and foreign aid were implemented as the natural instruments of balance of payments policy. An OECD consortium, founded in 1961 to institutionalize foreign borrowing on concessionary terms, carried through debt rescheduling in 1965 and 1978–80. Considerable exchange rate adjustments (urged by the IMF), however, were undertaken in 1970 and in the second half of the 1970s as the public sector credit policy became increasingly inflationary and macroeconomic targets overambitious. Despite a short liberalization era with a relatively generous supply of foreign exchange and relaxation of controls which occurred after the devaluation of 1970, the main principles of planning and economic policy remained unchanged until the debt crisis of 1978.[26]

The inward-looking ISI strategy was quite successful insofar as growth rates remained high. The étatist-oriented policy collapsed after the first oil shock of 1973–74, the deterioration of the domestic political scene when domestic inflation and foreign borrowing increased beyond sustainable levels and foreign lending to Turkey finally dried up. In due course, an external debt crisis became inevitable in 1978. An important factor that tended to make the étatist policy unsustainable and contributed to its breakdown was the excessive increase in real wages, a result of the liberalization of the labour market and the legalization of labour unions which the 1961 constitution guaranteed.[27]

During the 1929–80 era, Turkish development strategies were dominated by import-substitution with two short periods of relaxed trade controls in 1950–53 and 1970–73. As far as the ISI policies and the national planning of the 1960s and the 1970s are concerned, it is important to point out the link between the OECD and Turkey. These policies, by and large, were endorsed by the OECD. Since 1961, the OECD consortium was the number one financier of development in Turkey. Apparently, OECD views, which are reflected in the regularly published OECD *Economic Surveys for Turkey*, have been important to Turkish governments as they have formulated and implemented development policies.[28]

Derviş *et al.*[29] and Chenery *et al.*[30] evaluate the impact of the import-substitution measures of the 1960s and 1970s. They suggest that ISI policies made a remarkable contribution to the GDP growth rate especially during the 1960s. In that sense, they support the view that early import-substitution (1960s for the Turkish case) may exploit natural advantages and be highly efficient, but sooner or later these advantages would be exhausted. It is suggested that Turkey should have reached this stage in the 1970s.

The national planning years of the 1960s and 1970s mark an intensive import-substitution drive in Turkey, which was mainly implemented through effective quantitative restrictions and a deliberate policy of overvalued foreign currency regime. In retrospect, three sub-periods can be roughly identified (see Table 1.6). Although import-substitution was primarily adopted by the first five-year plan (1963–67) as a means of reaching the industrialization goal, by the time of the second five-year plan (1968–72) the motivation for inward-looking import-substitution policies stemmed much more from balance of payments difficulties.[31]

Persistent balance of payments deficits throughout the 1960s and most of the 1970s created a severe debt problem in the late 1970s.

Table 1.6 Stages of ISI, 1963–80

	Average annual growth rate (%)				
Period	*GNP*	*Agriculture*	*Manufacturing industry*	*Imp./ GNP*	*Exp./ imp.*
1963–70 (a)	6.4	2.6	10.4	6.8	0.68
1971–77 (b)	7.2	4.3	10.1	10.9	0.45
1978–80 (c)	0.5	2.4	–2.7	9.4	0.43

(a) Positive ISI financed with domestic savings.
(b) Negative ISI financed with foreign deficit.
(c) Economic crisis years.
Sources: Pamuk (1984, Table 1, p. 53); SPO, *Annual Programmes*.

From 1962 to 1970, the current account deficit was largely covered by concessionary loans from the OECD consortium. The debt rescheduling in 1965 was also undertaken by the consortium. During 1971–73 Turkey had, mainly as a result of the rapidly increasing remittances from migrant workers, a small current account surplus and had accumulated large foreign exchange reserves. However, in 1973–74 with the oil price shock, related adverse conditions and much more expansionary fiscal and monetary policies,[32] the need for foreign financing became critical. Foreign exchange reserves were drawn down during 1974–76, oil facility loans were obtained from the IMF and short-term loans from the Euro-markets, and exchange controls were tightened. A serious crop failure in 1977 with weak foreign markets for Turkish agricultural exports intensified the problems and in the autumn of 1977 the country was unable to repay its debt. After negotiations with the IMF and the OECD consortium, a stabilization programme was adopted in early 1978. The programme, the IMF Accord of 1978, was intended to last two years; it included credits from the IMF and the OECD consortium, reduction of public expenditure in real terms, price increases on the products of the SEEs, import restrictions and export promotion, and devaluation of the TL.[33] The impact of the 1978 stabilization programme is clear from Table 1.7. The government's policies were obviously not successful and when the 1979 oil shock promised to bring a further deterioration, the Social Democrat government, after losing the senate elections, resigned.

As seen, the period 1974–79 was one of external shocks, expansionary macro-economic policies, and political instability.[34] Economic

Table 1.7 Real GDP, Domestic Absorption, Foreign Trade and GNP, 1977–84 (per cent, over previous year)

Category	*1977*	*1978*	*1979*	*1980*	*1981*	*1982*	*1983*	*1984*
Population	2.0	2.0	2.0	2.2	2.3	2.3	2.4	2.6
GDP (a)	5.1	4.4	–0.7	–1.6	3.7	4.5	4.0	6.1
Agriculture	–1.1	2.5	2.8	1.8	0.0	6.4	–0.2	3.6
Manufacturing	7.2	3.7	–5.2	–6.3	9.2	5.5	10.3	5.5
Services	5.7	3.9	–0.3	0.8	4.2	4.1	4.5	5.7
GDP per capita	3.1	2.4	–2.7	–3.8	1.4	2.2	1.6	3.5
Domestic absorption (a)	6.0	–4.4	–2.2	–0.6	0.8	1.4	4.5	7.7
Private consumption	4.9	0.4	–1.9	–4.5	–0.9	3.5	6.2	10.4
General government cons.	4.4	9.8	1.6	8.8	–0.4	1.1	2.7	0.0
Fixed gross investment	6.9	–9.8	–3.6	–9.9	2.0	3.3	2.7	0.2
Domestic absorption per cap.	4.0	–6.4	–4.2	–2.8	–1.5	–0.9	2.0	4.9
Exports (b)	–17.7	14.1	–9.6	4.2	85.4	40.0	13.7	19.8
Imports (b)	4.2	–33.5	–6.8	2.5	14.8	7.5	17.1	27.7
GNP (a)	4.7	3.2	–1.5	–1.7	3.7	4.5	3.8	5.9
GNP per capita	2.7	1.2	–3.5	–3.9	1.3	2.2	1.3	3.3

(a) At constant 1980 prices.
(b) Goods and non-factor services at constant 1980 prices.
Source: World Bank, *World Tables*, 1989.

policy-making was not consistent, stable or rational during this period. In a period when global growth was low, the Turkish economy was quite slow to adjust. Despite unfavourable external circumstances, successive Turkish governments attempted to maintain or even accelerate the economic growth rates achieved during the earlier period. Although the growth rates were about 7 per cent in the three years immediately following the 1974 oil price shock, the growth process soon proved to be temporary due to those strategies based on inflationary policies, heavy borrowing, and postponement of the structural adjustment measures called for by changing world factor price. The country's economic performance deteriorated rapidly after 1976, resulting in an external debt crisis in 1978.[35]

The 1980s: market orientation and export-led growth (ELG)

A turning point in Turkish economic policy came in January 1980 when the government announced an economic reform programme. This followed several unsuccessful attempts in 1978–79 and several failed IMF programmes. The inward-looking ISI strategy was replaced by an outward-oriented ELG strategy. The economic reform programme, primarily, consisted of the following objectives and arrangements which have been realized to a certain extent:

- abandonment of an inward-oriented ISI strategy, and replacement with an outward-oriented one based on a more market-based economy;
- reduction of direct government intervention in the manufacturing sector;
- lowering of barriers to foreign direct investment;
- broad-based price liberalization, including a realistic and flexible determination of exchange and interest rates;
- gradual import liberalization;
- tight monetary controls and discipline to restrain domestic absorption and reduce the inflation rate;
- financial sector reform; by the end of the 1980s there were only a few restrictions remaining on the financial markets;
- public enterprise reform to reduce their heavy burden on the economy and improve their efficiency;

- encouraging privatization and limiting the extent of public enterprises;
- deregulation and rationalization of the public investment programme;
- export drive strategy; that is, more effective export promotion measures to encourage rapid export growth;
- steps to an improved external debt management and increased creditworthiness.

An overall evaluation of the above objectives of the 1980 reform programme simply reflects a transition experience from an inward-looking economy to an outward and more market-based one. Accordingly, the programme has brought some radical changes to the Turkish economy. Like previous liberalization episodes (1950–53 and 1970–73), that of 1980 was characterized by a devaluation of the domestic currency (in January 1980 the government devalued the TL from 47 to 70 per US dollar and the exchange rate has been adjusted on a daily basis since May 1981) and the institution of a macroeconomic stabilization programme. However, what distinguishes the 1980 reform programme from earlier liberalization attempts is that, '... for the first time the Turkish government demonstrated that it would use economic policies to create a more liberal market-oriented economy ...'.[36]

The 1980 programme was, at the time, presented as the government's own initiative and nothing to do with the IMF or the World Bank.[37] However, developments after the 1982 debt crisis suggested a great many similarities between the economic reform programmes for indebted countries imposed by the IMF and World Bank and Turkey's on the following issues:[38]

a) IMF conditionality on getting any kind of rescheduling agreement based on Paris Club negotiations;
b) a similar procedure has also been applied to World Bank-originated structural adjustment lendings (SALs);
c) the commercial banks only made new arrangements with those countries which were confirmed to be credible by the IMF and/or the World Bank.

Almost two decades after the introduction of the economic reform package in 1980, we are in a position to evaluate the results more objectively. Turkey's macro-economic performance indicators suggest a series of puzzles during the 1980s. First of all, Turkey is one of the few countries that managed to maintain high GNP growth after rescheduling foreign debts in the rather unfavourable global economic environment of the 1980s. Her real GNP grew by about 5 per cent on average between 1981 and 1990 (see Table 1.8).

The eighties witnessed a fundamental change in the composition of GDP in favour of industry. Industry's share rose considerably during the first half of the 1980s but stagnated during the second half. In addition, the country's export earnings have increased considerably (see Table 1.8). There is little doubt that one of the most successful outcomes of the 1980 Turkish economic reform programme was the remarkable growth in exports.[39] As a result of continual real depreciations, output recovery was driven mainly by exports until 1986–87. While many of the countries with debt problems chose to run large non-interest current account (NICA) surpluses, mainly by cutting expenditures and growth, Turkey opted for a high-growth strategy with less NICA surpluses known as 'growth-oriented debt strategy'.[40] This strategy sought to improve the debt–output ratio through output growth and permitted running lower external surpluses. Although this exchange rate policy raised the debt–output ratio through capital loses, it lowered the debt–exports ratio by increasing exports. Mainly due to this policy, Turkey's creditworthiness was restored, and the country was distinguished from most debtor countries whose debt–exports ratio rose in line with their debt–output ratios. During the 1980–88 period, the exchange rate strategy was actively used for export promotion. Turkey's export performance was impressive, especially in the first half of the 1980s. A combination of the following factors can explain such a successful export performance:

a) substantial real depreciation of the TL;
b) the introduction of new export-promotion schemes and the improvement of existing ones;
c) a significant reduction in domestic demand and the shift of production from domestic to foreign markets.

Table 1.8 Some Key Macroeconomic Indicators, the 1980s

	1975	*1980*	*1983*	*1985*	*1987*	*1988*	*1989*
Real GNP growth (%)	8.0	-1.1	3.3	5.1	7.5	3.6	1.9
Inflation rate[1] (%)	10.1	107.2	30.5	43.2	32.0	68.3	69.6
Total GFI[2] / GNP (%)	21.5	19.6	18.9	20.0	24.6	26.1	22.5
Total DS[2] / GNP (%)	19.6	16.0	16.5	18.9	23.9	27.2	22.1
PSBR[3] / GNP (%)	4.7	8.8	4.9	3.6	6.1	4.8	5.3
Export / import ratio (%)	29.6	36.8	62.0	70.2	72.0	81.4	73.6
Export[4] / GNP	2.9	4.2	9.2	11.7	11.6	12.8	10.7
Import[5] / GNP	10.0	11.6	15.3	17.0	16.5	15.8	14.7
Indust. exp. / total exports	35.9	36.0	63.9	75.3	79.1	76.7	78.2
CAD[6] (billion $)	-1.65	-3.41	-1.92	-1.01	-0.81	1.6	1.0
Int. reserves[7] (billion $)	1.2	1.21	2.1	3.28	5.21	6.43	9.3
TED[8] / GNP (%)	8.0	23.5	29.6	37.4	46.1	44.8	38.4
STD[8] / TED (%)	–	–	12.4	18.7	18.9	15.8	13.8
Debt service[8] (billion $)	–	–	-3.83	-4.22	-5.52	-7.16	-7.17
FDI[9] permits (million $)	–	97	103	235	655	821	1 512
FDI[9] Realizations (mill. $)	–	18	46	99	106	354	663

[1] Average annual change in wholesale price index.
[2] GFI: Gross fixed investment; DS: Domestic Savings
[3] PSBR: Public sector borrowing requirement.
[4] Exports of goods (fob).
[5] Imports of goods (cif).
[6] CAD: Current account deficit.
[7] Foreign exchange and gold reserves (net).
[8] TED: Total external debt; STD: Short-term external debt; Debt Service: External debt service (principal + interest).
[9] FDI: Foreign direct investments.

Source: SPO; SIS.

The policy of persistent real depreciation until late 1988 was an essential component of the high-growth strategy that Turkey opted for to solve her debt problem. The spectacular growth in exports, the outward-orientation of the Turkish economy, and expansion of production in tradables relative to non-tradables are some of the achievements of the 1980 post-liberalization period for which the exchange rate policy is to be credited. Starting in late 1988, however, as macroeconomic developments showed a discomforting resemblance to the Latin American experience, the Turkish government implicitly started to use the exchange rate as part of an anti-inflationary strategy, without committing itself to an explicit plan.[41] Some exogenous factors together with the endogenous ones worsened economic conditions in the domestic market in the second half of the 1980s.[42]

The fight against inflation was given top priority in the 1980 adjustment programme. With the help of restrictive monetary and fiscal policies, inflation fell to 30 per cent in the following years but these policies were relaxed after 1983 and especially 1987 due to electoral considerations. In the end, inflation accelerated and hovered around 60 to 70 per cent in the 1988–90 period (see Table 1.8). The view that the major cause of this outcome is the growing public sector deficit is generally accepted. It is also suggested that the Turkish authorities, during the 1980s, have used inflation tax (seigniorage) to finance the huge fiscal deficits.[43]

The years since 1986, however, have been marked by uncertainty in macroeconomic policies. During the last years of this period, real wages increased, the TL appreciated in real terms and exports stagnated. This dimension of the adjustment programme has also been stressed and evaluated in the recent literature. At first, the increasing competitiveness of Turkish politics made fiscal discipline of the economy a major victim especially after 1987.[44] Fiscal deficits have been one of the major characteristics of the economy in the 1980s (see Table 1.8). The fiscal situation of the economy during the second half of the 1980s has remained unstable despite the initial squeeze on fiscal balances in the early 1980s.[45] The inconsistency of the underlying fiscal policy with the exchange rate policy and other fields of liberalization programme became increasingly obvious after 1986–87 when Turkey started to transfer net income abroad (see Table 1.8).

One of the major objectives of the liberalization programme was to bring a lasting solution to the chronic balance of payments problem through switching the productive capacity of the economy into the tradables sector. While this requires, in the short run, the output level of tradables to expand relative to that of non-tradables, sustaining export-led growth in the longer run, needs increased fixed capital formation in the traded goods sector.[46] Despite the achievements in the sectoral composition of production, a capacity increase in tradables has been missing. The view that the favourable export performance of Turkey in the 1980s appears not to have generated an increase in private investment in tradables is shared by many.[47] In short, the 1980 economic reform programme has fallen short of inducing the level of investment in the tradables sector required for the future growth of the economy. The growth in investments has been maintained mainly through public sector investment programmes, largely in non-tradables. It appears that symptoms of inconsistent policies, inflation and high real interest rates, and the lack of an efficient investment policy lie at the heart of the problem. It is also likely that high debt servicing requirements (especially in the second half of the 1980s) reduced investment levels in Turkey. The 1980 adjustment programme relied on the assumption that financial liberalization would stimulate private savings so that greater funds would be available for fixed productive investments. These, however, did not materialize. As mentioned above, the decline in private manufacturing investment should be taken very seriously, since the sustainability of outward orientation and liberalization strategies critically depends on investment growth. Uygur[48] suggests policy uncertainty as an important factor which prevented private investment from increasing in the 1980s. Additionally, Conway[49] econometrically shows that relative price uncertainty in the economic environment is significantly correlated with reduced real investments.

The 1980s witnessed unemployment rates fluctuating around 10–11 per cent although they reduced considerably during the second half of the 1980s. However, high real-wage increases in 1989 and 1990 put a damper on further reductions in unemployment. However, some[50] argue that officially published unemployment figures in Turkey are simply misleading. Hence, any comment based on these figures would be quite dubious. Kepenek,[51] with his own calculations, shows that the unemployment rate rose from 16.4 per cent in 1980 to 22.9 per cent in 1988. Put another way, the number of unemployed people rose from 2.8 million in 1980 to 4.8 million in 1988.

The functional and size distributions of income deteriorated between 1980 and 1988 although a relative improvement came in 1989 and 1990 when real agricultural prices and real manufacturing wages rose significantly.[52] In this respect, Boratav[53] suggests that agricultural income decreased considerably and that the agricultural terms of trade deteriorated 53 per cent between 1976 and 1986.

It is also true that compared with the first half of the 1980s the economy has been less stable in terms of macro-economic performance during the second half, especially after 1987. Real GNP slowed down in 1988 and 1989 as a result of a tightening of economic policy in 1988 aimed at containing rising budget deficits and strongly increasing inflation. In 1990, however, economic growth recovered to 9 per cent largely due to relaxing monetary and fiscal policies in 1989. Economic expansion came to a halt by the end of 1990 owing to the shock of events in the Gulf. Turkey's foreign borrowing and foreign debt increased remarkably in the second half of the decade. However, foreign exchange and gold reserves reached high levels in the late 1980s (see Table 1.8).

We, like many others, view the 1980 liberalization as the start of a fundamental and sustained liberalization. As Dornbusch[54] points out: '... The results of Turkish opening (and of accompanying domestic political and economic stabilization and reform) are altogether striking ...'.[55] The liberalization of imports and the capital account were, however, approached gradually and at later phases of the 1980 adjustment programme[56] nominal tariff rates were reduced remarkably; quantitative restrictions were abolished and bureaucratic controls over imports were also relaxed especially in and after 1983–84. However, the import liberalization process in the late 1980s led to an increase in the import of consumer goods. Besides, capital account liberalization appears to have contributed to the real appreciation of the TL.[57] In 1990, further import liberalization measures were introduced during a period of real exchange appreciation, with the result that there was a noticeable trade and current account deficit.

The two most significant features of the 1980s' adjustment process were the substantial capital inflows during the very early stages and the successful export drive. Although an overall evaluation of the 1980 economic reform programme is not an easy task, its impact can be assessed as a success despite the fact that the Turkish economy still has a number of structural problems including inflationary pressures and a high proportion of fiscal deficits. Most observers credit the reforms with a significant structural transformation of the economy and suggest that, even if there is a future macro-economic crisis, the move toward a more outer-oriented economic activity will persist.[58]

There is little doubt that the Turkish economy has achieved an impressive transformation from being inward-looking to outward-oriented. Exports rose from about $US3 billion in 1980 to about $US12 billion in 1988. It is worth noting that the export boom was mainly in manufactured products. In fact, Turkey is one of the few countries that managed to maintain high GNP growth rates in real terms after rescheduling her debts in the 1980s. Riedel,[59] among others, citing the Turkish reform programme implemented in the 1980s, argues that the outward orientation of trade can boost export growth rates of LDCs. It is also true that the early and favourable timing of Turkey's debt crisis (in 1978), a favourable political environment (political autonomy) during the 1980–83 period, and a generous international loan package launched in the early 1980s[60] by the creditors are factors that cannot be ignored in evaluating the success of the Turkish experience.

The reforms of the 1980s have already produced a remarkable payoff, although a number of structural economic difficulties remain. Krueger[61] argues that if successive Turkish governments had attempted to continue the policies of the late 1970s there is little doubt that real output would have continued to fall and that inflation would have accelerated further.

Economic performance of the 1990s and prospects for the future

From the mid-1980s, the Turkish economy experienced boom–recession fluctuations; starting with high annual rates of growth in 1986 and 1987, real GNP slowed down in 1988 and 1989 as a result of a tightening of economic policy in 1988 aimed at restraining rising public sector deficits and strongly accelerating inflation. Due to the policy-induced downturn of economic activity real GNP growth fell to below 2 per cent in 1989 (see Table 1.8).

Although only modest success was registered on the inflation front in 1989, monetary and fiscal policies were relaxed again in the course of that year; particularly, public sector wages (which had been eroded by high inflation in earlier years) increased quite dramatically. Strong real wage increases were also recorded in the private sector, fostering household consumption. In 1990, Turkey experienced a boom in economic activity which was further boosted by the widening public sector deficit. Economic growth recovered remarkably in 1990, pushing the current external balance back into a considerable deficit (see Table 1.9).

However, economic expansion came to a halt by the end of 1990, hit by the events in the Gulf. Real GNP fell in early 1991 and recovered only mildly during the rest of the year. In addition to its direct contractionary effects, the Gulf crisis brought uncertainty to the economy and pessimistic expectations which resulted in adverse effects on demand and production decisions. Later that year domestic political events culminating in early general elections in October 1991 created renewed uncertainty about the future course of economic policy. Economic expansion slowed to an average annual rate of 0.3 per cent in 1991 against the government's target of 5.9 per cent. Inflation, however, continued to worsen in 1991, along with a sharp increase in the public sector borrowing requirement (PSBR) (see Table 1.9).

GDP growth was floating in 1992 and 1993, reflecting large real wage increases and lax macro-economic policies. By the end of 1993, the economy was overheating. Domestic demand rose by about 12 per cent in 1993, import volumes jumped by 36 per cent and GDP grew by 8.1 per cent. Following years of high fiscal deficits and inflation in excess of 50 per cent a year, a sharp deterioration in public sector (the PSBR was 12 per cent of GDP in 1993) and external deficits caused a loss of confidence in the TL and a financial crisis in early 1994. The process of Central Bank financing of the PSBR led to a loss of control over the money supply and the effects of this were intensified by wide-scale currency substitution which ultimately resulted in a sharp depreciation. An ambitious stabilization programme was introduced on 5 April 1994 to restore sound public sector finances through sharp cuts in government expendi-

Table 1.9 Some Key Macroeconomic Indicators, the 1990s

	1990	*1991*	*1992*	*1993*	*1994*	*1995*	*1996*	*1997*
Real GNP growth (%)	9.4	0.3	6.4	8.1	–6.1	8.0	7.1	8.0
Inflation rate[1] (%)	52.3	55.4	62.1	58.4	120.6	88.5	74.6	81.0
Total GFI[2] / GNP (%)	22.6	23.7	23.4	26.3	24.5	24.0	25.0	25.3
Total DS[2] / GNP (%)	22.0	21.4	21.6	22.7	23.1	22.1	20.0	20.1
PSBR[3] / GNP (%)	7.4	10.2	10.6	12.0	7.9	5.2	9.0	9.5
Export / Import ratio (%)	58.1	64.6	64.3	52.1	77.8	60.6	54.1	56.5
Export[4] / GNP	8.5	8.9	9.2	8.4	13.8	12.6	12.5	13.6
Import[5] / GNP	14.6	13.8	14.3	16.2	17.8	20.8	23.1	24.1
Indust. exp. / total exports	79.9	78.6	83.5	83.4	85.7	88.2	87.4	89.6
CAD[6] (billion $)	–2.6	0.25	–0.97	–6.43	2.63	–2.34	–2.4	–2.75
Int. reserves[7] (billion $)	11.4	12.3	15.3	17.8	16.5	23.9	25.0	27.1
TED[8] / GNP (%)	32.2	33.2	34.7	37.0	50.1	42.6	43.2	42.2*
STD[8] / TED (%)	19.4	18.1	22.8	27.5	17.2	21.4	25.7	25.4
Debt service[8] (billion $)	7.3	7.5	8.3	9.2	9.4	10.0	9.9	4.7**
FDI[9] permits (million $)	1 861	1 967	1 820	2 063	1 478	2 938	3 837	1 077***
FDI[9] realizations (mill. $)	700	783	779	622	559	772	612	245**

* Ratio of debt stock as of end of June to estimated GNP for the whole year.
** January–June period.
*** January–September period.
(1) Average annual change in wholesale price index.
(2) GFI: Gross fixed investment; DS: Domestic savings.
(3) PSBR: Public sector borrowing requirement.
(4) Exports of goods (fob).
(5) Imports of goods (cif).
(6) CAD: Current account deficit.
(7) Foreign exchange and gold reserves (net).
(8) TED: Total external debt; STD: Short-term external debt; Debt service: external debt service (principal + interest).
(9) FDI: Foreign direct investments.
Source: SPO; SIS.

ture, special tax measures, and, in the longer term, through structural reforms. Following this financial crisis the economy entered a depression. Real GNP fell by 6.1 per cent. Inflation was higher than before, and the TL depreciated sharply in real terms.[62]

It is also possible to argue that uncontrolled and ambitious financial liberalization was the main cause of the financial crisis in 1994. In addition to the further liberalization of the current account, major steps had been taken towards capital account liberalization since 1989. All limits regarding the export and import of Turkish currency and all limits on purchasing foreign currencies had been lifted; persons resident in Turkey were allowed to purchase and transfer foreign securities; persons resident abroad were allowed to purchase, sell and transfer Turkish securities; residents in Turkey, including the private sector and the SEEs were allowed to obtain foreign credits directly provided that these credits were used through banks or private financial institutions. These changes made it easier for foreign capital to exploit arbitrage opportunities stemming from interest rate differences.[63]

Turkish financial liberalization was not accorded with fiscal consolidation in the late 1980s. Fiscal and monetary policies were relaxed especially from 1987 onwards due to electoral considerations. Large and persistent fiscal deficits together with the liberalization of capital account transactions adversely affected internal and external balances causing a serious crisis in money, capital and foreign exchange markets at the beginning of 1994. Measures the government put into effect on 5 April 1994 aimed at stabilizing the economy were short-sighted, and it was clear at the beginning of 1995 that the programme aimed at getting out of the crisis with a hot-money policy (this would suggest that policy-makers had not learnt from past experiences!) rather than aiming at some longer-term achievements by designing a programme including structural reforms, privatization, and fiscal tightening. The TL began to appreciate, and the real exchange rates returned to pre-1994 levels. Real private consumption and investment continued to increase during 1995 and 1996. The external deficit was 4.6 of GDP in 1995. It fell somewhat in 1996, but was still high.[64]

The Turkish economy has enjoyed high GNP growth rates since 1995, although high inflation rates and structural problems have remained unresolved. As we write during early 1999 the Turkish economy has witnessed a new recession in recent months stemming from both the 'global recession' and the internal dynamics of the economy itself. While the process of forming a new government to carry Turkey to the general elections in April 1999 is still on, the near future prospects for the economy look gloomy. The major challenge facing the new government will be to put the macroeconomic balances in order so as to be able to overcome the ongoing recession, also to establish a credible strategy for achieving sustainable internal and external deficits (also achieving manageable internal and external debts), lower inflation and sustainable economic growth in the medium term. A viable medium-term stabilization and structural reform programme will require vigorous structural reform, *inter alia* reform of the deficit-ridden social security system, rationalization of the loss-making SEEs, accelerated privatization, and a widening of the tax base. Although entry into the EU Customs Union on 1 January 1996 was a unique opportunity to open up the economy to greater competition and to downsize the bloated and inefficient public sector in the middle term, the short-run consequences of the Customs Union have been a widening of the external deficits. There is little doubt that a more efficient public sector and more vigorous and sustained structural reform are the key missing factors.[65]

Concluding remarks

In this chapter we have presented a comprehensive overview of the Turkish economy in the postwar years, an era of struggle for the Turkish economy for rapid economic development. The country is a 'typical' middle-income country. Turkey was characterized by a rather closed economy with inward-oriented policies until the 1980s. In the late 1970s she found herself with a severe external debt problem stemming from the foreign exchange liquidity crisis with widespread shortages, negative growth and three-digit inflation rates. A turning point in Turkish economic policy came in January 1980 when the inward-looking economic strategy was replaced with an outward-oriented growth strategy based on export promotion. Almost two decades later, in 1998, Turkey has a relatively comfortable balance-of-payments situation, and holds significant foreign exchange reserves. Within the last 18 years the economy has achieved the transformation from an inward- to an outward-orientation with remarkable increases in exports. Yet, inflation remains high and substantial public sector budget deficits pose a real threat for the economy as a whole. Starting from the late 1980s, fiscal balances have come under increasing pressure due to heavy external transfers.

There is little doubt that the Turkish economy, compared to the first half of the 1980s, has been less successful in terms of macroeconomic performance in the late 1980s and the 1990s. As regards trade liberalization, the reforms of the 1980s and the 1990s have been sufficient to merit the status of a sustained liberalization. The import liberalization process in the late 1980s led, however, to an increase in imports of consumer goods.[66] Capital account liberalization, on the other hand, appears to have contributed to the real appreciation of the TL. In 1990, further import liberalization measures were introduced during a period of real exchange rate appreciation resulting in increasing trade deficits. In this respect, allowing residents uncontrolled access to international capital markets and short-term speculative capital flows proved to be very costly in 1994. It appears that Turkey needs to exercise some control over external capital flows in order to minimize their disruptive effects and gain greater autonomy to accomplish growth and stability.[67] Special care needs to be given to the design of external financial policies since mistakes in this area tend to be costly and difficult to reverse. We believe that restoring policy consistency should receive the top priority and the correcting action should come from the fiscal side. The main task of the exchange rate policy is that it needs to send credible and sustainable signals for continued outward orientation. There is little doubt that the future prospects and sustainability of the Turkish success depend critically on achieving optimal solutions to the stated problems.

Notes

1 Wagstaff, 1989.
2 Wagstaff, 1989.
3 Saraçoğlu, 1987.

4 For details see *World Development Report*, 1998/99.
5 In Chenery and Syrquin, 1975.
6 After Iraq's invasion of Kuwait in 1991, and the imposition of the international trade embargo, the cost to the Turkish economy is estimated by government sources to be around $US25 billion. Previously Iraq was exporting about a million barrels of oil daily through a pipeline in Turkey.
7 Boratav, 1988.
8 Hershlag, 1988.
9 Utkulu and Sevkal, 1997.
10 Hansen, 1991.
11 Hansen, 1991, p. 316.
12 Hershlag, 1988.
13 Hale, 1981.
14 Hansen, 1991.
15 Hansen, 1991; Hale, 1981; Rivkin, 1965.
16 Boratav, 1988.
17 Hershlag, 1988
18 Hershlag, 1988.
19 Krueger, 1974, notes that due to weather conditions, agricultural production decreased by about 20 per cent in 1954.
20 Krueger, 1974.
21 Baysan and Blitzer, 1991.
22 Hansen, 1991, ch. 11.
23 Baysan and Blitzer, 1991.
24 See Hale, 1981, Table 11.1.
25 See Hale, 1981, Table 11.2.
26 See Celasun, 1983; Hansen, 1991; Krueger, 1974.
27 Hansen, 1991.
28 At the time of the first five-year plan, the OECD, among other domestic and external groups and organizations, viewed import substitution and the policy of infant industries as a necessary initial stage in economic development and industrialization. For such views on the merits of import substitution policies, *see* 1963, 1966, 1967 and 1976 OECD *Economic Surveys for Turkey*.
29 Derviş *et al.*, 1981, pp. 93–4.
30 Chenery *et al.*, 1986, pp. 129–37.
31 Krueger, 1974.
32 Unlike many other countries, Turkey continued its fast growth policy despite the adverse global economic environment after the 1973–74 oil shock. This policy, however, proved to be too ambitious, and resulted in an external debt crisis in 1978.
33 See OECD *Economic Surveys for Turkey*, 1978; World Bank, 1982.
34 Between October 1973 and September 1980, seven governments (all coalitions) took office. The longest and shortest ones were 14 months and only ten days respectively.
35 Utkulu, 1995.

36 In a World Bank study on foreign trade liberalization, Baysan and Blitzer, 1991, focus on developments in the Turkish foreign trade sector between 1950 and 1984. They identify four attempts to liberalize trade, namely the years 1950, 1958, 1970 and 1980. The authors conclude that the liberalization was not sustained in the first three cases. Only the 1980 liberalization attempt is viewed as the start of a more fundamental and sustained liberalization. Unlike the earlier stabilization packages of the 1950s and the 1970s, the 1980 programme marked the beginning of a committed major programme of economic liberalization and trade reform. It is also worth noting that like all Turkey's previous liberalization episodes (that is, 1950–53 and 1970–73), its roots lay in balance-of-payments difficulties. During the late 1970s, inflation was accelerating, unemployment was rising, shortages were common, and labour unrest had reached crisis proportions. Even worse, political violence was widespread throughout the country. All these problems were becoming increasingly severe due to the economy's inability to adjust to higher world oil prices, a lack of incentives for exports, irrationality in the import-licensing system, poor performance by the SEEs, and political instability.

37 Wolff, 1987; Kirkpatrick and Öniş, 1991.

38 Arıcanlı and Rodrik, 1990b, refer to Turkey as '... a Baker Plan example before the Baker Plan ...'.

39 Rodrik (1988), for example, notes that 'fictional' exports played some role during the first half of the 1980s due to explicit export subsidization which fall outside the 'orthodox' policies. During the 1981–1985 period, the extent of over-invoicing averages out at 16 per cent, according to Rodrik's (1988) calculations. The key policies which played an important role in contributing to export performance were the active exchange rate policy, generous subsidization, the explosive political situation in the Middle East (especially the Iran–Iraq war), and austerity at home.

40 See van Wijnbergen *et al.*, 1992, p. 160.

41 Aşıkoğlu and Uçtum, 1992.

42 Kazgan, 1993.

43 For the same point, see especially Anand and van Wijnbergen, 1989.

44 Arıcanlı and Rodrik, 1990b.

45 Celasun, 1990.

46 Aşıkoğlu and Uçtum (1992) suggest that the behaviour of aggregate investment could mislead more than it could reveal for two reasons. First, what is more important is its breakdown into investment in traded and non-traded goods sectors. Second, an obvious characteristic of the Turkish economy is the significant role of the public sector in economic activity, particularly in fixed capital formation. Since the 1980 reform programme aimed at achieving an outward-looking transformation based primarily upon market forces, private fixed capital formation in traded (rather than non-traded) goods should be the investment category to be used in evaluating the post-1980 period.

47 See, among others, Arıcanlı and Rodrik, 1990b, Conway, 1990, 1991, and Uygur, 1993.
48 Uygur, 1993, p. 232.
49 Conway, 1991.
50 For example, Kepenek, 1990.
51 Kepenek, 1990.
52 Celasun, 1989; Uygur, 1993.
53 Boratav, 1990.
54 Dornbusch, 1992, p. 77.
55 Dornbusch, 1992, also provides a good account in favour of trade liberalization for LDCs.
56 Relying on the theoretical framework for policy options for reducing anti-export bias by Milner (1990, especially pp. 92–4), one can reasonably suggest that the Turkish government, during the 1980s, has utilized the following policy options: a) raising 'export subsidies', b) lowering the 'effective protection of importables'.
57 Akyüz (1993) warns that special attention needs to be given to the design of external financial policies, since mistakes in this area tend to be very costly and difficult to reverse. Allowing residents uncontrolled access to international capital markets has proved damaging in many developing countries, and short-term speculative capital flows have proved troublesome even for developed economies. Thus, most developing countries need to exercise some control over external capital flows in order to minimize their disruptive effects and gain greater policy autonomy to accomplish growth and stability. Akyüz cites the experience of Turkey following the liberalization of its capital account and the lifting of restrictions on private borrowing in August 1989. Turkey received about $US3 billion of short-term capital in 1990 compared to a net outflow of 2.3 billion in the year before, and its currency appreciated remarkably. Capital flows were reversed in early 1991 with the outbreak of the Gulf War and political uncertainty at home. Consequently, net short-term outflows reached $US3 billion in 1991, the currency depreciated sharply against the US dollar and foreign exchange reserves dropped. This evidence shows how short-term capital can be reversed easily. What is remarkable about this experience, as quoted by Akyüz, is that real domestic interest rates hardly differed between the two periods: the main difference was in the state of expectations and the direction of capital and exchange rate movements.
58 Krueger, 1992.
59 Riedel, 1991.
60 It is worth noting that during the period 1978–79, that is, before the economic reforms of 1980, the economic performance of Turkey was not much different from the typical pattern of severely indebted countries after 1982.
61 Krueger, 1992, p. 144.
62 See Table 1.9; also see various issues of OECD *Economic Surveys for Turkey*.

63 Uygur, 1993, p. 14; Güran, 1998, p. 3.
64 See also Selçuk, 1998.
65 For details see especially various issues of OECD *Economic Surveys for Turkey*.
66 See Uygur, 1993.
67 Akyüz, 1993.

References

Akyüz, Y., 'Does Financial Liberalisation Improve Trade Performance?', in M.R. Agosin and D. Tussie (eds) *Trade and Growth: New Dilemmas in Trade Policy* (New York: St. Martin's Press, 1993).

Anand, R. and S. van Wijnbergen, 'Inflation and the Financing of Government Expenditure: an Introductory Analysis with an Application to Turkey', *World Bank Economic Review*, Vol. 3, No. 1 (1989) 17–38.

Arıcanlı, T. and D. Rodrik (eds), *The Political Economy of Turkey: Debt Adjustment and Sustainability* (London: Macmillan, 1990a).

Arıcanlı, T. and D. Rodrik, 'An Overview of Turkey's Experience with Economic Liberalisation and Structural Adjustment', *World Development*, Vol. 18, No. 10 (1990b) 1343–50.

Aşıkoğlu, Y. and M. Uçtum, 'A Critical Evaluation of Exchange Rate Policy in Turkey', *World Development*, Vol. 20, No. 10 (1992) 1501–14.

Balazs, J., *Lessons of an Attempt at Stabilization: Turkey in the 1980s*, No. 63 (Budapest: Hungarian Scientific Council for World Economy, 1990).

Baysan, T. and C. Blitzer, 'Turkey's Trade Liberalisation in the 1980s and Prospects for Its Sustainability', in *The Political Economy of Turkey: Debt, Adjustment and Sustainability*, T. Arıcanlı and D. Rodrik (eds), (London: Macmillan, 1990).

—— and ——, 'Turkey', in *Liberalizing Foreign Trade: the Experience of New Zealand, Spain and Turkey*, Vol. 6, D. Papageorgiou, M. Michaely and A.M. Choksi (eds), A Research Project of the World Bank (Cambridge, MA: Basil Blackwell, 1991).

Boratav, K., *Stabilization and Adjustment Policies and Programmes: Turkey, Country Study, No. 5* (Helsinki: A WIDER Publication, 1987).

——, Türkiye İktisat Tarihi, 1908–1985 (*Turkish Economic History, 1908–1985*), (Istanbul: Gerçek Yayınevi, 1988).

——, 'Inter-Class and Intra-Class Relations of Distribution under Structural Adjustment: Turkey during the 1980s', in T. Arıcanlı and D. Rodrik (eds), *The Political Economy of Turkey: Debt, Adjustment and Sustainability* (London: Macmillan, 1990).

Celasun, M., *Sources of Industrial Growth and Structural Change: the Case of Turkey*, World Bank Staff Working Paper, No. 614 (Washington, DC, 1983).

——, 'Income Distribution and Employment Aspects of Turkey's Post-1980 Adjustment', *METU Studies in Development*, Vol. 16, Nos. 3–4 (1989) 1–32.

——, 'Fiscal Aspects of Adjustment in the 1980s', in T. Arıcanlı and D. Rodrik (eds), *The Political Economy of Turkey: Debt Adjustment and Sustainability* (London: Macmillan, 1990).

Central Bank of the Republic of Turkey, *Quarterly Bulletin* (various), Ankara.

Chenery, H. and M. Syrquin, *Patterns of Development: 1950–1970* (London: Oxford University Press, 1975).

Chenery, H., S. Robinson and M. Syrquin, *Industrialisation and Growth: a Comparative Study* (New York: Oxford University Press, 1986).

Conway, P., *Economic Shocks and Structural Adjustments: Turkey after 1973, Contributions to Economic Analysis*, No. 166, D.W. Jorgenson and J. Waelbroeck (eds of the series), (Amsterdam: North-Holland, 1987).

——, 'The Record on Private Investment in Turkey', in T. Arıcanlı and D. Rodrik (eds), *The Political Economy of Turkey: Debt, Adjustment and Sustainability* (London: Macmillan, 1990).

——, *Implications of Relative Price Uncertainty for Private Investment Expenditure in Turkey* (Mimeo, Department of Economics, University of North Carolina, 1991).

Derviş, K., J. de Melo and S. Robinson, *General Equilibrium Models for Development Policy* (Cambridge: Cambridge University Press, 1981).

Dornbusch, R., 'The Case for Trade Liberalisation in Developing Countries', *Journal of Economic Perspectives*, Vol. 6, No. 1, Winter (1992) 69–85.

Güran, N., *Public Sector Deficits and External Balance (The Turkish Experience in the Liberalisation Process)* (Mimeo, Dokuz Eylül University, Economics Department, Izmir, 1997).

Gürsoy, M., *World Economic Crises and Effects on the Turkish Economy (Dünyadaki Büyük Ekonomik Krizler ve Türkiye Ekonomisine Etkileri)* (Istanbul: Metiş Yayınları, 1989).

Hale, W., *The Political Economic Development of Modern Turkey* (London: Croom Helm, 1981).

Hansen, B., *Egypt and Turkey: the Political Economy of Poverty, Equity, and Growth*, A World Bank Comparative Study (Washington, DC: Oxford University Press, Published for the World Bank, 1991).

Hershlag, Z.Y., *The Contemporary Turkish Economy* (London: Routledge, 1988).

Kazgan, G., *Ekonomide Dışa* Açık Büyüme (*Outward-Oriented Growth of the Economy*), 2nd edition (Istanbul: Altın Kitaplar Yayınevi, 1988).

——, 'External Pressures and the New Policy Outlook', in C. Balkır and A.M. Williams (eds), *Turkey and Europe* (London: Pinter, 1993).

Kepenek, Y., *Türkiye Ekonomisi* (*The Economy of Turkey*) (Ankara: Verso Yayınevi, 1990).

Keyder, C., *State and Class in Turkey: a Study in Capitalist Development*, (London: Verso, 1987). Turkish Translation by S. Tekay: *Türkiye'de Devlet ve Sınıflar* (Istanbul: İletişim, 1989).

Kirkpatrick, C. and Z. Öniş, 'Turkey', in P. Mosley, J. Harrigan and J. Toye (eds), *Aid and Power: the World Bank and Policy-based Lending*, Case Studies, Vol. 2 (London: Routledge, 1991).

Kopits, G., *Structural Reform, Stabilization and Growth in Turkey*, IMF Occasional Paper, No. 52, (1987).

Krueger, A., *Foreign Trade Regimes and Economic Development: Turkey* (New York: NBER, 1974).

——, *Economic Policy Reform in Developing Countries: the Kuznets Memorial Lectures at the Economic Growth Center*, Yale University (Oxford: Blackwell Publishers, 1992).

Kuruç, B. *et al.*, *Türkiye Ekonomisi: 1980–1985* (*The Economy of Turkey: 1980–1985*) 3rd edition (Ankara: Bilgi Yayınevi, 1987).

Milanovic, B., *Export Incentives and Turkish Manufacturing Exports: 1980–84*, World Bank Staff Paper, No. 768 (1986).

Milner, C., 'The Role of Import Liberalisation in Export Promotion', in C. Milner (ed.), *Export Promotion Strategies: Theory and Evidence from Developing Countries* (London: Harvester Wheatsheaf, 1990).

Nas, T.F. and M. Odekon (eds), *Liberalisation and the Turkish Economy, Contributions in Economics and Economic History*, No. 86 (New York: Greenwood Press, 1988).

—— and —— (eds), *Economics and Politics of Turkish Liberalisation* (London: Associated University Presses, 1992).

OECD, *Economic Surveys for Turkey* (various issues), Paris.

Pamuk, S., *Osmanlı Ekonomisi ve Dünya Kapitalizmi, 1820–1913* (*The Ottoman Economy and World Capitalism, 1820–1913*), (Ankara: Yurt Yayınevi, 1984).

Riedel, J., 'Strategy Wars: the State of Debate on Trade and Industrialisation in Developing Countries', in A. Koekkoek and L.B.M. Mennes (eds), *International Trade and Global Development: Essays in Honour of Jagdish Bhagwati* (London: Routledge, 1991).

Rivkin, M.D., *Area Development for National Growth: the Turkish Precedent* (New York: Praeger, 1965).

Rodrik, D., 'External Debt and Economic Performance in Turkey', in T.F. Nas and M. Odekon (eds), *Liberalisation and the Turkish Economy, Contributions in Economics and Economic History*, No. 86 (New York: Greenwood Press, 1988).

Saraçoğlu, R., 'Economic Stabilisation and Structural Adjustment: the Case of Turkey', in V. Corbo, M. Goldstein and M. Khan (eds), *Growth-Oriented Adjustment Programs*, Proceedings of a Symposium Held in Washington DC, 25–27 February 1987 (Washington, DC: IMF and World Bank, 1987).

Selçuk, F., 'A Brief Account of the Turkish Economy, 1987–1996', in L. Rittenberg (ed.), *The Political Economy of Turkey in the Post-Soviet Era: Going West and Looking East?* (London: Praeger Press, 1998).

Şenses, F., 'An Overview of Recent Turkish Experience with Economic Stabilisation and Liberalisation', in T.F. Nas and M. Odekon (eds), *Liberalisation and the Turkish Economy, Contributions in Economics and Economic History*, No. 86 (New York: Greenwood Press, 1988).

Singer, M., *The Economic Advance of Turkey, 1923–1960* (Ankara: Ayyıldız Yayınevi, 1977).

State Institute of Statistics (SIS), *Statistical Indicators* (various), Ankara.

State Planning Organisation (SPO), *Annual Programmes* (various), Ankara.

State Planning Organisation (SPO), *Five-year Plans* (various), Ankara.

State Planning Organisation (SPO), *Main Economic Indicators*, March 1998, Ankara.

Utkulu, U. (1995), 'LDC External Debt, Trade and Solvency of a Nation: Time-series Evidence for Turkey', PhD Thesis, Leicester University, Economics Department, UK.

Utkulu, U. and N. Sevkal, 'The Turkish Economy between 1923–1929 and the Ottoman Legacy', in *Honorary Book for Prof. Dr. Nezihe Sönmez* (Dokuz Eylül University, Public Finance Department, Izmir, 1997).

Uygur, E., 'Trade Policies and Economic Performance in Turkey in the 1980s', in M.R. Agosin and D. Tussie (eds), *Trade and Growth: New Dilemmas in Trade Policy* (New York: St. Martin's Press, 1993).

Wijnbergen, S. van, R. Anand, A. Chhibber and R. Rocha, *External Debt, Fiscal Policy and Sustainable Growth in Turkey* (Baltimore: World Bank, The Johns Hopkins University Press, 1992).

Wagstaff, J.M., *The Role of the Government in the Industrialisation of Turkey, 1938–1980*, Centre of Near and Middle Eastern Studies, School of Oriental and African Studies (SOAS), Occasional Paper, No. 2 (1989), University of London.

Wolff, P., *Stabilisation Policy and Structural Adjustment in Turkey, 1980–1985: the Role of the IMF and the World Bank in an Externally Supported Adjustment Process* (Berlin: The German Development Institute, 1987).

World Bank, *Turkey: Industrialisation and Trade Strategy*, World Bank Country Study (Washington, DC: The World Bank, 1982).

World Bank, *World Development Report, 1998/99* (Washington, DC: The World Bank, 1999).

World Bank, *World Tables, 1989* (Washington, DC: The World Bank, 1989).

Suggestions for further reading

1. For information on the Ottoman economy in the nineteenth century and the early twentieth century, see, among others, Gürsoy (1989), Kepenek (1990), Pamuk (1984) and Hershlag (1988).
2. For the global economic effects of the Great Depression on the Turkish economy during the 1930s, see Gürsoy (1989).
3. For a variety of explanations about the sources of inspiration of étatism, see Boratav (1988), Hershlag (1988), Kepenek (1990), Keyder (1987).
4. For a full account of the achievements of étatism, see, e.g., Hansen (1991) 324–37.
5. For a more detailed discussion of the 1958 Stabilisation Programme, see, e.g., Krueger (1974).
6. For some other reasons for reintroducing planning, see Kepenek (1990), Keyder (1987).
7. Baysan and Blitzer (1991), 289–95, argue that in 1958–60 the trade regime was inward oriented and restrictionist since the 1958 programmes were essentially correctional and were not aimed at permanently creating a more liberal trade regime. It is also true that the devaluation package had

some distortion-reducing elements, but the anti-export bias was maintained. There are a substantial number of books, conferences, and papers on this field either in English or Turkish. See, e.g., Aşıkoğlu and Uçtum (1992), Arıcanlı and Rodrik (1990a, 1990b), Balazs (1990), Baysan and Blitzer (1990), Boratav (1987, 1990), Kazgan (1988), Kopits (1987), Kirkpatrick and Öniş (1991), Krueger (1992), Kuruç *et al.* (1987), Milanovic (1986), Nas and Odekon (1988, 1992), Saraçoğlu (1987), Şenses (1988), Uygur (1993), Wolff (1987).

2
Sectoral Analysis of the Turkish Economy

Mehmet Haluk Köksal

Introduction

A country's economic structure is determined by the relative weight of each individual sector. According to ISIC (International Standard Industrial Classification) the agricultural, manufacturing, mining, energy and service sectors are the key ones to be examined if an economy is to be analyzed by dividing it into sectors.

Our study is divided along these traditional lines with agriculture being the first area to be examined, followed by industry and then services. This chapter maps Turkey's transition as she moves away from being agriculture-reliant and rural-based, to being more and more industrialized and urban-based.

Agriculture

In 1923 agriculture accounted for 43 per cent of Gross National Product (GNP), a share that remained about the same until 1963. During the last thirty years, however, it has dropped dramatically, standing at 13 per cent in 1997 with the lion's share of GNP going instead to industry and the service sector.

Despite this shift, around 40 per cent of the economically active population is employed in agriculture.[1] There is a great range in agricultural product and income between the regions due to differences in the climate, the characteristics and distribution of land, the usage of machinery, fertilizers and irrigation, and the characteristics of labour. Thus the structure of the agricultural sector causes not only economic problems due to its very low income levels and unequal income distribution, but social and political problems too.

Usage of agricultural land

According to the 1991 General Agriculture Census, around 21.1 million hectares or 31.9 per cent of the total land can be used for agricultural purposes. Forest covers 31.9 per cent and pasture 18.7 per cent, the land unsuitable for agriculture is 17.1 per cent and unused arable land 3.1 per cent.

Sown area accounts for 73.5 per cent of total cultivated land. Land left fallow decreased from 27.9 per cent in 1980 to 14.9 per cent as a result of measures adopted after 1982. Fruit trees cover 11.1 per cent and the vegetable sowing area takes up 2.8 per cent of total cultivated land.

The total number of households employed in agriculture was around four million in 1991, and average land size per household decreased from 5.75 hectares in 1980 to 5.16 hectares in 1991.

Agricultural enterprises operating only on their own land account for 92.6 per cent of the total, and these were operating on 89.3 per cent of the total land in 1991. A decade before, the percentage of enterprises using their own land was 90.5 and the ratio of land they used to total land was 86.7.[2]

Size of enterprises

The size of agricultural enterprises and the changes in these data over time are important for explaining the structure of the agricultural sector although the relative size, characteristics, natural structure of the land, and climate conditions affect the volume of production and income gained.

As shown in Table 2.1, the size of most agricultural enterprises is less than ten hectares and these small enterprises as a whole account for only a small proportion of total agricultural land. The number of enterprises operating on 50 or more hectares has gradually decreased over time, and most of them are in south-eastern Turkey where the land is less fertile than in other regions. There are some initiatives for increasing agricultural productivity in southern Turkey[3] such as the Southeastern Anatolian Project, or GAP project, which is a multifaceted integrated regional development project established on the Tigris and Euphrates rivers, covering a series of dams, hydroelectric power generators, and irrigation establishments.

Table 2.1 Distribution of Agricultural Enterprise According to Scale (percentages)
A: Number of enterprises B: Relative size of enterprises

Scale of enterprise	*1952*		*1963*		*1970*		*1980*		*1991*	
(Decare)*	A	B	A	B	A	B	A	B	A	B
1–20	30.6	4.3	40.9	7.0	44.4	8.0	28.0	3.9	34.9	5.6
21–50	31.5	14.3	27.8	17.3	28.2	18.7	32.5	15.7	32.1	16.5
51–100	21.9	20.7	18.1	23.9	15.7	22.0	21.0	21.4	17.9	19.9
101–200	10.3	19.3	9.4	23.7	7.7	21.5	11.9	24.0	9.6	21.0
201–500	4.2	16.6	3.2	17.0	3.1	17.9	5.4	22.7	4.4	19.8
500 +	1.5	24.8	0.6	11.1	0.9	11.9	0.7	12.3	0.9	17.1

*1 decare = 1000 square metres
Source: 1952, 1963, 1970, 1980, and 1991 *General Agricultural Census*.

It aims at improving the regional economy especially through agriculture and providing important contributions to the national economy as a whole.

Small enterprises dominate Turkish agriculture and the distribution of enterprises according to scale shows great diversity, especially in some regions such as the southern and eastern. The number of households which do not have any land increased between 1981–91. Around 300 000 households work either permanently or part-time on other farmers' land. These kinds of household can generally find work during the summertime – harvest time – but are unemployed during the rest of the year.

Usage of inputs, production and productivity

The agricultural labour force of around nine million did not change during the 1960–97 period. However, the ratio of labour in agriculture to total labour reduced from 75 per cent to 40 per cent during the same period. This finding is important for two reasons: first, agriculture transfers excess labour to other sectors; second, it is clear that productivity per worker has risen since significant increases in agricultural production were realized after 1960.

Agricultural land has remained at around 24 million hectares since 1960. Land gained through the usage of tractors started at the beginning and finished at the end of the 1950s. Therefore, the increase in agricultural production after the 1960s can be put down to improving the quality of land and increasing the usage of other inputs, apart from improving labour productivity.

The majority of the land belonging to agricultural enterprises is over-fragmented due to the inheritance laws where land is divided to enable it to be passed from generation to generation. Having over-fragmented land causes a waste of resources and time and difficulties in production planning and usage of equipment.

Another significant factor affecting agricultural land and, therefore, its productivity is soil erosion and pollution. Urbanization has also resulted in the fertile plains next to big settlements being used for housing in place of agriculture.

The usage of fertilizers and the extent of irrigated land increased between 1965–70. The number of tractors drastically rose between 1970–75. The usage of tractors and combine harvesters as indicators of mechanization in Turkish agriculture increased after 1980 with the facilitation of imports. During the 1980s agricultural inputs rose steadily, but since the state largely abolished agricultural subsidies while remaining in control of price fixing, this resulted in the price of produce decreasing in real terms and farmers being unable to find the necessary capital for investments.

Field crops account for around 60 per cent of total agricultural production, animal husbandry around 30 per cent, forestry 7–8 per cent, and fishery products 1–2 per cent. These percentages have not changed much year by year apart from the percentage of fishery products which has been gradually increasing in recent years.

The developments in some field crops are given in Table 2.3. Wheat, the fundamental indicator of cereals, is accepted as the

Table 2.2 Usage of Some Selected Inputs in Agriculture

Year	*Tractors*	*Combine harvesters*	*Fertilizers (000 tons)*	*Irrigated land (000 hectares)*
1955	40 282	5 618	—	—
1965	54 668	6 540	—	—
1970	105 865	8 568	—	1 914
1975	243 066	11 245	3 691	—
1980	436 369	13 667	5 967	2 706
1985	583 974	13 615	7 251	3 303
1990	692 454	11 741	9 509	3 900
1997	775 442	12 706	9 165	4 555

Source: Economic and Social Indicators (1950–1998), SPO, Ankara, 1997.

Table 2.3 Area Sown and Production of Selected Field Crops

Year	*A: Area sown (000 hectares)*								*B: Production (000 tons)*					
	Wheat		*Cotton*		*Sugar beet*		*Tobacco*		*Sunflowers*		*Lentils*		*Chickpeas*	
	A	B	A	B	A	B	A	B	A	B	A	B	A	B
1950	4 477	3 871	448	118	50	885	128	93	—	—	51	42	76	85
1960	7 700	8 450	621	175	202	4 384	189	139	137	123	104	98	86	97
1965	7 900	8 500	685	325	157	3 421	222	132	160	160	100	90	85	89
1970	8 600	10 000	527	400	123	4 253	328	149	360	375	108	92	100	109
1975	9 250	14 750	670	480	214	6 948	241	199	418	488	124	135	140	172
1980	9 020	16 500	671	500	269	6 766	222	228	575	750	191	195	240	275
1985	9 350	17 000	660	518	322	9 830	176	170	643	800	597	618	399	400
1990	9 450	20 000	641	654	379	13 985	320	296	716	860	906	846	890	860
1997	9 340	18 650	721	831	472	18 400	288	286	550	900	560	515	721	720

Sources: *Statistical Indicators (1923–1995)*, SIS, Ankara, 1996; *1997 Statistical Yearbook of Turkey*, SIS, Ankara, 1998.

symbol of agricultural development in Turkey. Annual wheat production doubled between 1960–97 and the wheat-sown area gradually increased in the same period. Both the area sown and production volume for cotton and tobacco rose between 1960–95. The production of sugar beet, which is an important industrial crop, increased fourfold in line with the increases in domestic sugar production at the beginning of the 1980s. The area sown for and production of lentils and chickpeas multiplied after the 1980s since they were in demand from export markets. In the same way, the sunflower production volume showed important developments between 1960–97.

Productivity as evaluated by yield per unit of land is an indicator of the development level in agriculture. Productivity increases can be accomplished through the correct use of fertilizer, quality seeds, appropriate equipment, irrigation and spraying, but the effective usage of such modern inputs for improving productivity depends on improving agricultural prices. The widespread usage of modern inputs in Turkey started in the 1960s although initiatives for agricultural developments started in 1923, the same year as the foundation of the republic. The productivity developments for some selected field crops are shown in Table 2.4.

Wheat productivity is far behind the world average although wheat consumption per person is very high. Likewise the productivity levels for tobacco and cotton are lower than the world average.

Table 2.4 Productivity of Selected Field Crops (kg/hectare)

Year	*Wheat*	*Cotton*	*Sugar beet*	*Tobacco*	*Sunflowers*	*Lentils*	*Chickpeas*
1925	344	437	1 752	849	—	393	645
1950	865	264	16 781	785	—	838	1 111
1960	1 097	283	21 608	735	898	942	1 121
1965	1 076	474	21 689	596	1 000	900	1 047
1970	1 163	758	34 348	456	1 042	852	1 090
1974	1 595	716	32 389	828	1 167	1 084	1 229
1980	1 829	744	25 119	1 024	1 304	1 021	1 146
1985	1 818	785	30 436	964	1 244	1 035	1 003
1990	2 116	1 021	36 819	924	1 021	934	966
1997	1 997	1 152	39 424	988	1 607	920	1 000

Sources: *Statistical Indicators* (1923–1995), SIS, Ankara, 1996; *1997 Statistical Yearbook of Turkey*, SIS, Ankara, 1998.

However, the levels for sugar beet are similar to the world average and for sunflowers marginally in excess of them.

Animal husbandry provides and increases the income of many small farming families. Furthermore, it supplies the raw materials for some food and clothing industries. However, animal husbandry accounts for around 20 per cent of total agricultural income although it is more than 50 per cent in developed countries. The importance of animal husbandry declined after 1980 due to the domestic trade rates developing against agriculture, the amount of pasture and meadow area being reduced by extensive usage, and the migration of farmers from eastern and south-eastern Turkey to western parts of the country. Productivity for animal husbandry is determined by the production volume per animal. The number of animals milked is 27 million head and milk production was ten million tons in 1997. The number of animals slaughtered was around ten million and meat production was 516 000 tons in the same year.

Forest area covers 25 per cent of the total land and the number of forest villages is high. However, the equipment and techniques used in production are very primitive. Ignorance causes devastation of vast swathes of forested area every year whilst the amount of forest is insufficient compared to the total land area.

Turkey has the potential to step up its production of fishery products since it is surrounded by sea on three sides and has many lakes and rivers. However, fishing and fish-farming has only started to be developed in recent years. Sea pollution poses a significant danger and refrigeration and deep-freezing establishments are insufficient. Fishery production was around 2 per cent of total agricultural production with 430 000 tons in 1997.

Foreign trade of agricultural products

Turkish exports were mainly made up of agricultural products until recent years. Traditional agricultural products, such as cotton, tobacco and dried fruits accounted for around 80 per cent of total exports from the foundation of the republic to the 1960s, dropping to 60–70 per cent during the 1970s.

The export of agricultural products started to decline as a result of the economic liberalization policies pursued at the beginning of the 1980s. The structure of Turkish exports drastically changed in favour of manufacturing and the rate of agricultural products in

Table 2.5 Export Shares by Main Sector (percentage)

Years	*Agriculture*	*Industry*	*Mining*
1960	76.0	17.9	6.1
1965	75.9	19.6	4.5
1970	75.2	17.1	7.7
1975	56.6	35.9	7.5
1980	57.4	36.0	6.6
1985	21.6	75.3	3.1
1990	17.4	79.9	2.5
1997	8.8	89.6	1.6

Source: *Economic and Social Indicators (1950–1998)*, SPO, December 1997.

total exports, which was 57 per cent in 1980, dropped to 18 per cent in 1987, 15 per cent in 1992 and 10 per cent in 1997. The change from an agricultural to a manufacturing orientation in Turkish exports is mainly the result of practising economic policies which give greater importance to manufacturing and deliberately neglect the agricultural sector.

The import of agricultural products increased commensurate with the free trade being practised after 1980. When there was no progress in the export of agricultural products, increasing imports caused significant changes in the foreign trade of agricultural products. The substitution rate of exports to imports decreased from 1500 per cent at the beginning of the 1980s to 100 per cent today.[4] As a result, Turkey became an importer of agricultural products.

Energy

Energy, one of the key indicators of economic and social development is of critical importance for countries with limited energy resources like Turkey that need to meet their domestic energy requirement through imports. There is a close relationship between energy consumption per person and the development level of any country – therefore, increasing total and individual energy consumption to be able to support economic and social development targets has been determined as one of the main objectives of Turkey's energy policy. There has been an almost equal increase both in energy consumption and gross national product (GNP) within the last twenty years. The rate of energy consumption increase to GNP has been 1.08 during this term.[5] Energy consumption per person in Turkey is a little more than the world average; it is a quarter of France's, and a fifth of Britain's and Germany's. Electricity consumption per person in Turkey is around the same as the world average; it is one-sixth of France's and one fifth of Britain's and Germany's.

The structure and development of the energy sector

From the primary energy resource variation aspect Turkey is a rather rich country. Lignite (brown coal) and hydraulic energy are important resources and also petroleum, coal, asphalt, natural gas, geothermal energy, wood, animal and vegetable waste and solar energy as primary resources, and electricity, coke and briquette as secondary resources, are produced for consumption. The country's energy resources at the end of 1996 are given in Table 2.6.

Table 2.6 Turkey's Primary Energy Reserves (at the end of 1996)

Resources	*Visible*	*Provable*	*Possible*	*Total*
Coal (million tons)	428*	449	249	1 126
Lignite (million tons)	7 339	626	110	8 075**
Asphalt	45	29	8	82
Bitumen	555	1 086		1 641
Hydraulic				
GWh/year	123 799			123 799
MW/year	35 045			35 045
Raw petroleum (million tons)	48.4			48.8
Natural gas (billion m^3)	8.8			8.8
Nuclear resources				
Natural uranium	9 129			9 129
Thorium	380 000			380 000
Geothermal (MW/year)				
Electricity	200		4 300	4 500
Thermal	2 250		28 850	31 100
Solar (million tons of oil equivalent)				
Electricity				8.8
Heat				26.4

* Including ready reserve

** It becomes 8375 million tons together with 300 million tons determined and potential resources

Source: World Energy Council, *Turkish National Assembly 1996 Energy Report*.

Turkey's coal resources together with geothermal and hydraulic energy potential amount to 1 per cent of world resources. However, petroleum and natural gas reserves are very limited. Therefore, despite having every kind of energy resource Turkey's resources are insufficient in terms of quantity and quality.

Domestic energy production does not meet the consumption rate and this shortfall is made up by energy imports, the value of which in total supply is gradually increasing. For example, while the share of imports in total supply was 32 per cent in 1970, it increased to 59 per cent in 1990 and 64 per cent in 1997. The share of petroleum in total supply has changed and it is estimated that while the share of petroleum in total supply was 82 per cent in 1988[6] it will drop to 53–55 per cent in 2000 due to the increase in the consumption of coal and natural gas. In parallel with the increase in imports, the share of domestic energy production in total supply has decreased. For example, while the rate of domestic production/total supply was 72 per cent in 1970, it dropped to 48 per cent in 1990 and 44 per cent in 1997. The share of exports within domestic production was 0.7 per cent in 1970; it increased to 9 per cent in 1990 and 11 per cent in 1992, thereafter settling at an average of 7 per cent. Table 2.7 shows the general energy balance in Turkey since 1970.

Primary energy resources

The production of primary energy resources in terms of tons of petrol equivalent during 1970–97 is given in Table 2.8. A striking point in the table is the change in the production composition. Wood took first place and lignite second in front of petroleum during the period 1976–84, while wood was in first place and petroleum second in the total production in 1970. From 1984–97 lignite took first place and wood and petroleum second and third respectively. Another noteworthy point in the table is that the share of primary resources in total resources changed in the 1980s when new energy types started to be employed. In 1997 the share of lignite is 42 per cent, wood 20 per cent, petroleum 13 per cent, hydraulic 12 per cent, coal 5 per cent, animal and vegetable waste 5 per cent, while in 1970 the share of wood in total production was 27 per cent, petroleum 26 per cent, coal 20 per cent, animal and vegetable waste 15 per cent, lignite 12 per cent, hydraulic 2 per cent and asphalt 1 per cent.

Table 2.7 General Energy Balance by Year (thousand tons of oil equivalent)

Year	*Domestic production*	*Import*	*Export*	*Total energy supply*	*Used in transformation and energy sectors*	*Final energy consumption*	*Energy consumption per person*
1970	14 355	6 375	106	20 050	2 476	17 574	554
1975	16 138	11 020	728	25 485	3 688	21 797	653
1980	17 298	15 031	301	31 913	4 465	27 448	718
1985	20 144	19 030	1 833	37 247	5 678	31 569	759
1990	25 123	30 936	2 104	52 632	11 377	41 256	938
1995	26 255	39 779	1 947	63 180	13 703	49 477	1 016
1997	27 536	46 053	1 630	71 754	16 319	56 435	1 117

Note: Total energy supply includes changes in the inventory and statistical mistakes as well as domestic production, import and export figures.
Source: Turkey's 7th Energy Congress, *Energy Statistics*, 1997.

Table 2.8 The Production of Primary Energy Resources (Thousand tons of oil equivalent)

Year	*Coal*	*Lignite*	*Asphalt*	*Petroleum*	*Natural gas*	*Hydraulic*	*Geothermal*		*Solar*	*Wood*	*Animal and vegetable waste*	*Total*
							Electricity	*Heat*				
1970	2 790	1 735	15	3 719	–	261	–	–	–	3 845	2 128	14 493
1976	2 826	3 006	190	2 725	14	720	–	–	–	4 420	2 530	16 430
1980	2 195	3 738	240	2 447	21	976	–	–	–	4 730	2 953	17 298
1984	2 216	6 498	97	2 191	36	1 155	19	–	–	5 177	2 755	20 144
1986	2 151	8 949	261	2 514	416	1 021	38	–	5	5 271	2 609	23 234
1989	2 027	10 564	179	3 020	158	1 543	54	5	16	5 345	2 504	24 267
1995	1 319	10 735	29	3 692	166	3 057	74	64	52	5 512	1 556	26 255
1997	1 341	11 598	13	3 630	228	3 424	71	127	80	5 512	1 512	27 536

Sources: *Statistical Indicators 1923–1995*, SIS Publication No. 1883, Ankara, 1996; Turkey's 7th Energy Congress, *Energy Statistics, 1997*.

These changes in the composition of consumption occurred in parallel with the use of new energy resources such as natural gas, geothermal heat, and solar energy. It can be seen from Table 2.9 that since 1970 the traditional primary energy resources have been losing their importance with the appearance of the new ones.

Electric energy

The installed capacity of electricity power plants, which is important for the development of the country as a secondary energy resource is given in Table 2.10. It is seen that the installed capacity showed a 19 012 MW increase from 1970 to 1996. The installed capacity of 21 889 MW in 1997 is met by 11 786 MW thermal resources and 10 103 MW hydraulic resources. Lignite power stations started to make up most of the thermal capacity after 1980. Natural gas power stations, which started to operate since 1985, have increased their share and the importance of lignite power stations has subsequently decreased. To be able to adequately meet the demand for electricity which is expected to be 290 million MW/year in 2010 and 547 million MW/year in 2020, a 43 000 MW/year capacity increase until 2010 is required, and an additional 44 000 MW/year – on top of the previous capacity increase – until 2020 is needed.

This implies that an annual 3500–4000 MW installed power addition into the system is required until 2020, or an annual investment of US$3.4–4 billion. This amount rises to US$4.5–5 billion when the additional investments necessary to link the extra power to the transmission and distribution system are taken into consideration.

Manufacturing

Turkey has taken major steps in manufacturing during the last 30 years, especially after the 1980s when import substitution industrialization was abandoned and the export-oriented development strategy implemented. While the share of manufacturing in GNP was 17 per cent in 1970 it became 24.3 per cent in 1997 with around 17 per cent of the working population being employed in it. These figures indicate that although manufacturing has improved, agriculture still has great importance in total employment.

The share of fixed capital investment in manufacturing decreased in the years when the manufacturing production volume rose.

Table 2.9 Consumption of Primary Energy Resources (Thousand tons of oil equivalent)

Year	*Coal*	*Lignite*	*Asphalt*	*Petroleum*	*Natural gas*	*Electricity*	*Geothermal heat*	*Solar energy*	*Wood*	*Animal and vegetable waste*	*Other*	*Total*
1970	1 008	1 370	15	6 675	0	622	0	0	3 845	2 128	1 155	16 818
1976	789	2 278	190	12 953	14	1 366	0	0	4 420	2 530	1 345	25 885
1980	622	2 757	240	12 911	21	1 727	0	0	4 730	2 953	1 487	27 448
1984	903	4 117	96	14 163	36	2 336	0	0	5 177	2 755	1 986	31 569
1986	942	4 230	260	16 011	42	2 715	0	5	5 271	2 609	2 200	34 285
1989	1 590	5 372	175	18 957	410	3 627	5	16	5 345	2 504	2 053	40 054
1995	1 979	3 678	28	24 943	3 035	5 652	64	52	5 512	1 556	2 978	49 477
1997	3 944	4 039	12	26 288	4 271	7 355	127	80	5 512	1 512	3 295	56 435

Source: Turkey's 7th Energy Congress, *Energy Statistics*, 1997.

Table 2.10 The Development of Installed Electricity Power Capacity (MW)

Year	*Thermo-electricity*	*Hydraulic electricity*	*Total*
1970	1 509.5	725.4	2 234.9
1975	2 407.0	1 779.6	4 186.6
1980	2 987.9	2 130.8	5 118.7
1985	5 244.3	3 874.8	9 119.1
1990	9 550.8	6 764.3	16 315.1
1995	11 089.0	9 862.8	20 951.8
1996	11 311.8	9 934.8	21 246.6
1997	11 786.0	10 103.0	21 889.0

Source: World Energy Council Turkish National Assembly, *1996 Energy Report*, 1997.

Simultaneously, the share of investment goods imported reduced. Therefore, increases in the value added were accomplished by increasing the rate of capacity utilization and curtailing domestic demand.[7]

Size of enterprise

The relative weight of small and large enterprises can give an idea about the technological level, competition structure, capital accumulation and creation of employment in the sector.

According to Table 2.11, the share of small- and medium-sized enterprises (SMEs, or KOBİs) (1–99 employees) in manufacturing is 99 per cent, and small enterprises with 1–49 employees comprise 98.4 per cent of total manufacturing enterprises. Therefore, it could be said that the Turkish manufacturing industry is based on KOBİs. However, the rate of increase in the number of large enterprises

Table 2.11 The Distribution of Manufacturing Enterprises According to Size

Year	*(1–9)*	*%*	*(10–49)*	*%*	*(50–99)*	*%*	*(100+)*	*%*	*Total*
1970	170 479	97.3	3 391	1.9	604	0.3	825	0.5	175 299
1980	177 159	95.3	6 573	3.5	627	0.5	1 194	0.6	185 853
1985	183 106	94.5	8 033	4.1	1 128	0.6	1 483	0.8	193 750
1992	185 458	94.3	7 973	4.1	1 406	0.7	1 827	0.9	196 664

Source: *SIS General Industry and Enterprises Census 1992.*

with 100 plus employees has recently been higher than that in the number of KOBİs.

According to Table 2.12, KOBİs provide 53.4 per cent of total employment while the large enterprises employed 46.6 per cent of total labour in manufacturing in 1992. It can be concluded that KOBİs have a vital role in creating new jobs in Turkish manufacturing.

The importance of public and private enterprises in manufacturing

In the Turkish economy, public and private enterprises function together in every sector. Public enterprises relatively dominated Turkish manufacturing until the beginning of the 1980s. One of the main characteristics of the industrialization policy pursued after 1980 was the importance it placed on the private sector in the industrialization process. Consequently, the privatization of public enterprises by selling them to private domestic and foreign investors and making manufacturing depend on private enterprises was accepted as the principle. Public enterprises function in 23 sub-sectors and do not produce leather and fur, glass and glass products, or plastic products. However, in oil refining there is a public enterprise monopoly. From the data reflecting the percentage of the number of enterprises, annual average numbers of employees and value added between the public and private sector in Table 2.13, it is seen that the relative importance of public enterprises in manufacturing has lessened over time.

The distribution of value-added percentages between the public and private sub-sectors is given in Table 2.14. According to the data,

Table 2.12 The Distribution of Employment According to Size of Enterprise

Size of Enterprise	*1970* %	*1980* %	*1985* %	*1992* %
Very small (1–9 employees)	39	38	36	35.5
Small (10–49 employees)	9	11	12	11.5
Medium-sized (50–99 employees)	5	5	5	6.4
Large (100+ employees)	47	46	47	46.6

Source: SIS General Industry and Enterprises Census 1992.

Table 2.13 The Relative Importance of Public and Private Enterprises in Manufacturing

	1970		*1980*		*1985*		*1990*		*1993*	
	Public	*Private*	*Public*	*Private*	*Public*	*Private*	*Public*	*Private*	*Public*	*Private*
Number of enterprises	5.26	94.73	4.68	95.31	3.68	96.31	4.62	95.37	3.84	96.15
Annual average number of employees	36.79	63.20	36.49	63.50	29.79	70.21	24.39	75.60	21.79	78.20
Value added	54.27	45.72	40.40	59.59	88.02	61.97	31.27	68.72	25.57	74.43

Source: *Statistical Indicators (1923–1995)*, SIS, Ankara, 1996.

Table 2.14 The Distribution of Value-Added Percentages between the Public and Private Sectors in Sub-Manufacturing Sectors

Sub-manufacturing sectors	*1985*		*1987*		*1994*	
	Public	*Private*	*Public*	*Private*	*Public*	*Private*
Food, beverages, tobacco	61.45	38.55	52.47	47.53	30.00	70.00
Textile, apparel, leather	10.09	89.91	9.28	90.72	72.90	27.10
Wood and wood cork products	50.40	49.60	37.88	62.12	13.13	86.87
Paper and paper products, printing	39.40	60.60	24.03	75.97	17.12	82.88
Chemicals and of petroleum, coal, rubber and plastics	61.82	38.18	53.14	46.86	55.45	44.55
Non-metallic mineral products	14.86	85.14	14.34	85.66	5.09	94.91
Basic metal products	43.16	56.84	43.86	56.14	50.17	49.83
Fabricated metal products	12.15	87.85	8.60	91.40	5.02	94.98
Other manufacturing industries	–	100.00	–	100.00	9.82	90.18

Source: *1981 Statistical Yearbook of Turkey*, 100th Year Special Edition, SIS, Ankara, 1981.

the private sector creates more value-added than the public sector especially in food, beverages, tobacco, textiles, apparel and leather, wood and wood products, paper and paper products, non-metallic mineral products and basic manufactured products.

The public sector reduced its fixed investments in manufacturing after 1980. It realized 2.9 per cent at current prices in 1997 while the share of the public sector's fixed investments in manufacturing was 19.8 per cent in 1970 and then increased to 27.2 per cent in 1975. However, it started reducing afterwards. The private sector made 38.8 per cent of its fixed investments in manufacturing in 1970 and 43.3 per cent in 1975. Nevertheless, it shrank to 24.5 per cent in 1997.

Production of major manufactured products

Production of some selected manufactured products is shown in Table 2.15.

It can be seen that the production of major manufactured products shows an increase year by year although decreases in some products are observed in some years. It is interesting to note that the production of most of the manufactured products greatly increased after the 1980s.

Capacity utilization

Capacity utilization in manufacturing has gradually improved with the most remarkable improvements being achieved in non-metallic minerals, textiles, ready-to-wear apparel and leather, and wood or cork products. The private sector has made bigger improvements than the public sector in the same sub-manufacturing sectors. The distribution of capacity utilization percentages between public and private sectors in the sub-manufacturing sectors is given in Table 2.16.

Foreign trade of manufactured products

Turkey was regarded as an agricultural country until the 1980s when she changed the amount and structure of her exports. The export of manufactured products has increased and the share of manufacturing in GNP has continuously grown while the export of agricultural products has decreased since 1980. This can be seen as an indication of the country progressing towards industrialization. However, an important part of the main manufacturing products is related to agriculture-oriented products. The share of agriculture-oriented sub-sectors in total manufacturing exports, which was 20.3 billion dollars in 1995, is 15.7 per cent. The chief export products are textiles, tobacco, apparel, iron and steel, all kinds of machinery and mechanical equipment, and vehicles while the chief import items are chemicals, paper and paper-related products, iron and steel, all kinds of machinery and mechanical equipment, and vehicles.

Significantly, the ratio of capital and intermediate goods to total import value is high although the import value of consumer goods increased recently. Existing manufacturing is heavily dependent on the import of capital and intermediate goods. However, Turkey is making significant progress in producing consumer goods.

Table 2.15 Production of Some Selected Manufactured Products

Years	Steel ingot (000 tons)	Blistered copper (tons)	Glass and glassware (000 tons)	Cement (000 tons)	Sugar (000 tons)	Cotton textiles (000 metres)	Woollen textiles (000 metres)
1960	310	16 075	—	2 038	643	527 106	19 598
1970	1 600	18 951	160	6 734	592	610 000	26 500
1980	2 380	15 937	199	12 581	868	734 872	46 990
1985	4 884	33 505	611	17 581	1 286	960 000	52 000
1990	9 322	25 168	490	24 416	1 289	1 061 000	60 500
1995	12 745	26 065	506	33 143	1 375	1 210 000	69 500
1997	13 750	33 000	740	36 500	2 050	1 360 000	71 000

Years	Cars	Buses	Trucks	Refrigerators	Washing Machines	Television (colour)
1968	—	525	9 543	87 826	51 951	—
1970	—	805	6 434	126 508	60 009	—
1973	46 855	1 247	11 810	293 636	97 187	—
1980	29 114	1 475	7 584	629 049	231 099	—
1985	60 360	1 703	14 351	487 767	344 848	1 016 616
1990	166 222	1 663	16 679	986 574	743 957	1 994 621
1995	222 145	1 201	19 172	1 662 835	865 747	1 859 333
1997	236 419	3 448	43 618	1 945 920	1 481 934	4 657 007

Sources: *Main Economic Indicators*, SPO, January 1999; *Statistical Yearbook of Turkey 1998*, SIS, December 1997; *Economic and Social Indicators (1950–1998)*, SIS, December 1997.

Table 2.16 The Distribution of Capacity Utilization (Weighted by Production Values)

Sub-manufacturing sectors	*1978*		*1983*		*1987*		*1992*		*1995*		*1996*	
	Public	*Private*	*Public*	*Private*	*Public*	*Private*	*Public*	*Private*	*Public*	*Private*	*Public*	*Private*
Food, beverages, tobacco	71.1	61.7	63.5	58.8	77.9	73.0	74.6	67.0	70.4	72.8	73.1	71.8
Textile, apparel, leather	75.3	61.6	70.3	64.3	84.5	82.3	74.6	79.5	63.3	83.5	60.8	83.7
Forestry products	72.6	58.5	74.0	54.5	84.7	75.9	68.5	72.1	60.4	74.4	42.0	79.2
Paper and paper products	71.1	62.4	65.0	61.0	83.7	82.0	81.4	75.5	82.9	81.6	70.3	79.9
Chemicals	66.7	56.7	71.5	58.8	85.4	74.2	78.5	73.5	85.9	78.2	84.4	75.3
Soil products	62.0	58.6	78.0	57.5	82.1	86.4	70.5	88.5	75.4	87.7	70.2	87.6
Basic metal	66.0	58.7	60.5	54.5	67.0	74.8	86.9	77.9	79.1	75.9	89.6	80.0
Machinery	67.1	56.8	71.5	58.0	71.1	74.0	57.0	75.3	58.4	72.7	81.7	69.8
Other manufacturing	00.0	60.4	77.5	60.3	00.0	65.7	68.2	59.3	50.0	69.2	70.0	72.0
Total	70.6	60.2	67.5	59.3	80.7	76.8	77.8	75.6	80.5	77.9	82.0	76.5

Source: *Economic and Social Indicators (1950–1998)*, SPO, Ankara, 1997.
Note: For 1978 and 1983 capacity utilization rates refer to simple (unweighted) averages.

Mining

Mining can be regarded as an important source of capital accumulation when it is utilized properly although it requires large-scale research and investment. Mining has been vital for establishing the metallurgy sector and helping the development of agriculture by providing the necessary minerals for fertilizers in Turkey.

The share of mining in GNP was 1.4 per cent at producers' prices in 1997. Around 0.8 per cent of the active population worked in the mining sector in 1997.

Mining production

Mining was carried out by foreign companies before the establishment of the republic. After 1932 it was put under state control. Great importance was given to the private sector in parallel with the economic policy applied after 1945. In 1979, the main mines, especially lignite and iron were taken under state control due to a law nationalizing mines. The mines which were nationalized before were left to their ex-owners by legislating a new mining law in 1983. Therefore, it can be said that mining has been the subject of privatization and nationalization discussions for many years.

Mining sector production rates were constant during the 1970s, increased in the first years of the 1980s and have since remained constant.

Table 2.17 Mining Production (thousand tons)

Year	*Lignite*	*Coal*	*Chrome*	*Iron ore*	*Crude oil*	*Boron*
1950	1 214	4 360	422	233	—	—
1960	3 866	6 317	591	797	375	97
1965	6 350	7 019	585	1 545	1 532	196
1970	8 772	7 608	772	2 949	3 541	523
1975	11 856	8 360	952	2 359	3 095	964
1980	16 997	6 598	550	2 578	2 370	1 333
1985	39 437	7 260	876	3 994	2 109	1 543
1990	46 892	5 628	1 204	4 924	3 753	2 062
1995	56 031	3 377	2 080	4 931	3 515	1 768
1996	57 532	3 581	1 279	6 279	3 499	2 400

Sources: *Statistical Indicators (1923–1995)*, SIS, Ankara, 1996; *1997 Statistical Yearbook of Turkey*, SIS, Ankara, 1998.

Although the private sector owns the majority of mining enterprises this does not imply that mining is based on private enterprise. On the contrary, the public sector has a clear advantage in that its mines are generally larger than the privately owned ones, a situation which, overall, has enabled it to employ larger numbers of people and make more sales. Also, the public sector has a relative predominance when it comes to technology and capital investment.

Development in the production rate of the mining sector can be explained with the increases in the fixed investments in the sector. The share of mining in total fixed investments changed between 2–3 per cent during the 1970s. It rose above 5 per cent in the first half of the 1980s together with increases in production and gradually dropped to a level of 1.3 per cent. It can be said that the production increase became constant or changed depending on the capacity utilization during the years in which fixed investments in the mining sector decreased.

Construction

Construction is one of the most important sectors in Turkey. The need for infrastructure and public services as a developing country and also the rapid increase in the population and urbanization make the construction sector vital for the economy.

The share of construction in GNP was 5.9 per cent in 1997 with around 5.5 per cent of the active population employed in the sector. The distribution of total buildings was 94.3 per cent for housing, 2.9 per cent for commercial, 1.4 per cent for industrial, 0.2 per cent for medical, social and cultural, and 1.2 per cent for other purposes in 1997. The share of the public sector in total buildings is negligible and increasingly lessening.

The majority of buildings are made of brick and reinforced concrete. Around 40 per cent of construction is in cities whose population is more than 100 000 with the bigger cities taking the highest proportion of construction. This causes two awry developments. First, the model of 'build and sell' (*yap-sat*) dominates housing construction in the bigger cities. This provokes land speculation which increases the economic rent. Second, the shanty towns (*gecekondu*) around the big cities have become a kind of settlement.

Table 2.18 The Distribution of Buildings by Purpose of Usage (percentage)

Year	*Residential buildings*	*Commercial*	*Industrial*	*Medical, social and cultural*	*Others*
1970	74.3	13.3	2.4	0.4	9.6
1975	76.0	17.0	2.2	0.4	4.4
1980	88.9	6.1	1.7	0.4	2.9
1985	86.0	6.8	2.6	0.8	3.8
1990	88.7	4.5	3.2	0.7	3.0
1996	88.0	4.3	3.4	0.8	4.5
1997	94.3	2.9	1.4	0.2	1.2

Sources: Statistical Indicators (1923–1995), SIS, Ankara, 1996; *Statistical Yearbook of Turkey 1998*, SIS Publication No. 2240, Ankara, January 1999.

The construction sector progressed well in parallel with the development of the country during the 1970s but was affected by the recession in the economy caused by the world oil crisis at the end of the 1970s and beginning of the 1980s.

The share of housing in total fixed investments was 26.8 per cent at current prices in 1970 and did not change very much until 1987. It reached the level of 27.9 per cent in 1987, went to above 30 per cent afterwards and became 29.9 per cent in 1997.

The biggest share of construction investments during 1970–97 was made in the industrialized Marmara region with 31.57 per cent. Eastern Turkey received the least, with just 3.8 per cent.[8]

Table 2.19 Production of Residential Housing According to Type of Permit

Year	*Construction permits*	*Occupancy permits*
1970	154 825	71 589
1980	203 989	139 207
1985	259 187	118 205
1987	497 674	191 109
1990	381 408	232 018
1993	548 129	269 695
1997	458 000	273 000

Source: Economic and Social Indicators (1950–1998), SPO, Ankara, 1997.

Construction carried out by Turkish constructors in foreign countries is very important for the national economy. During the last thirty years Turkish constructors have done 35 billion dollars business overseas. The sectoral activities first started in North African, Middle Eastern and Gulf countries after the 1973 oil crisis when the members of OPEC decided to allocate surplus financial resources to infrastructure and construction investments. Between 1981–87 the Turkish construction services sector faced some serious difficulties in these countries since they have been directly or indirectly negatively affected by political and economic developments. After 1990, the construction services sector changed its target to countries with natural gas projects and to housing projects for Russian soldiers returning from East Germany. Former Soviet Union countries are today an important market for the sector. The Turkish construction services sector overseas employs a total of 54 000 people, of which most are Turkish.

Tourism

Tourism is an important sector for the Turkish economy with its forward and backward economic linkages to other sectors, injection of foreign currency into the economy, and contribution to employment. The share of tourism income in GNP was 0.6 per cent in 1973, and became 5 per cent in 1997. The rate of tourism income to total export income was 13 per cent in 1973, and reached 28.3 per cent in 1997. The rate of tourism income to the foreign trade deficit was 22 per cent in 1973, and reached 43 per cent in 1997. It is clear from the data that the Turkish tourism sector has advanced in leaps and bounds over the 1970–98 period.

The supply side of tourism

The supply elements of tourism have a somewhat complex structure since the end product emerges as resultant services by bringing together a number of products and services, sometimes from other sectors. Therefore, the supply side of Turkish tourism should be studied through physical facilities, infrastructure, and the structure and nature of employment.

One of the primary supply elements which has a direct relation to total demand within physical facilities, is lodging establishments.

The number of establishments, rooms and beds has continuously increased, especially after 1982. There was a lull after 1992 but facilities started to increase again in 1997. Table 2.20 below gives an idea about the developments in the lodging facilities. In addition, the total number of lodging establishments run with municipality accreditation was 8406 and their bed capacity 606 000 in 1997.

Although the number of quality bed capacity is around 250 000, more than 90 per cent of it is in hotels and holiday villages and 82 per cent is concentrated in the Mediterranean, Marmara and Aegean regions.

Infrastructure in almost every touristic zone is either non-existent or insufficient and is an important restriction on the economic benefits expected from the sector. Investments in infrastructure are being made with political pressure in order to remove short-term problems instead of acting on priorities. Moreover, with domestic migration and demand for summer housing, the infrastructure systems can not meet the demand. This problem has recently reached a level at which it affects demand from those tourists expecting upscale services.

Also, the background of the workforce directly affects the quality level of the services offered in the sector. The level of education and the skills, attitudes and behaviour of the people employed in it affect the characteristics and consequently the competition position of the services offered. Around 85 per cent of employers in the sector have not had any professional education and it seems that

Table 2.20 The Number of Lodging Establishments, Rooms and Beds

	Lodging facilities with tourism investment incentives			*Lodging facilities with tourism enterprise incentives*		
Year	*Establishments*	*Rooms*	*Beds*	*Establishments*	*Rooms*	*Beds*
1976	227	12 802	26 068	439	24 983	47 307
1980	267	13 019	26 288	511	28 992	56 044
1985	501	34 251	71 521	689	41 351	85 995
1990	1 921	156 702	325 515	1 260	83 953	173 227
1992	1 938	148 017	309 139	1 498	105 476	219 940
1995	1 334	96 517	202 483	1 793	135 436	280 463
1996	1 309	96 592	202 631	1 886	145 493	301 524
1997	1 402	110 866	236 632	1 193	151 055	313 293

Source: Ministry of Tourism.

educational institutions can not meet the demand for professional employees in the short term. In addition, entrepreneurs, employees and managers without an education related to the sector and seasonal activities reduce the level of service quality.

The natural structure of the country gives it the chance to capitalize on all kinds of touristic activity. However, in the places where lodging facilities are concentrated the natural surroundings and environment are starting to be destroyed.

The demand side of tourism

Demand from domestic and foreign tourists started rapidly increasing at the end of the 1980s and reached a total of 67 million overnight stays in 1996.

However, it is more interesting to study foreign demand due to the important role of exchange inflows in the development of the country. In 1970, 724 000 tourists visited Turkey and left a $52 million income. In 1980 around one million tourists came and this resulted in a $326 million income. In 1990, Turkey hosted over five million tourists and earned a $3.2 billion income. Turkey took 17th place among the countries attracting the most tourists with 9.7 million visitors and a $7.2 billion income in 1997. Almost 80 per cent of total foreign tourism demand stayed in three provinces – Istanbul, Antalya and Muğla. These figures are explained in detail in Table 2.21.

Table 2.21 Tourism Activities, Revenues and Expenditures

Years	*Number of tourist arrivals*	*Number of citizens travelling abroad*	*Tourism revenues (million $)*	*Tourism expenditures (million $)*
1950	36 372	—	2	8
1963	198 841	41 833	8	21
1970	724 784	515 992	52	48
1980	1 057 364	1 324 159	326	104
1985	2 190 217	1 848 702	1 094	324
1990	5 397 748	2 937 546	3 225	520
1995	7 747 389	4 045 143	4 955	911
1997	9 700 000	4 700 000	7 500	2 000

Source: *Economic and Social Indicators (1950–1998)*, SIS, December 1997.

Investments

During the 1970s technical infrastructure investments, marinas and lodging facilities which are called example facilities were made by the state. The share of tourism investments in total fixed investments realized under 1 per cent. The tourism investment incentive law was put into effect in 1982 to develop the sector and bring some necessary regulations. Through the incentives given by the state, bed capacity rapidly increased while most modern and quality touristic facilities were built during these years. The share of tourism investments in total fixed investments reached 1.3 per cent in 1985 and 3.9 per cent in 1989. In the first half of the 1990s, marketing and promotion were given special importance to increase the occupancy rate. In parallel with the increase of supply capacity, the efforts to provide a qualified workforce increased. In the second half of 1990, apart from the diversification of tourism activities and mass market tourism, different market segments were concentrated on. Promotion activities were increased in Japan, the US, Canada, the Asia-Pacific region, former Soviet Union countries and the Gulf states, as well as in traditional markets such as Britain, Germany and France. The share of tourism investment in total fixed investment dropped to 2.1 per cent in 1998.

The banking sector

The Turkish financial system between 1923–80 has some common characteristics compared to the post-1980 liberalization period. Because of the importance of the banking sector in the financial sector, developments in it will be discussed within the banking sector. This will be done by dividing the developments in the banking sector into two periods.

General overview of the banking sector before 1980

Prior to 1980 the banking system was the foundation of the Turkish financial system; it played the role of the financial system with responsibility for carrying out all money transactions, instead of becoming specialized banks. The lending of medium- and long-term funds by the banks delayed the establishment of a stock exchange market in Turkey. Only the existence of money markets in the financial system, and the control of most of the money movements by the banks caused an increase in the activities of illegal lending organizations.[9] The loan sharks who more easily collected the funds than the regular banks and not enough organized money and capital markets created a difficult situation for the banks. Therefore, the banks wanted to work like the loan sharks who wanted to enter the money market with the tools of the capital market. This led to a competition war and resulted in the crisis in the Turkish financial system. This prompted a guided interest policy to start and be practised under the leadership of the public banks.

The public sector was accustomed to dominating the banking system through the Central Bank of Turkey and other large public banks. The banking sector had an oligopolistic nature far removed from competition. For example, in 1979 six large banks were controlling 63.4 per cent of total credits and 73.1 per cent of total deposits and these banks had 66.6 per cent of total assets.

The banks in Turkey chose to have excessive numbers of branches, even several in the same town and along the same street. They preferred working with labour-intensive methods without installing labour-saving automation equipment.

Trading and industrial corporations had to use excessive bank credits instead of providing necessary funds through supplying shares and securities due to the fact that a stock exchange had not yet been established and the interest rates on credits remained lower than the inflation rate. Banks either established new trading and industrial corporations or became partners of existing corporations in order to increase interest income which they shared with industrialists and traders. Consequently the affiliates and subsidiaries of banks reached an important level during this term.

Table 2.22 The Number of Banks and Branches

Years	*1924*	*1930*	*1958*	*1965*	*1975*	*1980*	*1985*	*1990*	*1993*	*1997*
Banks	35	61	62	49	43	44	51	66	70	72
Branches	439	424	1 653	1 981	4 605	5 975	6 292	6 584	6 250	6 819

Source: The Union of Turkish Banks, various reports.

Doing transactions and having assets in terms of foreign currency for banks has been strictly stipulated by law since the country went through the foreign currency crisis in the late 1970s. Neither could the equities of banks be increased to a sufficient level nor could an efficient supervision and auditing system be established. Enough capital capacity could not be provided and the deterioration in the asset balance could not be prevented, therefore, some banks had to stop their activities.

The resources of the Central Bank have been used to provide credits to the sectors given priority as if those resources belonged to a development and investment bank.

Developments in the banking sector after 1980

The banking system was one of the areas affected by the serious changes in economic policy after 1980. The main aim of the financial aspects of the 1980 economic policy was to strengthen the regulative effects of the market mechanism and to remove the conditions restricting competition in the sector. The first step in this direction was to permit the establishment of new domestic and foreign banks. The number of banks became 72 in 1997, while it was 43 in 1980. The banks started giving more importance to the services of foreign exchange and trade due to the increase in the volume of foreign trade after 1980. In addition to traditional banking services, they offered new international finance methods such as factoring, leasing, and export credit insurance.

The main purpose of the interest rate policy pursued after 1980 was to set deposit and credit interest rates free and apply positive real interest rates. These practices caused a rise in the interest rates. Banks first competed with loan sharks and then with each other for obtaining funds. Increases in the interest rates were in line with inflation rate increases and this was one of the main reasons for high inflation. Increased interest rates pushed the banks into reducing their personnel and other costs and moving away from having extensive branches. On the other hand, increase in the interest rates changed the deposit composition of banks towards the fixed rate deposit and foreign currency deposit accounts. As a result, average costs of deposits increased dramatically.

The Stock Exchange Market law came into force on 30 July 1981 and a Stock Exchange Council was formed according to this law.

The Stock Exchange Council, which is responsible for regulating, auditing and developing the stock exchange market, constituted the legal structure of the market by issuing official procedures. During the years after enforcing the law, new organizations functioning in the stock exchange market such as intermediary organizations, investment partnerships, and investment funds were established. The size of transactions was not really large enough during the first few years but has been gradually increasing with the entrance of new investors, especially foreign ones.

The Interbank Money Market was established on 2 April 1986 with the aim of efficient usage of resources in the banking system. Through the Central Bank the banks with a cash surplus in the short term met the banks with a short-term cash deficit in the Interbank Money Market. In this way, money movements within each bank could be traced, the liquidity requirement of the economy could be determined by taking the total reserve of the system into consideration, the additional money emission requirement could be substantially reduced and the fluctuations in the interest rates could be anticipated daily and within the same day.

As an application of the stabilization program which was enforced on 24 January 1980, the foreign exchange regime, which had been strictly stipulated for a long time, was liberalized and real foreign exchange rates were put into practice. The banks were authorized to have foreign currency and to carry out transactions in terms of foreign currency. In parallel with the liberalization of the foreign exchange regime the Interbank Foreign Exchange Market was activated within the Central Bank in order to help determine foreign exchange rates under free market conditions.

Another important institutional development was the establishment of a Gold Equivalent in the Foreign Currency Market on 28 March 1989. However, this market ended its activities with the establishment of the Istanbul Gold Market on 26 July 1995.

The banking system

The magnitude of the system's balance sheet increased to $96.6 billion at the end of 1997 while it was $52.8 billion at the end of 1996.[10] The private deposit banks have the largest percentage in the system with 53.3 per cent, followed by the public deposit banks with 35.2 per cent. The development and investment banks and foreign capital deposit banks have a small percentage with 5.3 per cent and 4.2 per cent respectively.

Banks help economic activities not only by transferring funds to individuals and companies who demand credits but also by creating nominal money. Therefore, the banks are the organizations serving society and substantially affecting economic activities. In order to reflect this characteristic of the Turkish banking sector, Table 2.23 shows some selected accounts of its consolidated balance sheet and their percentage in GNP.

The ratio of total assets to GNP which shows the share of the Turkish banking sector in the economy increased during the years 1986–96. While the ratio of total assets to GNP was 41 per cent in 1990 it realized 60 per cent in 1996, figures which clearly identify the position of the banking sector in the Turkish economy.

The equities of the Turkish banking sector amounted to $8.6 billion in 1997. In the same year the share of foreign capital deposit banks in total equities was 10.3 per cent, private deposit banks 10.2 per cent, public deposit banks 5.7 per cent and development and investment banks 15.1 per cent.

The Central Bank of Turkey

The Central Bank is the last credit organization to remain at the centre of the financial system. There are several reasons for this, the

Table 2.23 The Percentage of Some Selected Accounts in GNP

Years	*Total Assets* *GNP*	*Total Credits* *GNP*	*Total Deposits* *GNP*
1986	50.91	22.50	30.90
1987	57.36	24.94	32.21
1988	54.25	21.48	29.71
1989	45.76	19.39	26.37
1990	41.40	19.54	27.00
1991	45.82	20.17	27.00
1992	49.38	20.70	27.24
1993	49.93	21.20	25.61
1994	51.63	20.28	32.67
1995	52.23	22.20	33.93
1996	59.23	25.52	40.63

Source: Compiled from data from the Union of Turkish Banks and the SPO.

Table 2.24 The Equities Structure in the Turkish Banking System

	1986	*1987*	*1988*	*1989*	*1990*	*1991*	*1992*	*1993*	*1994*	*1995*	*1996*
Paid-up capital	59	60	50	45	44	50	49	41	42	37	37
Reserve funds	11	10	13	13	11	11	11	10	10	11	10
Allowances for possible loss	3	4	6	2	2	2	2	1	2	2	1
Revaluation	11	9	11	21	23	21	24	19	27	25	21
(Loss)	–1	–1	–2	–1	–3	–9	–16	0	–7	–6	–1
Profit	17	18	22	20	23	25	30	29	26	31	32

Source: Compiled from data from the Union of Turkish Banks.

first being that the Central Bank produces the high-powered money which is the core of the money in circulation. Second, the Central Bank is responsible for the execution of the money-credit policy and the usage of the policy tools related to it. Third, the Central Bank identifies the amount of bank notes to be issued by determining the needs of the economy. Fourth, it also meets the liquidity requirements of the banks.

Directly or indirectly the Central Bank of Turkey has financial relationships with all parts of the economy. It gathers funds from domestic and foreign resources and generally transfers them directly to the public sector and indirectly to the private sector through deposit banks and development and investment banks. The Bank has strong and extensive relations with the public sector. It gives credits to the treasury and public organizations and enterprises. The public sector borrowing requirement is generally financed by the Central Bank.

Notes

1 *Statistical Yearbook of Turkey: 1998*, Ankara, SIS, 1999, p. 263.
2 *General Agriculture Census, 1980*, SIS, Publication No. 1028, Ankara.
3 *South-Eastern Anatolia Project*, Turkish Chambers of Industry, Commerce and Sea Commerce Report, Publication No. 258, Ankara, 1993, p. 1.
4 Ahmet Şahinöz, 'Agriculture Sector', in *Turkish Economy: Sectoral Analysis*, Ankara, 1998, p. 101.
5 Ömer Kuleli and Murat Gültekingil, 'Energy', When the Century Finishes: the Republican Era, *The Encyclopedia of Turkey*, İletişim, İstanbul, c. 1995, p. 472.
6 Ibid., p. 472.
7 Yakup Kepenek, Nurhan Yentürk, *Turkish Economy*, 7th Edition, Remzi Kitabevi, 1995, p. 323.
8 'Construction', *The Turkish Economy on the 75th Anniversary of the Republic*, Dünya Newspaper Special Supplement, 1998.
9 Here 'lending organizations' means those individuals and organizations collecting funds from people and lending them to companies or individuals at high interest rates, otherwise known as 'loan sharks'.
10 The Prime Ministry of Turkey, Treasury Under-secretariat, the Board of Bank Auditors *The Turkish Banking System – 1998* Report.

Selected references

Aruoba, Çelik, and Cem Alpar (eds), 'Türkiye Ekonomi Kurumu', *Türkiye Ekonomisi 'Sektörel Gelişmeler'* (Ankara: Özyurt Matbaacılık, 1992).

Boratav, Korkut, *Türkiye İktisat Tarihi 1908–1985* (Istanbul: Gerçek Yayınevi, 1987).

Boratav, Korkut and Ergun Türkcan (eds), *Türkiye'de Sanayileşmenin Yeni Boyutları ve Kit'ler*, 3. Baskı (Ankara: Türkiye Ekonomik ve Toplumsul Tarih Vakfı, 1993).

Dinler, Zeynel, *Tarım Ekonomisi*, 4. Baskı (Bursa: Ekin Kitabevi, 1996).

Dünya Ekonomi-Politika, *Gazetesi Cumhuriyetin 75inci Yılında Türkiye Ekonomisi* (Istanbul: Dünya Yayımcılık, 1998).

Eren, Aslan, *Türkiye'nin Ekonomik Yapısının Analizi* (Izmir: Bilgehan Basımevi, 1989).

Eser, Uğur, *Türkiye'de Sanayileşme* (Ankara: İmge Kitabevi, 1993).

Karluk, Rıdvan, *Türkiye Ekonomisi: Tarihsel Gelişim Yapısal ve Sosyal Değişim*, 5. Baskı (Istanbul: Beta Yayınevi, 1997).

Kepenek, Yakup, and Nurhan Yentürk, *Türkiye Ekonomisi*, 7. Baskı (Istanbul: Remzi Kitabevi, 1995).

Kılıçbay, Ahmet, *Türk Ekonomisi: Modeller, Politikalar, Stratejiler*, 2. Baskı (Ankara: Türkiye İş Bankası Kültür Yayınları, 1985).

Oktav, Mete, Günal Önce, Alican Kavas and Mustafa Tanyeri, *Orta ve Küçük İşletmelerde İhracata Yönelik Pazarlama Sorunları ve Çözüm Önerileri*, Türkiye Odalar ve Borsalar Birliği, Yayın No. 176 (Ankara: 1990).

Şahin, Hüseyin, *Türkiye Ekonomisi: Tarihsel Gelişimi-Bugünkü Durumu*, 4. Baskı (Bursa: Ezgi Kitabevi, 1997).

Şahinöz, Ahmet, 'Türkiye Ekonomi Kurumu', *Türkiye Ekonomisi: Sektörel Analiz* (Ankara: Turhan Kitabevi, 1998).

Dünya Ekonomi-Politika, *Gazetesi Cumhuriyetin 75inci Yılında Türkiye Ekonomisi* (Istanbul: Dünya Yayımcılık, 1998).

İletişim Yayınları, *Yüzyıl Biterken Cumhuriyet Dönemi Türkiye Ansiklopedisi*, Istanbul.

3
An Overview of Turkey's Urbanization

Naci Sevkal

Introduction

The pace of urbanization in many developing countries (LDCs) between 1950 and 1970 was remarkable and was a trend that was often accompanied by dramatic social and economic changes. Migration from rural to urban regions as the force behind rapid urbanization was influenced by certain global developments.

First, the spread of advances in medicine in the years following the Second World War caused sharp decreases in mortality rates in LDCs. With high fertility rates remaining the same, especially in rural areas, this caused rapid population growth.

Second, the world economy experienced an unprecedented boom in the period between 1950–70. LDCs, too, benefited from the resultant expansion of the global economy as demand for the traditional export goods, that is, raw materials and agricultural produce increased.

These favourable global economic conditions raised hopes in the LDCs that they could also become developed. Development strategies devised by Western scholars and 'international' organizations like the World Bank also supported these hopes. Import-substitution strategy was seen as the magic formula for industrialization and, therefore, development, and was adopted by many LDCs.

Import substitution, that is, domestic production of previously imported goods, brought growing industrialization to many LDCs. This alone meant an increase in the importance of cities since industrialization is an urban phenomenon rather than rural. Coupled with a surplus population in rural areas, most of the LDCs saw large-scale migration to urban areas. Large economic centres, especially, started to grow rapidly.

By the 1970s, such LDCs had long been faced with urban problems such as housing, employment, city management, and so on. Growing research interest in 'third world urbanization' produced a sizeable literature on the matter. Initial hopes that development through industrialization would solve the 'temporary' problems of urbanization started to crumble with the first oil crisis in 1973. The first and second oil crises in the 1970s signified both the end of sustained economic growth in the world, and the vanishing hopes of development through industrialization in many LDCs.

Worst hit by the global economic recession, many LDCs were left with growing urban problems and no direction for economic development. However, the World Bank-led economic policy-makers were quick to come up with new strategies. These policies were originally introduced to solve the LDCs' debt crisis and in the early 1980s were formulated as a new development strategy called 'export-led growth'.

This new development strategy came as a package of neoliberal policies. Its basic principles were privatization, decreasing government expenditures mainly on welfare, and increasing exports through the exchange rate mechanism. Most of these policies were by no means unique to LDCs; they were implemented in developed countries as well. However, the effect of decreasing already meagre welfare spending was devastating for the urban masses in LDCs. Apart from raising false hopes of benefiting some, most urban dwellers faced deteriorating living conditions throughout the 1980s.

The 1990s brought little change to the living conditions of the urban population of LDCs. Instead, the catastrophic consequences of growing urbanization in these countries became more pronounced as the number of megacities grew. A new economic approach has yet to replace the discredited neoliberal policies of the 1980s. Many LDCs lost faith in miraculous development strategies, after being left with the gigantic urban problems of today.

Turkey, under the impact of the above-mentioned global trends, shares some urbanization characteristics with many LDCs although, of course, country-specific conditions and history play an important role in urbanization.

The following pages give a narrative of the general course of the development of urbanization in Turkey. References to statistics are kept to a minimum. Such detail is abundant in urbanization literature. The aim is to give an overview of Turkey's experience, but issues such as city management, employment and environmental degradation are not included as they require a more detailed discussion. After some background information, demographic change, regional disparities, and housing are treated in the urbanization context since the 1970s.

Turkey's experience

The Republic of Turkey was founded out of the Ottoman Empire in the Anatolian heartland in 1923, and today the country covers an area of 780 576 sq km. The Anatolian peninsula, an extension of the Asian continent towards Europe, forms the largest part of its territory, whilst Thrace, the European part of Turkey, divided from Asia by the Straits, comprises only a small proportion of its territory, and is located in the east of the Balkan peninsula.

The Republic of Turkey was overwhelmingly a rural country in 1923. Within a span of 75 years, not only has the country's population risen from 13 648 000 to 62 867 000, but the percentage of the urban population has increased from 24.2 to 64.69.[1] This dramatic change has taken place alongside a socio-economic transformation.

In the inherited territories there were two big cities, both ports, Istanbul and Izmir, and some medium-sized cities. Istanbul, the capital of the Ottoman Empire, was the biggest city of the new republic as well. Izmir was the second largest as a busy export centre.

In 1923, the capital was transferred to Ankara, a town in Central Anatolia with 20 000 inhabitants. Turkey first saw rapid urbanization in Ankara as the new capital's population increased within a couple of years. However, an increase in urbanization at the national level had to wait until the end of the Second World War.

The world-wide economic boom after the Second World War had its impact on Istanbul and Izmir as already established economic centres, and to a certain degree on Ankara as the centre of government. The volume of trade in both imports and exports, particularly in Istanbul and then in Izmir, rose considerably. Ankara, too, benefited from increasing economic activities because many private companies set up offices in this city for lobbying purposes.

The same period also saw increases in private manufacturing investments. These were mostly concentrated in Istanbul with some in Izmir. Wealth accumulated in some hands during the war through profiteering combined with foreign funds from Marshall Aid helped to finance these investments. These growing manufacturing investments were mainly directed towards import-substituting industries.

Although the newly established manufacturing companies were producing a range of goods, in fact production was in the form of assembling parts. This kind of production had to rely on know-how, investment goods, intermediate goods and so forth, all imported from abroad. Furthermore, the production targeted a domestic market protected by high tariffs.[2]

Like any other example of this sort, one of the consequences of these developments was increasing demand for labour, and rural Turkey was ready to meet this demand. There had been increases in the growth rate of the population in rural areas, and the advent of tractors in great numbers as part of the Marshall Aid Programme created a labour surplus in agriculture. Added to this picture, extensive road building, with the help of the US Aid, replaced the railway-oriented transport policy and thus facilitated mobility.[3]

Between 1950–70, Turkey experienced rural to urban migration on an unprecedented scale. Initially Istanbul, subsequently Ankara, Izmir and some other medium-sized cities grew rapidly. The most visible sign of growth was the change in city landscapes as migrants took matters into their hands and built their own homes in the absence of any public housing measures. Another sign was that marginalized labour engaging in various trades as migrants with expectations of building better lives in cities exceeded available employment opportunities. Cities were in the course of transformation.

Migrants gradually expanded their foothold in the cities despite the initial hostility of city authorities and native urban dwellers. By the early 1970s, migrants, however much they differed from the former city dwellers, had firmly established themselves in cities. By this time they formed a considerable proportion of city populations that no political party could ignore. Of course, such a transformation was not a painless process.

Cultural conflict arose between migrants and the urban élite when the former became a fact of life in the cities in the early 1970s. In these years, this tension manifested itself at every level of daily life. The food and music of the migrants were accused of not being sophisticated enough to be urban. For instance, migrants developed a new *genre* which was neither like their original rural music nor similar to that of the cities. This music, generally with extremely sad lyrics, was first heard in minibuses (*dolmuş*),[4] and labelled *dolmuş* music. *Dolmuş* music, later erroneously called *arabesk* after arabesque because of its similarity to Arabian music, created its own stars. However, the state radio and television closed their doors to this music during its long broadcast monopoly.

Food and music aside, however, more serious social conflicts were brewing. The growing urban population has changed the political process drastically. (Political process here is meant in the broader sense beyond party politics.) This process had been less volatile when the majority of the country's population lived in rural areas. There was at that time no serious threat to the political system and any such opposition could easily be contained within the system. Rapid urbanization has not only changed the physical environment of the cities, it has altered deeper social structures as well.

Conflicting social interests could be met to a certain extent within a growing economy; or, any hopes towards a better standard of living could be kept alive as long as national development rhetoric convinced people that their demands would be met. Therefore, any downturn in the national economy created destabilizing social consequences originating from urban areas.

Demography

The population continued to grow after the 1970s. However, far-reaching changes started to take shape in terms of the age structure of the population as well as fertility and death rates (*see* Table 3.1 and Figure 3.1).

The average annual growth rate of the population in the period 1970–90 remained above 2 per cent. Despite some fluctuations, the average annual growth rate had always been between 2 and 3 per cent with the exception of the Second World War years (*see* Figure 3.1). Without the impact of extraordinary conditions

Table 3.1 Life Expectancy

Years	*Life expectancy at birth (years)*	*Infant mortality per 1000 live births*
1950–55	44	235
1955–60	43	206
1960–65	52	185
1965–70	55	158
1970–75	58	140
1975–80	61	111
1980–85	63	83
1985–90	66	65
1990–95	67	51

Source: SPO (State Planning Organization).

the average annual growth rate dropped for the first time below 2 per cent between 1990 and 1997. According to demographers this signifies a turning point in the population growth rate trend.

Higher population growth rates stemmed from high fertility rates combined with low mortality rates following a relative improvement in health care in rural areas after the Second World War. On the other hand, Turkey has been a special case with low fertility rates in urban areas since the turn of the century.[5] The urban population grew slowly until 1950. The link between urban population growth and migration is evident especially in the period 1950–60. These are the years during which Turkey saw the highest annual population growth rate and the fastest growth in urban population.[6]

The decline in fertility rates started as early as 1950 and has accelerated since the 1970s. Nevertheless, population growth has continued, although at a decreasing rate, because of increasing life expectancy and better health care.[7] Another aspect of fertility rates is their regional variation. Urban areas have had lower rates than rural areas. Also, fertility rates in eastern regions have exceeded western regions.[8]

For many years characterized by a young population, Turkey is on the threshold of having an ageing population. According to projections, the proportion of youth will not increase, and the age structure will be changed in favour of older age groups. Also, the total population will stabilize at 98.4 million in 2050, mostly living in urban areas.[9]

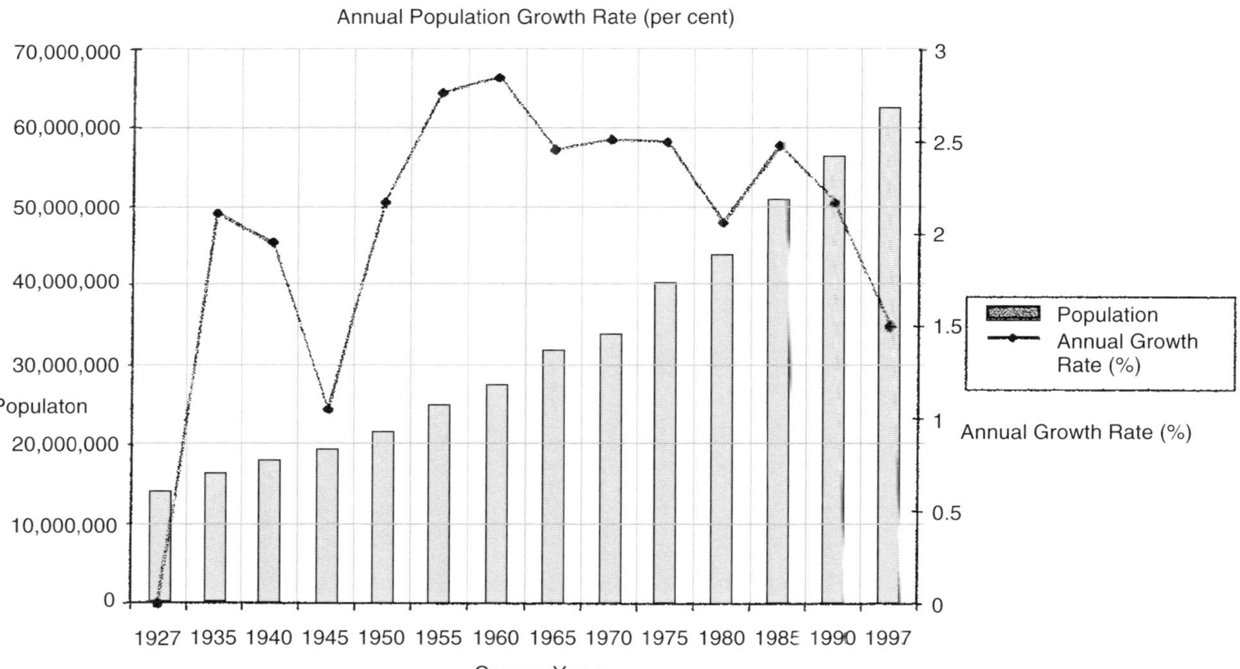

Source: SIS

Figure 3.1 Annual Population Growth Rate (per cent)

This decrease in population growth and the changing age structure will have far-reaching consequences on education and employment. A proportionally stabilized youthful population will give way to improved quality in education. However, increases in the workforce may lead to higher unemployment rates.[10]

It can be concluded that the interaction between demographic structure and urbanization changed direction in the 1970s and that higher population growth in rural areas, among other factors, had contributed to rapid urbanization until then. After that time urbanization started to increase its influence on the demographic structure through lowering fertility rates and raising life expectancy.

Regional Disparities

Turkey has seven geographical regions. These regions often show socio-economic as well as physical differences. They are the Marmara and Aegean in the west, the Mediterranean in the south, the Black Sea in the north, Central Anatolia, South East Anatolia, and East Anatolia.

The east–west divide, a legacy of the past, still exists despite some limited efforts at regional development. In the early 1970s the spatial distribution of economic activities took shape and since then there has not been any fundamental shift in regional roles. On the contrary, the more established regions have strengthened their positions, in most cases, at the expense of the other regions.

Istanbul, the biggest city, which is located in the Marmara Region in the north-west of the country, has always been an economic and cultural centre, therefore, private investments as well as most of the public investments have concentrated there and in the surrounding region. That region's share in the national economy is far greater than that of the rest of the country.

Izmir, the third biggest city, and the Aegean Region follows the Marmara Region as the second most developed region. Again, Izmir and its hinterland used to be an important economic centre in the nineteenth century. Izmir sustained its role during the republic as well. Also, the whole Aegean region appears to be the second most developed region.

Apart from these two regions, some others have relatively important cities. For instance, the capital, Ankara, and Turkey's second biggest city, in the Central Anatolian Region, attracted considerable investment and migrants. However, it created a limited economic impact on the Central Anatolian Region. The same is true for other regional centres which in most cases contributed very little to their region's development.

The economic crisis experienced in the mid- and late 1970s resulted in fundamental changes in economic policies. Under the influence of the world economy, the import-substitution strategy was replaced by the export-led development strategy in the early 1980s. This change has brought more emphasis on market mechanisms and the private sector. The share of the public sector in the national economy has always been large and this shift has not reduced the public sector's role despite the privatization efforts. However, it had implications for the spatial distribution of economic activities.

First, traditional centres strengthen their positions as economic centres. For instance, Istanbul's role increased remarkably. Second, small- and medium-sized firms (KOBİs[11]) flourished in different parts of the country engaged mainly in textiles and food processing and various other manufactured goods for both the domestic and foreign markets. Third, agricultural areas with export potential in parts of the Aegean and Mediterranean Regions increased their advantage. Fourth, investments in tourism rose sharply in the 1980s. All kinds of tourist facilities, hotels, restaurants, and so on mushroomed along the southern Aegean and western Mediterranean coastlines.

Existing regional disparities became increasingly evident with these developments during the 1980s and 1990s, and the distribution of income between regions and within regions has been worsening since the mid-80s. The Marmara and Aegean Regions saw increases in prosperity, followed by the Central Anatolian and Mediterranean Regions. The losers were the East and South-East Anatolian Regions and the Black Sea Region. There are, of course, economically vibrant cities in these regions like Trabzon on the Black Sea, Gaziantep, Kahramanmaraş, and Adıyaman in the south–east. Nevertheless, the overall picture is quite bleak. Furthermore, the continued fighting between the armed forces and Kurdish rebels in the Eastern and South–eastern Anatolian Regions since the mid-eighties disrupts the regional economy and displaces people.

Cities and the housing mess

a) Illegal housing

Housing is the most striking aspect of rapid urban growth. Housing conditions are the manifestation of the socio-economic situation of an urban area. Turkish cities faced the arrival of migrants in increasing numbers and inevitably experienced housing shortages from the very beginning. In the absence of any housing policies these migrants started to build their homes on vacant land on the periphery of cities without observing building regulations. In most cases public land was illegally occupied; and even in the rare circumstances when it was bought the land was illegally subdivided. The name *gecekondu* started to be used for such buildings – which were similar to *favelas* in Brazil, *ranchos* in Venezuela, and so forth. *Gecekondu,* literally meaning 'landed at night', was first humorously used to name buildings in squatter settlements to emphasize their illegality and rapid building process and was later established as a name. There was even some *Gecekondu* Legislation passed in 1966.

The first reaction of city authorities was to demolish *gecekondus*. However, destroyed buildings were re-erected. The bulldozing policy was not successful. *Gecekondus* gradually spread over many parts of cities and by the 1970s they had long been recognized by the city authorities. It was estimated that in 1980, some 23 per cent of the urban population lived in *gecekondus* which accounted for 21 per cent of the urban housing stock. Most of these, around two-thirds, were in Istanbul, Ankara, and Izmir.[12]

Although some analysts maintain that permissive *gecekondu* policies allowed low wages by reducing the cost of housing, others tend to see the matter as a failure of the administration. According to this view, inappropriate policies or the lack of them led to a chronic *gecekondu* problem.

Permissive policies can be related to political parties. Political parties quickly realized the importance of the electorate living in *gecekondu* areas after early attempts failed to prevent their spread. Demands for amenities such as piped water, electricity and paved roads were met. The disputed legal situation of *gecekondus* was resolved by 'amnesties' from time to time and most of the *gecekondus* were legalized, that is, owners were granted titles for their *gecekondus* through some rehabilitation of the existing building. Owners thus saw increases in the value of their property. This actually meant a transfer of urban rents to these people. One obvious result of these policies is mushrooming *gecekondus* before every election with the expectation of an 'amnesty'.

The legalization process and the shortage of vacant land transformed *gecekondu* building practice. They are now built by Mafia-type organizations for rent or to be sold for rent, while earlier *gecekondus* were mostly self-built.

Gecekondus are not the only type of illegal buildings, there are other ones too. These can be commercial buildings as well as housing. In this case there is no dispute over the ownership of the land – somebody owns it legally. Illegality arises from non-compliance with the building regulations either by erecting a building without a building permit, or changing the specifications of a building from those permitted. According to one estimate, more than half of the buildings in Istanbul are illegal. It would not be an unrealistic claim to say that other big cities are any different.

b) 'Legal' housing

Big cities not only attracted poor peasants but relatively better-off people as well. Although middle-income groups also faced housing problems in big cities this is a rather less studied area when compared to *gecekondu* research.

The main characteristic of middle-income housing has been the absence of a proper mortgage scheme.[13] Those available embraced only a small minority. The only exception is the Mass Housing Fund established in the early 1980s. After an initial success, this fund is also far from meeting the needs of these groups.

There are two main ways of having a legal house for middle-income groups. The first method is called the *yap-sat* process (literally: build and sell) whereby those who have a developed plot of land or an old house agree with a building contractor on the construction of a block of flats. The contractor builds the block, and gives a pre-agreed number of flats to the owner of the land. Agreement on the number of flats to be given to the owner varies depending on land prices in an area. The rest of the flats are sold by the contractor, in many cases before completion of the building, by instalment and a down-payment to cover the cost of construction.

The second method is forming a housing cooperative. Generally, people working in the same place get together and form a cooperative to buy a developed plot of land and find a building contractor. Members pay monthly instalments and a down-payment decided by the cooperative. This is still the method most used by middle-income groups to own a flat.

The first method was quite common until 1980 among urban dwellers owning developed land or an old house to be replaced by a larger block. Small- or medium-sized building contractors dominated this market. After 1980, both available land for such development decreased considerably, and the market was hit by the economic crisis.

The *yap-sat* process, although it lost momentum because of rocketing urban land prices and big companies' interest in the housing market, still exists. It transformed the urban landscape in Istanbul, Ankara and Izmir, and spread to other cities as well during the 1960s and 1970s. Most of the existing one- or two-storey buildings were replaced by five- to eight-storey blocks. Still today, these poorly designed and almost identical flats dominate urban landscapes in many cities, big or small and an average middle-income neighbourhood looks more or less the same in almost every city.

Both the *yap-sat* process and cooperatives contributed to the creation of multi-storey block dominated neighbourhoods. Low-density areas were replaced by high-rise blocks during the process. Increasing densities have strained the existing infrastructure causing traffic congestion, air and noise pollution and counters the claims that it is more economical to supply urban services to high-density settlements. Added to these, the lack of control over such buildings in so-called planned urban areas puts many lives at risk because almost the whole country is in an active earthquake zone.

As a result of five decades of rapid urbanization, the cities have changed beyond recognition. Urban landscapes have been shaped by illegal settlements ignoring all planning requirements, and so-called legal settlements have manipulated master plans for their own interests. Municipal councils became an arena of competing vested interests for urban rents. Municipal planning departments, unable to lead urban development, are reduced to distributing favours. That is how the physical urban fabric came to be irreparably destroyed in cities like Istanbul and Izmir which were established a couple of thousand years ago.

Conclusion

What has happened in the past fifty years is the massive movement of people from less desired places to more desired ones. In the course of this process, these more desired places became transformed into less desired ones, and the less desired ones are even still less desired. With the appropriate planning and practices adhered to it might take another fifty years to undo the previous half-century's damage. However, the World Bank's recent interest in urban matters may shorten this process: they might even come up with another 'brilliant strategy'.

Meanwhile, Turkey's rapid urbanization experience is a result of the development strategies it has adopted in the past fifty years. Turkish cities are the monuments of these 'strategies' and one might be right in thinking that 'development' created more problems than it solved when looking at them. It is an open question whether the targeted development level was achieved.

Notes

1 The State Institute of Statistics (SIS) accepts provincial and district centres as urban areas. However, the problem with this definition is that some district centres are very small and no more than villages with some government buildings.
2 Kepenek, 1990.
3 Rivkin, 1965.
4 The *Dolmuş* was the contribution of migrants to the city transport. Basically, it is a shared taxi for people travelling in the same direction in the absence of city buses. It could be anything from old American cars to minibuses. It first started between *gecekondu* areas and city centres but was soon discovered by the other city dwellers in formal neighbourhoods as the overstretched municipal transport services deteriorated. Now, they are mostly uniform minibuses which operate as city buses with marked stops and standardized fares.
5 Shorter, 1997.
6 Shorter, 1997.
7 Shorter, 1997.
8 Shorter, 1997; TÜSİAD, 1999.
9 Shorter, 1997; Güvenç, 1997.
10 Shorter, 1997; Güvenç 1997.
11 KOBİs are generally low-tech, labour-intensive companies employing up to 150 workers.
12 Danielson and Keleş, 1985.
13 In fact, chronic high inflation (currently running – October 1999 – at 60 per cent) for the last twenty years is the major obstacle for such schemes.

References

Danielson, M. and Keleş, R., *The Politics of Rapid Urbanization: Government and Growth in Turkey* (New York: Holmes and Meier, 1985).

Güvenç, M., 'Nüfus Bilgisi ve Türkiye'de Demografik Değişim' ('Population Information and the Demographic Change in Turkey'), *Birikim*, No. 101 (1997) 70–73.

Kepenek, Y., *Türkiye Ekonomisi* (*The Economy of Turkey*) (Ankara: Verso, 1990).

Rivkin, M.D., *Area Development for National Growth: the Turkish Precedent* (New York: Praeger, 1965).

Shorter, F.C., 'Türkiye'de Nüfus Bilgisi Konusunda Kriz Var', *Birikim*, No. 101 (1997) 74–86. See English original of the article: Shorter, F.C., 'The Crisis of Population Knowledge in Turkey', *New Perspectives on Turkey*, 12 (1995) 1–33.

State Institute of Statistics (SIS), *1990 Population Census, Administrative Division* (*Summary Tables*) (Ankara: State Institute of Statistics, Prime Ministry, Republic of Turkey, 1991).

State Institute of Statistics (SIS): *http://www.die.gov.tr*

State Planning Organization (SPO): *http://www.dpt.gov.tr*

TÜSİAD, *Türkiye'nin Fırsat Penceresi: Demografik Dönüşüm ve İzdüşümleri* (*Turkey's Window of Opportunity: Demographic Transformation and Projections*) (Istanbul: TÜSİAD (Association of Turkish Industrialists and Businessmen), 1999).

Suggestions for Further Reading

Danielson, M. and Keleş, R., *The Politics of Rapid Urbanization: Government and Growth in Turkey* (New York: Holmes and Meier, 1985), is a detailed study of the urbanization process in Turkey.

Keyder, Ç., *State and Class in Turkey: a Study of Capitalist Development* (UK: Verso, 1989), gives an excellent analysis of the Turkish development from a historical perspective.

4
Turkey's Mainstream Political Parties on the Centre-Right and Centre-Left

Ayşe Güneş-Ayata and Sencer Ayata

Introduction

The highly fragmented political party structure that reflects deep cleavages in political culture is a major source of instability in Turkey's politics and government. Despite the high number and the enormous variety of political parties, public opinion polls taken in early 1999 in the run-up to the April elections indicated that nearly one-third of the voters were undecided and because of their alienation from politics seemed reluctant to go to the ballot box on election day.[1] Expressing dissatisfaction with the existing state of party politics and blaming the party leaders for everything that goes wrong in the country is a very common theme in everyday discourse. The majority of the voters also tend to contend that there is in fact no political party that really deserves their vote. Voter alienation is congruent with various survey results that underline a similar decline in the respectability and prestige of the parliament as an institution. Dissatisfaction with the existing parties raises the hopes of politicians that aim to appeal to the discontented voters by means of founding a new party and this further increases fragmentation in the political party system.

The Turkish electoral system has both advantages and disadvantages for the representation of the political parties in the parliament. The practice of proportional representation based on large constituencies in the 1961–80 period has proved highly instrumental in the parliamentary representation of small parties, giving rise to the formation of successive coalition governments throughout the

1970s. Despite a 10 per cent threshold introduced after the 1981 Constitution to prevent political party fragmentation, in the 1995 general elections five parties, the biggest gaining only 21 per cent of the votes, were able to make their way into the parliament. Although their votes were substantial, the Turkish nationalist Nationalist Action Party (MHP) with 9 per cent and the Kurdish nationalist Peoples' Democracy Party (HADEP) with 4 per cent of the votes, could not pass the threshold. Similarly, after the 1999 elections two significant parties, the Republican Peoples' Party (CHP) and HADEP could not pass the threshold with 8.5 per cent and 4.4 per cent of the votes respectively. Nevertheless, the present parliament, which was renewed in April 1999, hosts five parties altogether. At present (October 1999) there is a coalition between three parties. The last session of parliament also had a series of coalition governments. In the course of only three and a half years the government changed hands four times, and two of these were highly vulnerable minority governments dependent on outside support for a vote of confidence.

This paper has an exclusive focus on the four mainstream political parties that have played a major role in Turkish politics since 1981; two of these are on the left, the Republican Peoples' Party and the Democratic Left Party (DSP), and two on the right, the Motherland Party (ANAP) and the True Path Party (DYP). The first part includes a brief account of their history and a discussion of their ideologies, organization and voting support, while the second involves an analysis of general trends and developments. We begin with the centre-right parties that have managed to pool greater votes than the centre-left and either ruled the country single-handedly or as major partners in coalition governments since 1983.

The centre-right

Although there was always one big leading party on the centre-right in the 30 years between 1950 and 1980, the peculiarity of the last 15 years was the severe competition between two ideologically similar centre-right parties of more or less equal electoral strength. ANAP and the DYP have confronted each other as government and opposition parties except for a very brief period in 1996 when they joined forces in a coalition government. The tug-of-war between them stems from both the deep-rooted personal hostilities among their leaders and the severe competition for power positions among party organizations that provide access to political, bureaucratic and economic resources.

ANAP was founded in 1983 by Turgut Özal, a former economy bureaucrat who was appointed as deputy prime minister by the military rulers in 1980 and who later became president (1989–93). Özal was known for his personal charisma, mediatic leadership style and a certain depth and breadth of vision. He was a man of new ideas, challenges and proposals, some novel and important and others premature and only half-baked, but almost all introduced and even implemented without serious calculation of the consequences. During the 1990–91 Gulf Crisis for instance, his move to send troops to northern Iraq to invade Mosul was prevented by the chief of staff who had to resign from his post to stop him. Ozal's relaxed attitudes in public life – such as giving interviews to journalists wearing pyjamas and visiting army units wearing shorts – was a source of bitter criticism for those who were used to associating stately manners with more ritualistic and ceremonial conduct. Also, the endless scandals in his family have occupied the media and aroused public indignation for years.

His successor, Mesut Yılmaz, on the other hand, is neither charismatic nor a man of great vision; on the contrary, he is highly conventional in his behaviour and leads a middle-class family life. Yılmaz is known to be a person of moderation, self-restraint and calculation. Some observers in the media tended to interpret the change of leadership from Özal to Yılmaz as 'the routinization of the charisma'. Indeed, the differences between the two leaders can be followed through the evolution of the party's ideology and organization.

In the first elections in which it took part in 1983, ANAP had a landslide victory getting 45 per cent of the votes and winning a clear majority in the National Assembly (parliament, TBMM) with 53 per cent of the seats. The party was also successful in the 1987 general elections having less votes but even more seats due to changes in the election law. In the 1991 elections, the first ones under Yılmaz's leadership, votes for the party decreased to 24 per cent, in 1995 to 19 per cent and in 1999 to 13.2 per cent. In the last two elections, the party's strongholds were the Black Sea Region,

Istanbul, and the inner parts of the Aegean and Mediterranean coasts.

Unlike both the major centre-right Justice Party (AP) of the 1960s and 1970s, and its present rival, the DYP, ANAP has been more successful in the cities than in the countryside. In the urban areas the party found its most ardent supporters among the upwardly mobile, business-minded, entrepreneurial middle classes and the self-employed.[2] Compared with its centre-right counterpart ANAP has greater support from both the youth and women.[3] In Özal's new political discourse urban groups and urban problems always received primacy, which, in fact indicated a radical break from the village-centred centre-right propaganda of the past.

The most outstanding aspect of ANAP ideology was its insistence on the opening up of Turkey to the world and the liberal restructuring policies aimed at reducing the role of the state in the economy.[4] Such policies have promoted the rise of the urban entrepreneurial and managerial middle classes and new consumption patterns and lifestyles based on the increased abundance of imported Western products. The globally oriented new middle class, the main propeller of ANAP in its early years, had a profound impact on social, political and cultural life in the country. The ANAP governments of the 1980s also emphasized export-led growth strategies, improvements in communications and the development of tourism.[5] Survey results indicate that the proportion of those who want full integration with the European Union (EU) are highest among ANAP voters.

Özal's claim of a synthesis of four major political currents was also an ideological novelty in Turkish politics; these included conservatism, nationalism, liberalism and social democracy. Later however, the liberal, conservative and the nationalist wings, if not necessarily the weaker social democrats, squabbled among themselves to get the upper hand in the party. The liberal imprint with a single-minded emphasis on the virtues of the market economy and the conservative stress on the significance of the family, religion and the national community have always remained powerful. The combination of economic liberalism with social conservatism in the neo-right fashion was the cornerstone of Özal's politics who was personally close to both the globally oriented economic élite as well as the Islamic tarikat networks. In the elections held immediately after the 1980 military intervention ANAP had almost universal support from the Islamist groups and communities. In government, Özal actively supported the tarikat networks by giving them representation in the party, diverting greater amounts from public resources to religious activities and appointing their members to influential positions in the bureaucracy and politics. With his departure for presidency and the rise of the Welfare Party (RP) in the early 1990s the religiously inspired votes have largely deserted the ANAP. Although the party's nationalist inscription had become more prominent with Mesut Yılmaz, its leader since 1991, the party could, as in the case of the 1995 elections, forge alliances with the Islamist networks and communities. The liberal and secular orientation of the ANAP has become more pronounced in the last few years as the party leadership tended to support the secularist groups and forces in their struggle against the Islamist threat.

Although the DYP was also founded in 1983, it claims direct descent from both the AP of the 1960s and 1970s and the Democrat Party (DP) of the 1950s. Since 1983, the DYP has changed leaders a number of times but the interim leaders of the pre-1987 period were only titular; it was obvious to everyone that Süleyman Demirel, the restricted 'natural leader' of the party, was holding the reins behind the scenes, waiting for the right moment to take over. The second major change in leadership was the election of Tansu Çiller to party leadership in 1993 when Demirel left the party to become Turkey's ninth president. The differences between the two DYP leaders were even more striking than those between Özal and Yılmaz.

Tansu Çiller, Turkey's first female prime minister, is an American-educated professor of economics, who is also known for her vast family fortune. Her election as the party leader has targeted the increased support of new constituencies among secularist groups, the professional middle classes, youth and women.[6] This objective was partly fulfilled in the 1995 elections as Çiller managed to become a role model for many educated and aspiring urban women and improved the image of the party among the educated strata. In her first years as prime minister, she received wide attention from the foreign media and the international public as a Westernized woman who achieved unrivalled political success by being elected as a female political party leader in what ultimately is a strongly patriarchal society. As the prime minister of the country for a brief period between 1993–1995, she followed Özal's path of opening up to the world, especially in her efforts towards signing the Customs Union Agreement with the EU.

The DP–AP–DYP tradition in Turkish politics is known for its emphasis on 'national will', a concept underlying a strongly majoritarian view of democracy, based on the nationalist and religious values of the Sunni population of Anatolia generally expressed through a language of loyalty to 'the flag and the Koran'. In his political strategy Demirel took it for granted that the national will was naturally on the side of the centre-right tradition in Turkish politics, and more specifically always on the side of his own party. He used the same concept to emphasize the supremacy of elected bodies over appointed ones, when two governments under his premiership were toppled by the military, first in 1971 and then in 1980.[7] As argued by Levy[8] such discourse facilitates appeal to the masses on a populist basis. Finally, nationalism beyond a rhetoric of patriotism and defence of traditional values and communities was a powerful ideological weapon used against the rising left in the 1970s.

A major survey conducted in 1988 indicated that the DYP had its principal stronghold among the vast Anatolian village population and the traditional middle class of artisans, shopkeepers and merchants in the small towns and cities and that it was weakest among the educated middle classes, bureaucrats and professionals. Similarly, DYP support was inversely correlated to education and age and especially under Demirel's leadership the party had very limited appeal to women. In the 1995 elections however, the DYP, compared with ANAP, had less of the religious and conservative, and more of the secular pro-Western middle-class votes.[9] This indicated that Çiller was indeed the right choice for the DYP to improve its image in cities although the votes of the party had declined from 27 per cent in 1991 to only 19 per cent in 1995, mainly as a result of heavy losses in the conservative Central and Eastern Anatolian provinces. Its votes were further reduced in 1999, resulting in the DYP barely passing the threshold with 12.3 per cent. These votes were shifting to the Islamist RP and its successor, the Virtue Party (FP).

The decline of the centre-right

Besides being divided, the major threat facing the centre-right parties is losing votes to the radical right, including both its religious and nationalist variants. The total ratio of centre-right votes has declined dramatically from 55 per cent in 1987, to 51.2 per cent in 1991, to 38.8 per cent in 1995 and this trend was further continued in 1999, to 25.5 per cent. The fragmentation and the decline in the centre-right is seen as a major source of increasing political instability in Turkey.

The rural countryside used to be the stronghold of the centre-right since the 1950s; this readily available vote bank always guaranteed power for these parties when the majority of the population lived in rural areas. However, as the rural–urban population ratio reversed in the last three decades the centre-right parties began to lose ground first against the left and then the radical right. What underlies the growing alienation of the migrant population from the centre-right parties was their failure to address problems such as poverty, unemployment and absence of social security.

Changes in social class structure also had a profound impact on the organization and ideology of the centre-right parties which have always been closer to business groups and represented their interests in politics. In the last two decades the locus of wealth and power within the Turkish bourgeoisie has shifted from local merchants, the major bearers of traditional norms and values, to a new globally oriented bourgeoisie of large holding companies with diverse investments in commerce, industry and services. The new Western-educated metropolitan bourgeoisie has adopted new values and lifestyles, often radically different from those of the working population, and as a highly distinctive community they hold strongly 'anti-populist' values which tend to discard the redistributive mechanisms in traditional society and clientelistic relations in politics. As the emerging dominant group in Turkey, the new big bourgeoisie argues for a smaller state, privatization, reduced spending on agricultural subsidies and welfare, and policies aiming at keeping labour costs low. For the centre parties it became increasingly difficult to balance the interests of the big bourgeoisie with the majority population. Furthermore, as these parties became increasingly subservient to the demands of the big metropolitan bourgeoisie, the so-called Anatolian capital of small- and medium-scale entrepreneurs tended to turn to political Islam.

The neo-liberal restructuring policies of Turgut Özal promoted a new ethos centred on individualism, competition, and acquisition of status on the basis of consumption and the display of wealth. In the context of rapidly growing and differentiating cities, the rich, forming their own segregated communities are increasingly isolated from the rest of society. The leading centre-right politicians are primarily influenced by the values, views and lifestyles of this particular stratum thus becoming less sensitive to the everyday problems of common people.

What really epitomized this fundamental change in orientation in Turkish politics was Özal's well-known statement, 'I like rich people', which signalled the radical break from the traditional communitarian ideology of the centre-right tradition. In the provincial Anatolian setting, despite marked inequalities in wealth and prestige, the poor and the rich lived close to each other sharing a common set of values based on the Islamic religion; according to these the notables who expected deference from their subordinates had to attend to their needs when they were desperate. Thus, the centre-right political discourse until Özal tended to emphasize 'sympathy' for the poor and conceived politics as 'servicing the people'. The religious conservatism of Özal, by contrast, was similar to the ideology of the new right in the Western countries, in that it was largely devoid of an egalitarian social and economic content. In the 1990s the ideology of communitarian egalitarianism was adopted and developed mainly by the Islamist RP.

A third major problem area facing the centre-right is the rise of the religious and nationalist right.[10] Since its inception, the centre-right tradition in Turkish politics underlined close affinity with the traditional culture of the people. Although the centre-right parties have not opposed secularism, in the sense of the separation of state and religion, they nevertheless promoted policies towards increasing religiosity in society and the consolidation of the power of religious communities and institutions. During the Cold War years, the strengthening of religious and nationalist identities was used as part of a strategy to combat 'the Communist threat'. Since the 1950s, the centre-right parties have tended to see both the nationalist and the Islamist movements as their allies and companions, rather than rivals.

In the 1990s, both the nationalist and religious right won increased votes at the expense of the centre-right; for instance the combined votes of the RP and the MHP have increased from 16 per cent in 1991 to 30 per cent in 1995. The total votes of the extreme right came to 33.3 per cent in 1999. For the centre-right parties it became increasingly difficult to contain these two tendencies within their organizational and ideological framework as they themselves turned more liberal and both the nationalist and Islamist right more radical. The nationalist and especially the religious right were able to build a vast mass following through revitalizing solidaristic and redistributive community networks among the recent migrants to cities, a practice that the centre-right parties have long tended to abandon.

As the left ceased to be perceived as a major threat in the 1980s and 1990s, the essentially anti-Communist nationalist right of the 1970s began to emphasize ethnic Turkishness against the Kurdish nationalist movement. The religious right on the other hand has continued to Islamize society and institutions with increased zeal. For the centre-right parties however, it was not possible either to compete with the nationalist right in shoring up chauvinistic and racist sentiments or indeed with the Islamists in politicizing Islam. On both fronts they were bound to lose against those who were more radical.

The centre-left

Until the 1980s the centre-left was represented by the CHP which, except for brief spells in power, was the major contender party in the parliament. When political party life had resumed with the return of civilian rule in 1983, the CHP was split as its former leader Bülent Ecevit founded the DSP and the vast majority of the party members joined the Social Democratic Peoples' Party (SHP), headed by Erdal İnönü, a professor of physics and the son of İsmet İnönü, the second president of Turkey and the leader of the CHP for 33 years between 1938 and 1972. The Social Democratic Party had experienced two mergers, first, in 1985, with the Peoples' Party (HP) and then, in 1994, with the Republican Peoples' Party which was opened in 1992. Since İnönü, the SHP and the CHP had two interim leaders and is at present under the leadership of Deniz Baykal.

As indicated by Tachau[11] the parties on the centre-left have a strong leadership tradition. Bülent Ecevit, a journalist by profession, was first elected as a member of parliament from the CHP in 1957. He is a charismatic politician with a romantic touch and a poetic style of speech that proved highly effective in mobilizing the masses. Under his leadership the CHP was able to defeat its major centre-right rival, the AP, for the first time in 27 years since 1950. Ecevit has a reputation for his honesty, determination and intellectual consistency and, despite his uniquely élitist family background, he was identified with a folk hero, 'Karaoğlan'. He is also recognized as an ardent defender of national interest as epitomized by his moves as prime minister during both the Cyprus conflict in the summer of 1974, and the abduction of the Kurdish guerrilla leader Öcalan in February, 1999.

Erdal İnönü on the other hand, had neither deep emotional nor idealistic commitment to a political movement nor was he a person of great ambitions in politics; rather, he tended to define his role as one of responding to a call and performing a duty. He knew well that he was representing a party of extremely divergent interests and what was expected of him was to hold the party together in the difficult days following military rule in the early 1980s. As an earnest, moderate and easy-going person İnönü was loved and respected even by those who did not vote for him. Despite fierce opposition from Deniz Baykal, who challenged his leadership three times in the party congresses, he was able to retain his position for ten years between 1983 and 1993. Despite his bright academic background, Baykal has a reputation as a hard-core professional politician and a master of tactics in factional politics. In the first elections that he entered as the leader of the left in 1995, the CHP witnessed a big election defeat, only able to pass the threshold with a tiny fraction of the votes and since then Baykal has done little to show that he can be a leader of some breadth and vision. Contrary to this defeat, the Democratic Left Party with the leadership of Ecevit was paving its way to an election victory by being the bigger party of the left.

Mango[12] argues that the left–right divide in Turkey that often reflects a major tension between the modern secular groups and the religious conservative masses is essentially cultural in nature. The CHP gets most of its support from the secular urban middle classes and the members of the minority Alevi sect. Since 1983, however, Bülent Ecevit, has adopted a more critical stance *vis-à-vis* the élitist contempt for the religious customs and beliefs of ordinary Muslims that used to characterize some sections of the left in Turkey.[13] The

CHP, on the other hand, had made the defence of secularism against the increasing encroachment of Islam in public life and institutions the number one issue on its agenda. The conception of secularism and the nature of relations with Islamic groups and communities remain an area where the two centre-left parties have slightly divergent views.

Though both centre-left parties initially opposed the neo-liberal restructuring policies, economic issues hardly took priority on their agenda. Mainly for the SHP/CHP political issues such as constitutional reform, the rights of individuals, civil liberties, secularism and democratization have always occupied a central place in ideology and propaganda. The CHP seemed more responsive to the demands of collectivities such as ethnic groups and women. Ecevit, on the other hand, emphasized the interests of corporate groups such as farmers, artisans and workers while strongly arguing against any notion of giving cultural autonomy to the Kurds, identifying ethnonationalism as a major threat to the unitary nature of the state. In his view the Kurdish problem is one of regional underdevelopment, not cultural but fundamentally socio-economic in nature. In foreign policy too, slight differences in orientation are identifiable. While the SHP–CHP strongly committed itself to the Customs Union Agreement with the EU when it was in power between 1991–95, the DSP seemed hesitant, and in government it opposed the terms that the EU wanted to stipulate for Turkey.

The votes of the two parties have significantly varied over time. In the 1987 elections the SHP, under the leadership of Erdal İnönü, had 24.8 per cent of the votes whereas the DSP remained at a mere 9 per cent and thus unable to pass the threshold. In the 1995 elections however, the pattern was reversed as the CHP which only had 10.75 per cent of the votes lagged behind the DSP, that peaked with 14.64 per cent of the votes. In the 1999 elections this reversal was further strengthened when the CHP could not pass the threshold with 8.6 per cent and the DSP became the biggest party with 22.1 per cent. Since 1983, the total votes cast for the centre-left parties has ranged from one-third of the total to a quarter.

SHP support was highest among the university-educated urban professional middle classes and the youth.[14] The CHP still retains 'relatively' higher support among university graduates, but it has become a party of the middle-age group, largely unable to attract new votes.

On the other hand, both centre-left parties have their strongholds in the cities. Men predominate among the CHP voters, whereas amongst the housewives the DSP tends to score higher. On the other hand, the Alevis have so far showed a clear preference for the CHP and as its votes diminished gradually throughout the 1990s the support from the minority sect has indeed become the single most important factor sustaining the party. Another significant difference in terms of the electoral basis is that the DSP is closer to the poorer and the relatively less-educated sections of the population; for instance, 88.4 per cent of DSP supporters believe that their party defends the interests of the unprivileged better than the others. CHP support is by contrast relatively more élitist. Both centre-right parties get their votes from people who are particularly sensitive about defending the secular regime in Turkey. Geographically, the centre-left electoral support is more western than eastern, more coastal than inland and more urban than rural. Finally, Kurdish support is higher for the CHP and Sunni support higher for the DSP.[15]

The differences in party organization however are considerable. The DSP's weak party organization is highly submissive to the leader and its function is largely one of electioneering. The CHP, by contrast has a highly elaborate and extensive party organization reaching almost every single corner of the country; it has been able to enforce mergers, select its own leaders, determine its candidates and initiate a multitude of activities. However, as the SHP/CHP votes tended to diminish and as the party stayed away from power for most of the time in the last two decades, the clientelistic networks of the party have lost much of their previous vigour and effectiveness. The party's access to resources was confined mainly to the municipalities under its control.[16]

The centre-left: similarities and differences

The centre-left, too, suffers seriously from being divided. Once separated, the parties emphasize their differences, often exaggerating them, and this leads to continuous strife, tension and squabbles that eventually prove damaging for them both. Secondly, the centre-left parties now find it increasingly difficult to define their distinctive identities *vis-à-vis* the centre-right as they have tended to move ideologically towards the centre.[17]

In the last few years the CHP began to argue for a 'new left', emphasizing dialogue and compromise between divergent social groups' interests in society, rapid economic growth and increased integration with the world economy. In the CHP manifestos, income redistribution and social welfare-oriented policies have gradually receded into the background. Thus, in the case of the CHP the move to the centre has been more in the sphere of economic policy. The DSP, by contrast, has moved closer to the centre in cultural terms; this involves giving more premium to nationalist sentiments and adopting a more tolerant attitude towards religious activity and moderate Islamist groups. In both cases the move to the centre was reinforced by government experience.

Both centre-left parties have weak ties with intellectuals, voluntary associations and new social movements such as feminism and environmentalism. This significantly deprives them of access to new ideas, resources and social groups that could add fresh fuel to the enthusiasm of the existing party organizations.

Identity politics began to have an impact on the Turkish political scene in the last two decades mainly in the form of Islamic revivalism, Kurdish ethnicity, and ethno-nationalism. Although the Islamist movement has not penetrated centre-left politics in any significant way, the Alevi revivalism that grew as a reaction to it has; the members of the minority sect were heavily represented in both centre-left parties and especially the SHP/CHP. Both the DSP and CHP argue that the state should recognize the Alevi as a distinctive community, though neither has taken important steps in this direction when they have been in power. Rather, the Alevi community is considered as a vote bank that should not be alienated. Similarly, various Kurdish groups and intellectuals have also sought refuge in the SHP/CHP which have subscribed to more liberal views on ethnic identities. The CHP, however, is caught up in a major dilemma; while it argues for increased scope for multiculturalism and the urgent need for democratization, it becomes too closely associated with minorities which poses the threat of being thought of as a party of marginal groups.

Another problem facing the Turkish left is that of leadership and the balance of power between the leader and the party organization. In both centre-left parties, the gradual weakening of the party organization *vis-à-vis* the leaders creates frustration among the rank and file. The classical branch parties, as typified by social democratic ones in Europe, do not exist in Turkey. The DSP, with a member–voter ratio of only 1:20, is simply a leader party; whereas the ratio is as high as 1:2 in the case of the CHP, many of its members have weak membership loyalties.

New actors in Turkey's politics

The mainstream political parties have a number of common problems that seem to lie at the basis of their relative decline and the general erosion of the legitimacy of party politics since the 1980s. This tendency has become more marked as actors and institutions other than political parties began to play a more influential role in strategic decision-making in relation to the fundamental policy issues. Although the new actors are indeed many, the present discussion takes into account only the following: the international actors and forces, the military, big business and the media.

The recent literature on globalization emphasizes the changing functions and declining role of individual states both in the international arena and in domestic politics. For instance, especially since the 1980s the power and discretion of governments over various economic and domestic policy issues were considerably reduced. As interaction with the outside world tended to grow and intensify the USA, the EU, individual European states, the International Monetary Fund (IMF), transnational corporations and international networks of voluntary organizations began to exert greater influence on government policy and public opinion in Turkey. The growing encounters between the international actors and the increased technicality and complexity of the transactions tended to bypass individual political parties, which also tended to get less interested in most foreign policy issues.

Public opinion polls indicate that the military is the most trustworthy and dependable institution in the country while they rank the political parties among the lowest. Since the transition to a multi-party system the military has attempted three coups (1960, 1971, 1980) assuming direct rule in the first and last ones. Although the military leaders always justified their intervention as restoring order and democracy in the country, and indeed returned the country to civilian rule shortly afterwards[18] the shadow of the military over Turkish politics is deeply felt especially in times of political crisis. Political fragmentation, weak governments, the threat of political Islam, terror, and conflicts in international relations with Turkey's immediate neighbours such as Greece tend to shore up the military influence in politics. In the last few years the platform used by the military to impose its policy priorities has been the National Security Council where the military high command meets the president, the prime minister and the ministers in charge of security affairs. On many important issues the public looks to the decisions of this powerful institution of the state rather than the executive organs of the political parties. The implication of course is that in the case of most serious issues, political parties have little influence and are seen as quite incapable of offering viable solutions.

Another crucial institution is the media and particularly television; in a matter of only five or six years the number of private TV channels has exceeded twenty and in a society where written media has limited appeal the visual media has emerged as the most influential institution shaping public opinion. Most private TV channels have a clear preference for sensational news, polarized viewpoints and reporting on the personal characteristics of political party leaders. The attitude in the visual media towards party politics is on the whole highly negative often involving systematic attempts to discredit both politicians and political party activity in the eyes of the wider public. The personalistic emphasis and the leader-centred nature of reporting on the visual media have reinforced the power of the party leaders who use it as a chance to appeal to the voters directly, thereby significantly ignoring the party organizations.

Organized business groups have also increased their influence in politics. In addition to lobbying and the exercise of pressure group politics, business interests are voiced mainly through the media, which in recent years has come under their absolute control. The effect of mass media on politics was most obvious in the case of economic policy matters; issues such as falling real wages, growing income and wealth disparities, and reductions in social welfare expenditure were practically censored and political parties that attempted to criticize the negative consequences of neo-liberal restructuring polices were silenced by the powerful media groups.

Conclusion

As to problems that stem directly from the political parties themselves, it is possible to underline factionalism and fragmentation, decline in party democracy, rampant corruption and the demise of ideology. Almost all the parties of the centre are affected by the negative consequences of internal power struggles and factionalism which threaten the unity of the party and divert the energy of the members to non-productive activities. To the outsider, political party activity then appears futile and devoid of purpose, even proving difficult to understand.

The internal power struggles as well as the squabbles between parties are an outcome of the intense competition for control over key bureaucratic, political and government positions that often bring individuals and political groups tangible material benefits. Since benefits are maximized when the resources are distributed among a smaller number of people others are necessarily excluded, and the latter often emerge as political rivals. The other side of the coin is that holding political office depends significantly on the effective mobilization of public resources to buy political support.[19] The rampant corruption in Turkish politics has its origins in the extreme politicization of rent distribution that has gained new pace with the privatization of public enterprises.[20] In the eyes of the wider public, party politics is thus perceived as an essentially corrupt activity involving promotion of the material interests of individual politicians and/or political groups.

A major criticism directed against the 1995 parliament was that most of the MPs were appointed by the leaders, instead of being truly elected by the party or the voters. The leaders prefer to reward their most loyal supporters with whom they form executive inner circles in the party, and, provided that the party is in power, in the cabinet too. Especially in the case of the DSP, as well as for a number of members of parliament in the other three parties, extreme dependence on the leaders tends to restrict free debate and discussion in the party. Those who do not comply with their leaders can survive either by joining the opposition forces in the party or simply by changing parties. As new recruits are often rewarded with material benefits the negative image of party politics as an essentially corrupt activity is thereby reinforced;[21] Güneş-Ayata, 1994).

Although both centre-left parties have a relatively cleaner record on corruption, the DSP has a distinctively good reputation; this stems from the weakness of clientelism in this particular party where the leadership has crushed all factions and opposition groups, also, however, undermining democracy in the party.

In the 1970s, the ideological differences between left and right was the major axis of party politics. The growing polarization in society with escalating tensions, conflict and violent clashes between left and right was suppressed by the military. The mainstream left and right political parties of the 1980s and 1990s emphasized dialogue and compromise in their relations with each other and they often joined forces in a number of coalition governments. The end of the Cold War and the rise of neo-liberalism have also contributed to this process; as ideological differences tended to wane, ethnic, national and religious identity politics began to take priority. In the 1995 general elections the Islamist RP, the Turkish nationalist Nationalist Action Party (MHP) and the Kurdish nationalist Peoples' Democratic Party (HADEP) together managed to get 34 per cent of the votes.

The structural deficiencies and the electoral decline of the centre-right and centre-left parties are indicators of the difficulties that these parties face in adapting to changing conditions in their environment and the serious decline in their efficiency and legitimacy. Can these parties overcome such problems, or, in other words, are they capable of self-reform? It seems possible to identify various positive changes in this particular direction. The general public is growing increasingly more conscious, sensitive and responsive to corruption incidences and their roots in party politics. On the other hand, urban new middle-class people frustrated about the existing state of party politics, are looking for ways to mount pressure on political parties by means of getting organized in civil associations. New groups can bring new vigour to politics through introducing new ideas, visions and forms of participation. Finally, the loss of strength and the erosion of a good image in public, make a growing number of politicians recognize the urgency of self-reform. The current situation however is one where the discrepancy between the present performance of the mainstream political parties and what is expected of them tends to increase.

Notes

1 Voting is compulsory.
2 KONDA, 1988.
3 TÜSES, 1996.
4 Heper, 1990.
5 Ergüder, 1991.
6 Arat, 1998.
7 Acar, 1991.
8 Levy, 1991.
9 TÜSES, 1996.
10 Bora, 1994.
11 Tachau, 1991.
12 Mango, 1991.
13 Erdoğan, 1992.
14 Kalaycıoğlu, 1994; KONDA, 1988.
15 Tuncer, 1996.
16 Köksal and Kara, 1989.
17 Yıldırım, 1996.
18 Hale, 1994.
19 Ayata, 1993.
20 Öniş, 1997.
21 Turan, 1988b.

References

Acar, Feride, 'The True Path Party, 1983–1989', in Metin Heper and Jacob M. Landau (eds), *Political Parties and Democracy in Turkey* (London: I.B. Tauris, 1991).

Arat, Yeşim, 'A Woman Prime Minister in Turkey: Did It Matter', *Women and Politics*, Vol. 19, No. 4. (1988).

Ayata, Sencer, 'Artık Solda Siyaset Yapmak Paralı Adamın İşi', *İktisat Dergisi*, Eylül, (1993).

Bora, Tanıl, 'Türkiye Sağının İdeolojik ve Siyasi Bunalımı: Oynak Merkez – 'Merkez'siz Oynaklık', *Birikim*, No. 64. (1994).

Erdoğan, Necmi, 'Demokratik Sol ve Sosyal Demokrat Portreler', *Birikim*, No. 44. (1992).

Erel, Nursun and Ali Bilge, *Tansu Çiller'in Siyaset Romanı* (Ankara, Bilgi Yayınevi, 1994).

Ergüder, Üstün, 'The Motherland Party, 1983–1989', in Metin Heper and Jacob M. Landau (eds), *Political Parties and Democracy in Turkey* (London: I.B. Tauris, 1991).

Ergüder, Üstün and Richard I. Hofferbert, 'The 1983 General Elections in Turkey: Continuity or Change in Voting Patterns' in Metin Heper and Ahmet Evin (eds), *State, Democracy and the Military: Turkey in the 1980s* (Berlin and New York: de Gruyter, 1988).

Güneş-Ayata, Ayşe, 'Ideology, Social Bases, and Organizational Structure of the Post-1980 Political Parties', in Atila Eralp, Muharrem Tünay and Birol Yeşilada (eds), *The Political and Socioeconomic Transformation of Turkey* (Westport and London: Praeger, 1993).

——, 'Roots and Trends of Clientelism in Turkey', in Luis Roniger and Ayşe Güneş-Ayata (eds), *Democracy, Clientelism and Civil Society* (London: Lynne Rienner Publishers, 1994).

Hale, William, *Turkish Politics and the Military* (London: Routledge, 1994).

Heper, Metin, 'The State, Political Party and Society in post-1983 Turkey', *Journal of Comparative Politics*, Vol. 25, No. 3, Summer (1990).

Kalaycıoğlu, Ersin, 'Elections and Party References in Turkey: Changes and Continuities in the 1990s', *Comparative Political Studies*, Vol. 27, No. 3, October (1994).

Köksal, S. and N. Kara, (1989) 'Belediyeler ve Kentsel Gruplar', Ankara II. Ulusal Sosyal Bilimler Kongresi, 31 May–2 June 1989.

KONDA (1988) Political Parties in Turkey (the results of a public opinion poll conducted in 1988).

Levy, Avner, 'The Justice Party, 1961–1980', in Metin Heper and Jacob M. Landau (eds), *Political Parties and Democracy in Turkey* (London: I.B. Tauris, 1991).

Mango, Andrew, 'The Social Democratic Populist Party, 1983–1989', in Metin Heper and Jacob M. Landau (eds), *Political Parties and Democracy in Turkey* (London: I.B. Tauris, 1991).

Öniş, Ziya, 'The Political Economy of Islamic Resurgence in Turkey: the Rise of the Welfare Party in Perspective', *Third World Quarterly*, Vol. 18, No. 4 (1997).

Tachau, Frank, 'The Republican People's Party', in Metin Heper and Jacob M. Landau (eds), *Political Parties and Democracy in Turkey* (London: I.B. Tauris, 1991).

Tuncer, Erol, *24 Aralık 1995 Milletvekili Genel Seçimi: Sayısal ve Siyasal Değerlendirme* (Ankara: TESAV Yayınları, 1996).

Turan, İlter, 'Stages of Political Development in the Turkish Republic', in Ergun Özbudun (ed.), *Perspectives on Democracy in Turkey* (Ankara: Turkish Political Science Association, 1988).

——, 'Political Parties and the Party System in Post-1983 Turkey', in Metin Heper and Ahmet Evin (eds), *State, Democracy and the Military: Turkey in the 1980s* (Berlin and New York: de Gruyter, 1988b).

TÜSES, *Türkiye'de Siyasi Parti Seçmenlerinin Nitelikleri, Kimlikleri ve Eğilimleri*, Türkiye Sosyal Ekonomik Siyasal Araştırmalar Vakfı (1996).

Yıldırım, Erdoğan, 'CHP ve DSP: Sosyal Demokrasinin "Belirsizlik" Sorunu', *Birikim*, No. 81 (1996).

Suggestions for further reading

Ahmad, F., *The Making of Modern Turkey* (London, New York: Routledge, 1993).

Balım, Ç. *et al.* (eds), *Turkey: Political, Social and Economic Challenges in the 1990s* (London: E.J. Brill, 1995).

Dodd, C.H., *The Crisis of Turkish Democracy* (Huntingdon, Cambs.: The Eothen Press, 1990).

Eralp, A., Tünay M. and Yeşilada B., *The Political and Socioeconomic Transformation of Turkey* (Westport, CT, Praeger, 1993).

Finkel A. and N. Sirman (eds), *The Turkish State, Turkish Society* (London: Routledge, 1990).

Geyikdağı, M.Y., *Political Parties in Turkey* (New York: Praeger, 1984).

Güneş-Ayata, A., *CHP: Örgüt ve İdeoloji* (Ankara: Gündoğan, 1992).

Hale, W., *Turkish Politics and the Military* (London: Routledge, 1994).

Heper, M., 'The State, Political Party and Society in the Post-1983 Turkey', *Government and Opposition*, 25 (3), (1981) 321–33.

——, *The State Tradition in Turkey* (Beverly, North Humberside: The Eothen Press, 1981).

Heper, M. and A. Evin (eds), *State, Democracy and the Military, Turkey in the 1980s* (Berlin: Walter de Gruyter, 1988).

Heper, M. and J.M. Landau, *Political Parties and Democracy in Turkey* (New York: I.B. Tauris, 1991).

Kalaycıoğlu, E., 'Elections and Party Preferences in Turkey – Changes and Continuities in the 1990s', *Comparative Political Studies*, 27(3), (1994), 402–24.

Karpat, K., *Social Change and Politics in Turkey* (Leiden: Brill, 1973).

Özbudun, E., 'The Turkish Party System: Institutionalization, Polarization and Fragmentation', *Middle Eastern Studies*, 17(2), (1981), 228–40.

Özbudun, E., 'Turkey – How Far from Consolidation?', *Journal of Democracy*, 1996, 7(3), pp. 123–38.

Özbudun, E. (ed), *Perspectives on Democracy in Turkey* (Turkish Political Science Association, 1988).

Schuler, H., *Türkiye'de Sosyal Demokrasi: Particilik, Hemşehrilik, Alevilik* (İletişim Yayınları, 1999).

Tuncer, E., *24 Aralık Milletvekili Genel Seçimi: Sayısal ve Siyasal Değerlendirme* (Ankara: TESAV Yayınları, 1996).

Turan, İ., *Evolution of the Electoral Process in Politics in the Third Turkish Republic* (Boulder: Westview Press, 1994).

TÜSES, *Türkiye'de Siyasi Parti Seçmenlerinin Nitelikleri, Kimlikleri ve Eğilimleri* (Türkiye Sosyal Ekonomik Siyasal Araştırmalar Vakfı, 1996).

Weiker, W.F., *The Modernization of Turkey: from Atatürk to the Present Day* (New York: Holmes and Meier, 1981).

5
The Media in Turkey since 1970

D. Beybin Kejanlıoğlu

Introduction: what 'media' exactly?

The term, 'media', refers to several means of communication[1] which have not been classified according to a precise criterion due to the development and adaptation of media at different times. The oldest media (books, newspapers and magazines) are physical products, like records and tapes; an age-old film is also a product, yet cinema is a location; radios and televisions are the receiving equipment we use at home; and the new media, cable and satellite, are technologies of distribution.[2]

A further uncertainty arises from the regulations which consider some media together, such as radio and television under the rubric of *broadcasting*, and books, newspapers and magazines as *print media*. Among the print media, another classification depends upon the cycle of distribution, putting books in one category if they are 'irregular' and classifying newspapers and magazines as dailies, weeklies, monthlies, bi-monthlies, and so on, and calling them printed *press*.

The convergence of communication-information technologies and telecommunications further complicated such an incoherent field. Electronic publishing, teletext, videotex, teleconferencing are no longer new; interactive use of the Internet is common for some people and potentially for most people in the world, and a new technology under discussion is digital TV. It has become quite difficult to separate telecoms from broadcasting yet the predominance of economic imperatives has called into question the latter's cultural aspect.

Still, most of the analyses of the media are usually selective and focus on a few media. One of the widespread classifications is to distinguish media 'for' politics from entertainment.[3] Media 'for' politics include news and current affairs programmes on TV and political stories in the press. Even the scholars who endorse that the entertainment format is steeped in political implications, go on making such traditional distinctions for the specific perspective they adopt.[4] Whatever the reason, selectivity in analyzing the media is necessary for practical reasons.

All the above arguments imply that the media will be analyzed with their cultural, political and economic aspects. It is not easy to draw a map of the media in any particular country over any particular time span, and when we specify a country such as Turkey and a time span from the 1970s up to now, we start encountering further problems. The rest of this introductory part highlights specific problems in mapping out the media scene in Turkey and leads to a selectivity and outline of the chapter.

We are faced with three main problems. The first is that we cannot take all the media into consideration because the different classifications and exclusions of media both in academic and in general terms, the different social uses of different media, diversity of economic and technical factors, and regulatory diversification prevent us from such an attempt. 'Media' as an inclusive term has entered common usage in Turkish quite recently (*medya* in Turkish). Its usage in the singular as 'media' not 'medium' has not attracted attention except from academics and some publishers; a short-circuited debate has focused on whether to follow its translation from French as singular or from English as plural. Although the term is still regarded with distaste by some circles, it has acquired widespread usage[5] and sometimes is used to refer to television only. Such imprecision matters.

The printed press and broadcasting are the media that have most commonly attracted much attention making them a suitable choice for analysis. Film/cinema follows. Even if we exclude, for example, video tapes and pop music from the analysis by themselves, they should be included in the analysis of broadcasting and film/cinema. The same is true for the exclusion of cable and satellite: they would enter into the analysis of television by the backdoor.

The second problem is to feel content with selecting a few inclusive media fields. The problem arises from two contradictory trends. On the one hand, the diversity of social uses of other media can escape attention; on the other hand, it is difficult to separate these fields in Turkey in the 1990s with regard to economic trends – those of concentration. The first side of the problem can be partly solved by mentioning diverse uses when the flow of argument allows it. And the second side will be solved by taking the 'media industry' into account under a separate heading after dealing separately with books, printed press, film, radio and television (including video, cable and satellite which enter the analysis at certain points).

The third problem is related to the chosen time period – from the 1970s to the 1990s – because, historically, each medium has different stages of development in Turkey as in the rest of the world. A brief historical background can allow us to overcome this problem.

Thus, the plan of the chapter will be as follows: first, the cultural, economic and political aspects of the media until 1970 will be outlined in very broad terms. Different stages of their development will be included in this brief and general account. Then, the general trends in diverse media since 1970 will be taken into consideration. The media field in the nineties will be assessed through the 'media industry', focusing, particularly and necessarily, on the press and broadcasting. The last part will be a critical evaluation of 'media and society' in Turkey.

Media in Turkey before 1970: a brief historical account

One-party rule (Republican Peoples' Party, 1923–46)

By turning her face to the West the Republic of Turkey has from its very inception been involved in cultivating a 'new' culture. Under the presidency of Mustafa Kemal Atatürk, several radical attempts were made and several measures were taken in the cultural arena which would have an important influence on people's daily lives and which are still under discussion.

One of the chain of radical attempts was related to the alphabet and language which directly influenced publishers. In the first five years of the Republic (1923–28), approximately 5000 books were published, using the old (Arabic) alphabet, for one million readers, less than one-tenth of the population. The state was directly involved in publishing through the Ministry of Education.[6] In 1928, adoption of a new, Latin alphabet was ordered and publication of books in the old alphabet was strictly forbidden. Those were hard times for publishers and printers.

Under İsmet İnönü's presidency in the late 1930s and early 1940s, the Ministry of National Education played a decisive role in education; in fact, the cultural policy of the state gained a new impetus. Classic literary and philosophical texts were translated into Turkish and in 1950 their number reached 745. From 1939–46 publishers, authors and Ministry officials had a very good working relationship.[7] However, neither the late 1930s and 1940s, nor the first 15 years of the Republic saw favourable comments from the press. Courts, censorship, and suspension of publications were common practices.[8]

The prospect of film as an important medium for education, culture and propaganda in a newly established country with 90 per cent illiteracy was simply ignored. Interestingly, several films were shot during the war years or before the establishment of the Republic but no films were produced between 1924–28.[9] Until the mid-1940s, theatrical narration was dominant in Turkish films and import-based big family companies were dominant in the film industry.[10] All through these years there was control over films which became stricter after 1939 with a new legal document allowing state agents to check film scripts and films at every stage of production.[11]

In radio broadcasting, the state was an active agent even in its first ten years (1927–36) when a private company ran the business. Radio was initially regarded as an entertainment medium; from the 1930s onwards it acquired an educational role. In an attempt to spread Western classical music through establishing music schools, the Presidency's Philharmonic Band and so on, the state also intervened in radio which was mostly dependent upon disseminating music. In 1934, broadcasting Turkish music was even banned for some time.[12] Similar to book publishing, the period between 1939–45 is generally regarded as the 'good days' of radio broadcasting.

In sum, such an holistic attempt to educate people of different backgrounds from above or to cultivate a somewhat Westernized culture required the means of communication to be under the direct and strict control of the state. Community interaction was also provided by establishing 'public houses' in the cities, then in the rural areas, where not only exhibitions, concerts and courses on painting, language and so on, were organized but also where books were published and films shown. Such a policy on communication–education–culture would have setbacks after passing to the multi-party period but without the state losing anything of its role as controlling agent.

The multi-party period (1946/50–60), the military intervention of 1960 and afterwards

Winning the first multi-party elections in 1946, the Republican Peoples' Party continued to rule the country for four more years. Yet it was stricter than before and faced constant opposition from the Democrat Party (DP). The 1950s witnessed three general elections (1950, 1954 and 1957), all of which resulted in the victory of the DP even though it steadily lost public support in the course of its years in government. The party defended religion and economic liberalism in its rhetoric, but after the first few years in office it started to be restrictive and even repressive in its policies. The military intervention of 1960 severely punished the leading figures of the DP. A new constitution was prepared and passed under military rule. The 1961 Constitution is generally regarded as Turkey's most democratic constitution, yet the lack of democratic consensus and popular support in preparing it made it one of the most significant subjects for criticism throughout the 1960s and ended with amendments in the early 1970s.

The DP government's tolerance towards the press lasted for two years. From 1952 onwards and especially after 1954, new restrictive laws and their implementation set the relationship of the government to the press.[13] The most important development for the press under the multi-party regime of those years was its industrialization. The newspapers became 'mass entertainment media'[14] and similar trends were observed in book publishing: cheap pocket book series were published and detective Mayk Hammer's stories became best-sellers.[15]

The 1961 Constitution brought 'press freedom'; however, before the 1962 general elections, a new law provided that the press had no right to criticize military decisions and actions especially against the DP. Moreover, the restrictive Penal Law was still in force. In the 1960s, both books and newspapers proliferated with varied contents. An important development in the press was the establishment of a distribution duopoly. Press dependence on the government continued as was manifest in its revenues, 56 per cent of which came from official ads in 1969.[16]

The film industry in Turkey entered into a new phase from 1946 onwards. It was based on an increase in Turkish film production and cinemas in Anatolia, and the regional distribution of Turkish films in Anatolian markets. The dominance of regional distributors was established in the mid-1950s and this system of film-making based on the demands of distributors continued up to the late 1970s.[17] A star system for films was established both because of the demands of the regional distributors and of a general trend towards consumer entertainment as also observed in books and newspapers. The only exception to film-making's dependency on distributors' demands was the attempts of official bodies which aimed primarily at producing educational films or documentaries.[18] The democratic environment of the 1960s had no direct positive effect on cinema; the same restrictions and controls were applied.

In radio, the DP's rhetoric was echoed in the introduction of religious programmes and advertisements. From the late 1940s onwards, the American supply of radio programmes was also evident. However, what made radio a crucial subject in the 1950s was its extensive use as a propaganda medium by the government. Those years in broadcasting history in Turkey are labelled a period of 'partisan radio'.[19] Leading DP figures were judged by the military regime because of their use of the state radio along with other crimes. Consequently, the most democratic attempt for the media in the 1960s was in broadcasting. Following an article in the constitution, a new broadcasting law was passed in 1963 and an independent public corporation was established in 1964: Turkish Radio and Television Corporation (TRT). However, constitutional and legal guarantees were not sufficient in practising autonomy. TRT was subject to partisan use.[20] Another important development in this period was the introduction of television in 1968. It had not been planned beforehand and was started with technical aid from Germany and professional education mainly from Germany and Britain.[21]

In short, book publishing, the press and film enjoyed a somewhat restricted liberal regime; the state defined their independence. In the press laws, the Penal Law, the law of Police Duties and Responsibilities, and other related legal documents or in cases of national emergency, the state reserved the right to reduce their autonomy. A more indirect way of enforcing formal rules and unwritten rules of power politics was also used to intervene in their operation. In broadcasting the state not only intervened but was an active agent as well. Even after 1964, the autonomous public corporation could not be autonomous in practice; the rules of power politics dominated the broadcasting arena which would also be provided for legally in the early 1970s by the abolishment of TRT's autonomy.

The media in Turkey since 1970

The military intervention of 1971, which did not abolish the parliament, brought significant amendments to the 1961 Constitution and other laws, most of which restricted democratic freedoms and rights. The military intervention of 1980 was stricter and even today, the most undemocratic constitution ever seen in Turkey, that of 1982, is in force with few amendments. However, 'constitution' and 'law' do not seem to have been the source of legitimacy for the powerful.

Books

The political authorities in Turkey have long considered the *book* to be one of the most dangerous 'weapons' due to its importance in influencing people. Books did not lose their dangerous status even in the 1980s as was manifest in portraying terrorist groups with their books along with their arms in photographs published by national newspapers and on television.[22]

Publishing certain books and prints was banned at particular times. It was quite easy to be arrested for having dangerous books and prints at home or when carrying them with you. Burning books – a practice related to the dominance of repressive state organs at particular times – was not exceptional either. These actions were common during the military intervals and during some periods of democratic rule.

Despite such pressures on publishers, the period of the state of siege from spring 1971 to autumn 1973 witnessed a proliferation of books. The total number of books published was more than 6500 in 1971 and 1972, reaching almost 7500 in 1973, from approximately

200 publishers at the end of the state of siege. The total number of books decreased to 4318 in 1980.[23]

Coalition governments and social unrest symbolized the 1974–80 democratic period. Illustrative examples of the military regime's attitude towards books were the banning of 237 titles and the burning of 133 000 books.[24] Even the printers were arrested in those years. Similar hostile attitudes towards book publishers continued all through the 1980s.

However, there were also several attempts to develop publishing. One of them was to establish a publishers' cooperative which lasted 4–5 years yet published some books and journals. Another attempt was to open book clubs and make sales or send bonus books to members. Yet another attempt was the most permanent one: organizing book fairs. The first was in 1982 in Istanbul; it then became more comprehensive and started to be organized annually. In 1987, 104 publishers participated and 57 000 people visited the fair; the number of publishers increased to 237 and of visitors to 336 000 in 1994.[25] Today, the three main cities (Istanbul, Ankara, Izmir) have annual book fairs.

The 1980s were also the golden years for encyclopaedia publishing. Newly unemployed intellectuals (from universities and from TRT) worked on such initiatives. Moreover, in the 1980s, several inexperienced and unprofessional people entered the marginal publishing sector with some of them becoming opposition voices in Turkey. These publishers and some already established ones jointly organized interesting campaigns against political pressure.[26] Today, book publishing seems to be an unstable market full of small business ventures. However, in the last few years, the finance sector and big newspaper groups have started to increase their investments in this sector.

The publishing sector has no specific regulations. However, the Penal Law, the law on terrorism, the law on works of art, and the law on protecting children from harmful publications have all been applied to it. Copyright has only recently become a significant issue. Changing rates of value added tax, increasing paper costs, politically restrictive regulations and 'pirate' editions of books are among publishers' most important problems.[27]

According to the data provided from the General Directorate of Libraries, a branch of the Ministry of Culture, 7813 books were published in Turkey in 1995, a figure which increased to 9494 in 1996, each with an average print run of a thousand copies.[28] The data from the State Institute of Statistics, however, show the total number of books in 1996 as 8207, so we do not know the exact number of published books or precise information about their subjects. For instance, in 1996, 2391 books out of a total of 8207 were categorized as 'social sciences', 1690 as 'literature', and 1024 as 'general'![29] The most striking development in this period is an increase in the Islamist orientation of publishers, and accordingly in published religious material.

Newspapers and magazines

Under the state of siege, journalists were under the strict control of the state. Newspapers were ordered to cease operation 39 times, some for known, some for unknown periods. Although there were several legal investigations and court cases against journalists between 1974–80, decisions were delayed. The military coup of 1980 completed them along with the new ones; most of them ended with imprisonment: 82 writers, journalists and publishers were imprisoned.[30] The 1982 Constitution, the Press Law, and – similar to book publishing – the law on harmful publications, the Penal Law (and later the law on terrorism) constituted the legal framework within which the printed press operated. Furthermore, a series of government regulations in spring 1990 brought censorship to the press.[31]

There were also indirect control mechanisms. Although the role of official ads declined (56 per cent in 1969, 6.8 per cent in 1980), the control of paper input by the government still made the press dependent on the government. Especially in the late 1980s, Prime Minister Turgut Özal used this weapon against hostile press. For instance, after the big newspaper managers had agreed on increasing the newspaper sale price, the government announced an increase in the price of paper input the same day.[32] One ton of paper cost $US 276 in 1980 and $US 750 in 1989.[33]

Furthermore, oligopolization of the printed press was intentionally promoted by the government in the late 1980s. Cypriot businessman Asil Nadir entered the press sector through his personal ties with the government's leading figures, including members of the Özal family and their friends.[34] Since then, not only have marketing techniques become one of the major tools of the press, but also few big press groups have been left in the sector. There were six big groups in the late 1980s, declining to four in two or three years, and to three in 1994. The coalition government of the True Path Party and the Social Democratic Peoples' Party (SHP) (from 1991 onwards) also supported this condensed structure by providing credits for big press groups.

While the number of press groups has been declining, the number of newspapers and magazines has been increasing. The amount of newspapers with an average daily circulation over 10 000 was 11 in 1983, 14 in 1990 and 32 in 1997.[35] The motives behind this increase may be directly related to the big groups having invested heavily in new technology, enabling them to increase their opportunities to get more ads, a situation in sharp contrast to their attitudes to journalists who continue to have weak or no syndical rights.[36] The difference in newspaper prices is covered by the different prices of consumer goods they offer and that 'readers' can obtain through collecting a certain number of coupons. So, the increase in the daily circulation of national newspapers, from three million in the late 1970s to five–six million today, seems to be the result of such promotional activities.

The big newspaper groups had few magazines in the late 1970s yet this pattern started changing in the 1980s. Today, the major newspaper and publishing groups publish specialist magazines; they have even made agreements with foreign companies which have resulted in the proliferation of magazines with foreign brand names like *Marie Claire, Cosmopolitan, Penthouse, Esquire, Votre Beauté* and so forth. Three major press groups – Hürriyet, Sabah and Milliyet – are also dominant in periodicals along with broadcasting.[37]

There were 21 weekly periodicals, each with a circulation over 4000 (annual circulation 316 500) in June 1997. The themes of these weeklies range from people's lives and mostly sensational news, to automobiles, sports, economy and computers. Most of the magazines published in Turkey are monthlies (40 per cent), and those with an average circulation of over 10 000 amounted to 31 in July 1997. Women, cooking, health, fashion, youth, decoration, travel and economy are their leading themes.[38]

Film (and video)

National film-making has been declining from the late 1970s onwards. The chain of production–distribution–display in the film industry was broken and the film sector entered into crisis. Nevertheless, the crisis conditions had no effect on control. Different legal documents in 1977, 1979, 1983 and 1986 continued to restrictively define and set the parameters for film-making.[39]

The main indicators of the crisis were the decline in the number of viewers and cinemas. The total number of viewers in 1984 was 56.2 million; it decreased to 20.2 million in 1988 and to 11 million in 1994. Meanwhile, foreign releases increased from a 49 per cent share of the total in 1985 to 84 per cent in 1994. This was related to the entry into the Turkish film market of giant international distributors from 1989 onwards. The total number of cinemas was 460 in 1987 and 281 in 1993.[40] Although the number of cinemas started rising and reached 300 in 1996, the number of seats were declining because of the division of each big hall into smaller ones especially in big cities. The distribution of cinemas is uneven: in 1996, 29 per cent of cities had none, 30 per cent had only one, Istanbul had 83, Ankara 34, and Izmir 27.[41]

The spread of television viewing in the 1970s and the introduction of VCRs and videotapes into an unregulated market in the early 1980s had an important impact on the film industry.[42] However, video along with the advertising sector in the 1980s, and private television channels along with the music sector (videoclip) in the 1990s also provided jobs for staff previously from the film sector. Of course, these sectors have their specific conditions and operations which differ from film-making.

Under crisis conditions, and in spite of a steady decrease in the number of viewers and cinemas, the increase in the production of films can only be explained by the fact that filmmakers directed their attention to the video sector.[43] However, video lost its attractiveness in a few years both for producers because of the introduction of regulations and for viewers.

The number of films started declining from 1988 onwards and the following year foreign capital was allowed to intervene in the Turkish film market. Film releases started developing to the advantage of foreign films, mostly American, and to the advantage of giant film distributors, namely Warner Brothers, UIP, and Özen Film, a big Turkish company.[44] Foreign distributors initially supported Turkish films which would not have a chance of commercial success, then they also started controlling the management of the

Table 5.1 Total Number of Films Produced in the mid-1980s

Year	*No. of films*
1983	78
1984	126
1985	123
1986	184
1987	186
1988	117

cinemas. In 1993, only 11 out of a total of 83 Turkish films could be released.[45] In 1994, 72 films were shot and only 16 were shown, mostly for less time than their foreign competitors. Of the 16, eight were distributed as a result of their producers' relentless efforts, two had their distribution opportunity in Islamic circles, and only six were distributed by the giant distributors.[46]

Despite the individual successes of some Turkish films today the cinema system in Turkey is under the domination of a few distributors, two of which are giant trans-nationals. American cultural domination is apparent everywhere; still, in small Turkish cinemas one can see films of high technical quality without delay![47]

Radio

Recent developments have differentiated radio from television which used to be regulated together under the title of broadcasting. As a matter of fact, the regulatory environment of the 1970s and early 1980s was applied to both.

Radio broadcasting was under TRT monopoly in the early 1970s, with one nation-wide channel. However, in 1971 there were more than 70 radio stations for some schools and institutions. Among these, 'police radio' and 'meteorology radio' had a high rate of listeners. Moreover, there were American radio stations for the military personnel at the American bases in Turkey. Two more TRT radio channels started broadcasting in 1975.[48]

After the military intervention of 1971, a new director-general, who had a military background, was appointed to TRT. He tried to strengthen regional radio programmes to protect Turkey from harmful foreign broadcasts.[49] Later, TRT lost its legal autonomy and government control of radio has continued legally since 1972. Especially from the mid-1970s onwards, TRT has become a major arena for party politics. TRT's director-generals and other high positions have changed after every change of government. This has had disastrous effects on TRT's long-term planning.

There were two million receiver sets in the mid-1960s, 4.5 million in 1980, and today there are approximately ten million registered. Radio, especially studios in Istanbul and Ankara, improved technically and financially. In the 1970s, 25–34 per cent of programmes were educational/cultural and news; 4–5 per cent ads and the rest were Turkish and foreign classical and pop music.[50] After the military coup of 1980 and the 1983 broadcasting law, nothing changed much in radio broadcasting for a decade. One of the most important articles of the new law was to establish a high board for radio and television whose members were to be appointed mostly by civil and military bureaucrats. This board was to oversee broadcasting at a time when there were no private channels but a public broadcasting corporation under the influence of that day's government. Yet what was under discussion about the law was not such an issue as TRT's use by the government, mostly related to TV.

Local governments, mostly led by the opposition parties, announced their intention to open radio stations in 1989, yet their applications were refused by the central administrative and political authorities. However, in 1992, several illegal radio stations started broadcasting, following the pattern of private television stations. Turkey went through a private radio station boom. In the first three months of 1993, the Ministries of Transportation and Internal Affairs (Home Office) sent circular letters to the city governors to close the stations. So, all the private radio stations and some TV stations using terrestrial channels had to stop broadcasting for 3–4 months. There was much speculation about the reasons for this decision: (1) the official one was technical – the pollution of frequency bands; (2) another official announcement was political; (3) the most probable reason was to take measures against the dissemination of Islamist radios; (4) another one was the lobbying activities of producers in the music sector looking for copyright;[51] and (5) the last one was the government's manoeuvre to change the agenda.[52] Whichever the reason(s), a widespread public campaign erupted against this decision. An amendment to the 1982

Constitution was made in July 1993. Radio stations became constitutional but had to wait for the new broadcasting law to get licences and for frequencies to be allocated. The law has been in force since April 1994, most of the stations have been registered for getting licences, but frequencies have not yet been allocated!

Today, the total number of radio stations is more than 1200: 1056 local, 108 regional and 36 national stations, plus unregistered ones. It seems that radio has become the most significant local media. In their programming policy, all the private radio stations are heavily reliant on music and phone-ins.[53]

Television (plus cable TV and satellite broadcasting)

Being introduced in 1968, television broadcasting in Turkey not only arrived late but was also poor both technically and content-wise. Until the mid-1980s there was only one black and white channel. Colour TV came in 1984 and the second channel was introduced in 1985. After the three-year long military administration, the debate on broadcasting in parliament consisted of elected members of parliament (MPs) focusing on some of the articles in the 1983 broadcasting law instead of dealing with how to improve television broadcasting. Two main articles of the law were under discussion: one was about allocating 30 minutes a month to the government to present its activities on radio and TV, and the other was about broadcasting parliamentary activities only on radio not on TV.

While the opposition parties and most of the journalists were dealing with the government's extensive use of television for its own interests only and bias in the news, the government made several related attempts in communications directly influencing broadcasting. One of them was related to the article in the broadcasting law about presenting government activities on TV – it allowed the government to prepare such programmes but without using TRT's production facilities. Furthermore, TRT started buying and showing programmes produced outside TRT in 1985, a move that enabled independent production companies to flourish.[54] Although applications by the press groups to start broadcasting had been refused,[55] the state minister responsible for TRT announced that private channels would be allowed to operate if independent producers could supply sufficient programmes.

Other areas of conflict emerged before and after the 1989 local elections. Before them, opposition parties and especially the SHP applied several times to the High Election Board to stop TRT's biased broadcasts. For the first time in TRT's history, the Board cautioned TRT about its broadcasts. Consequently, TRT did not broadcast the programme on the government's activities which was scheduled a day before the elections. After the election victory for the opposition the conflict within the Motherland Party between liberals and conservatives became apparent. Prime Minister Özal changed the cabinet members and forced the director-general of TRT to resign. Interestingly, a company which would lead in the private TV initiative in Turkey the following year – and in which Özal's son had a share – was established in 1989.[56]

After the local elections another area of conflict erupted. The mayors of several cities and towns, mostly from the SHP, began retransmitting programmes received from the satellite channels on UHF frequencies. Not only the government but also the High Board of Radio and Television acted against these initiatives. However, the government and High Board conflicted with each other on another issue, cable TV. The government and the PTT went on cabling Ankara and Istanbul, and stated that it was a pilot project; yet the High Board and TRT defended a position that cable TV was violating TRT's monopoly. However, the crucial violation would come to the fore in 1990. A private TV channel, Star 1, commenced broadcasting via satellite. Its legality, transfer of TRT's personnel with high salaries, taking away TRT's revenues and audiences, and tax problems would occupy the agenda.[57]

Özal became President. The company which held the advantage of having the first private TV channel in Turkey started making plans for a second private channel. The SHP and True Path Party formed a coalition government. The company was not willing to include Özal's son in the second channel plans. A severe chain of conflicts was seen between the shareholders of Turkey's first private channel from the last days of 1991 onwards. Another chain was related to the launch of more TV channels. Two years later 20 national TV channels appeared.

A new radio-television broadcasting law was passed in 1994. It was shaped by the terms of the Council of Europe's Convention on Trans-frontier Television Broadcasting. What was forgotten, however, is that the Convention is about trans-frontier television broadcasting, which caused, for instance, 'broadcaster' to be defined as only television broadcaster.[58] The RTÜK (Radio and Television Supreme Board) was established by this law and consisted of nine members nominated by parliament (five nominated by the party/parties in power and four by opposition parties). It tried to overcome some of the problems in the law, like adding 'radio' to the definition of broadcaster, through issuing a set of regulations. The law is still in force full of mistakes.

The very first action the RTÜK took was to ask for its share of advertisement revenues from the private broadcasters. In its history of four and a half years, the RTÜK has published some regulations and taken actions against private radio and television stations – most of which were punitive – with the suspension of broadcasts becoming a common act. The RTÜK was quite late in auctioning the transmission frequencies, yet when it intended to do so in the last months of 1997 the National Security Board (military commanders constituted more than half its members) stopped it.[59] This means that all the private stations are operating without licences, and thus, according to one commentator,[60] they are still illegal.

The number of channels that can simultaneously transmit on UHF and VHF frequencies is limited and other countries do not use much of this technical capacity in order to secure technical quality. However, in Turkey this is not the case. Today, there are 261 registered commercial television channels in Turkey, 16 of which are national, 15 regional and 230 local. As there was no allocation, the major channels are available on microwave via a normal aerial as well as on cable and satellite. This has also resulted in low satellite viewing and cable subscription. Penetration of cable television was only 6.5 per cent in 1997 which is far behind western Europe's 26.3 per cent; over 1 500 000 households have been cabled and only a third subscribe. Therefore, it seems that broadcasting in Turkey does not only have technical problems but that it is also striving for regulation.[61]

Almost eight million of a total 12 112 000 households have at least one television set and the average viewing time per day is 300 minutes, compared to 180 minutes in Europe.[62] Research conducted during the week of 18–24 April 1998 through an analysis of the programme schedules of 12 major national television channels, including public broadcasters TRT1 and TRT2, showed that only 18 per cent of all programmes are foreign. However, it must be remembered that television genres were mostly Turkish adaptations of foreign ones. Among the total of 1624 (82 per cent) domestic programmes, news/discussions and entertainment programmes constituted almost half of the schedules.[63]

Media industry in Turkey in the 1990s

It was not possible to talk about a media industry in Turkey until the last decade. Of course, there have been newspaper barons who ran the print media as a family business; there have been regional film distributors for some time who dictated what kind of films to produce. However, they did not see themselves – and nor did anyone else see them – as big industrial businessmen. Everything changed in the late 1980s and 1990s. Earlier newspaper owners sold their companies to the new players who had interests in different sectors; then commercial broadcasting commenced. The new players extended their shares to cross-media ownership along with some other interests. Among their reasons for investing in the media sector the following can be listed: comprehension of all-powerful media, social control, decreasing the risk of capital in other sectors, getting credits from the state/government, having a pressure tool over the government, substituting ad spend, marketing, and financial transactions.[64] In fact, the figures do not give the exact amount of ads and ad spend, and are insufficient to understand the operations of the media industry. A lot of ads on each channel are by sister companies and are not paid for. '[A]ll television channels are big money losers but are useful in boosting newspaper sales or customers for non-media interests through relentless ads' and audience ratings.[65] They are also useful in putting pressure on the government to get credits or win bids in other sectors of the economy.[66]

Nevertheless, there was an advertising boom in the 1990s and the figures are as follows: Total ad-spend peaked in 1992 at $US1158 million, decreased sharply in 1994 – a year of economic stagnation – to $US382.8 million, and bounced back to reach $US1250 million in 1997.[67] The distribution of ad-spend among media also changed in the 1990s with television starting to take the lion's share: 41 per cent went to TV, 40 per cent to the press, 7 per cent to cinema, 7 per cent to outdoor media and 5 per cent to radio in 1997. The four big television stations' share of ad-spend ranges from 15 per cent to 25 per cent, which accounts for more than 80 per cent of all TV ad-spend.[68]

These big four groups have recently cooperated in many areas and taken similar measures (in ads, in stopping costly productions, in transfer of their staff, and so on) as all are facing big financial losses. The fifth big group has forwarded new outputs and been trying to change its conservative image. These media groups are commonly mentioned with the names of TV channels, ATV, Channel D, Star, Show and TGRT and of their owners. Their holding's interests in media and other sectors are shown in Table 5.2. The table also shows that the broadcasting law (such as limits on single investors and shareholders of private channels) has either not been implemented or that the industry has found gaps in the law through which to impose its interests.

Concluding remarks: what are the media 'for'?

When we talk about media industries we also talk about 'cultural industries' which are integrated into the general industrial structure as economic initiatives but which are at the same time producing cultural goods – thus they play an important role in 'organizing the images and discourses through which people make sense of the world'.[69] The media in Turkey since 1970 seems to be a story of a change from a poor media environment to the rapid industrialization of media and its increasing reliance on visual material, advertisements and consumption. People in Turkey have never become 'citizens' in the Western democratic sense of the word but have been converted into 'full-time consumers' rapidly and easily, something in which media have played the major role.

Meanwhile, there have been no changes in the authoritarian understanding of the state and its control. The constitution and the most important laws have been put into force directly or indirectly by the military. Big business interests are always safeguarded. 'Why not?' one might well ask in a country where they are the main supporters of the nationalist, statist discourse. Laws are for the powerless and the phrases 'to be lawful', 'to be legal' and 'to be accountable' mean nothing for the powerful of the day.

Table 5.2 Cross-Media Ownership in Turkey

Holding	*Media interests*	*Non-media interests*
Milliyet Gazetecilik Hürriyet Holding Owned by Aydın Doğan	*TV*: Kanal D (with Doğuş Group & Italian MediaSet) Bravo (cable) *Radio*: Radyo D, Hür FM *Newspaper*: *Milliyet, Hürriyet, Radikal, Meydan Posta, Fanatik* *Other*: Magazines, media marketing, TV production, distribution, news agencies, book publishing, D&R book and music stores (with Raks)	Automotive, banking, health, insurance, marketing, travel
Medya Holding Medi Group Owned by Dinç Bilgin	*TV*: ATV (with Çukurova Holding), Prima *Newspaper*: *Sabah, Yeni Yüzyıl, Takvim, Bugün, Fotomaç, Yeni Asır* *Other*: Magazines, media marketing, TV production, distribution, news agency, book publishing.	Mainly media, but through Çukurova Holding: Banking, finance, insurance, steel works
Prime Holding Rumeli Holding Owned by Cem Uzan	*TV*: Star, Kral *Radio*: Super FM, Kral FM, Metro FM Radio Blue *Other*: Production, marketing, advertising, printing	Banking, cement, construction, energy, finance, football (till 1998), telecoms

Table 5.2 Cross-Media Ownership in Turkey – *continued*

Holding	*Media interests*	*Non-media interests*
Holding in America & Europe Owned by Erol Aksoy	*TV*: ShowTV, Cine5 (+PlayboyTV), Maxi, SuperSport (subscription except ShowTV) *Radio*: Show Radyo, Radyo5 *Newspaper*: *Akşam*, *Güneş*, *Spor* *Other*: Magazines, tele-marketing, film & TV production, distribution	Banking, finance, insurance, marketing, manufacturing
İhlas Holding Owned by Enver Ören	*TV*: TGRT *Radio*: TGRT FM *Newspaper*: *Türkiye*, *Turkey* *Other*: Magazines, news agency, distribution	Automotive, banking, finance, food & soft drinks, health, home appliances, insurance, marketing, travel

Source: MDB Media Information Unit, *Mediascape Türkiye '98*, İLEF Ankara University and Konrad Adenauer Stiftung, 1998, 55. Adapted with minor adjustments.

Of course some problems occur between different business interests and different political parties. In such cases, the unwritten rules of power politics and arbitrariness dominate the political, administrative, economic and cultural agenda. Generally, business ventures in the media are also political ventures, which raises doubts about the new media magnates' intentions, especially when one considers the severe financial problems they face.

In short, the repressive role of the state, the organic cord tying the private sector to the state, the unwritten rules of power politics and the passive role of the public are the underlying features of politics in Turkey and they have direct implications on the media.

Notes

1 Here, the term 'media' is chosen to refer to means of communication. The term 'mass media' is not used not only because of the pejorative connotations of the term 'mass' (see Williams, 1958 and Bennett, 1982) but also because of the technological developments which have made the term obsolete.
2 Seymour-Ure, 1987, 283; Negrine, 1989, 231.
3 See Seymour-Ure, 1987.
4 For example, Negrine, 1989.
5 We even have a *Medya Plaza*, a *Medya Centre* and *Medya Towers* (they are not translated but are used in Turkish as they are given here). They are the big media companies' buildings in Istanbul.
6 Kaynardağ, 1985.
7 Kaynardağ, 1985, 2826–27.
8 Kabacalı, 1990: 110–58.
9 Özön, 1985.
10 Işığan, 1998.
11 Özön, 1985.
12 Kocabaşoğlu, 1980.
13 Kabacalı, 1990.
14 Şenyapılı, 1971; Oktay, 1987.
15 Kaynardağ, 1985.
16 Koloğlu, 1995.
17 Işığan, 1998.
18 Işığan, 1998.
19 Aksoy, 1960.
20 Şahin, 1974.
21 Öngören, 1982.
22 Kabacalı, 1996.

23 Kaynardağ, 1985.
24 Koloğlu, 1995.
25 Kabacalı, 1996.
26 Gürsoy, 1996.
27 Kabacalı, 1996; Sökmen, 1996.
28 MDB, 1998.
29 MDB, 1998.
30 Kabacalı, 1990.
31 Kabacalı, 1990.
32 Production of paper was dominated by the state-owned SEKA. The printed press had a privilege in the 'allocation' of paper; the rest was transferred to the market for textbook publishing. Thus, paper was subject to black market selling. Even the production of paper by the private sector did not solve this problem as the private sector preferred to produce expensive high quality paper (Kabacalı 1996).
33 Koloğlu, 1995.
34 Münir, 1993.
35 MDB, 1998.
36 Koloğlu, 1995.
37 Gür, 1995.
38 MDB, 1998.
39 Özön, 1985.
40 Işığan, 1998.
41 MDB, 1998.
42 There was a video boom. Today, more than half the households with a TV have a VCR (MDB, 1998).
43 Işığan, 1998, see Table 5.1.
44 Açar, 1996; Işığan, 1998.
45 Eryılmaz, 1996.
46 Işığan, 1998.
47 Açar, 1996.
48 Kocabaşoğlu, 1985.
49 Gülizar, 1985.
50 Kocaba şoğlu, 1985.
51 Aksoy and Robins, 1993.
52 Kejanlıoğlu, 1998a.
53 MDB, 1998.
54 Alemdar and Kaya, 1993; Çelenk, 1998.
55 Çaplı, 1990.
56 Kejanlıoğlu, 1998a.
57 Çaplı and Dündar, 1995.
58 For the details of other implications and translation mistakes, see Pekman, 1994.
59 Kejanlıoğlu, 1998b.
60 Batmaz, 1998.
61 MDB, 1998.
62 MDB, 1998.

63 MDB, 1998.
64 Tuncel, 1994.
65 MDB, 1998.
66 Moreover, television stations do not adhere to the location and time limits of ads imposed by law and even create new forms of presentation like the appearance and disappearance of images and brands in 2–3 seconds in nooks and corners of the TV screen during programmes.
67 MDB, 1998.
68 MDB, 1998.
69 Golding and Murdock, 1991.

References

Books, dissertations and articles

Açar, M., 'Türk Sinemasında Amerikan Hakimiyeti', *Yüzyıl Biterken Cumhuriyet Dönemi Türkiye Ansiklopedisi*, Vol. 14 (İstanbul: İletişim Yayınları, 1996), pp. 1186–9.

Aksoy, A. and K. Robins, '*Gecekondu*-Style Broadcasting in Turkey: a Confrontation of Cultural Values', *InterMedia*, Vol. 21, No. 3, June–July (1993), 15–17.

Aksoy, M., *Partizan Radyo ve DP* (Ankara: Forum, 1960).

Alemdar, K. and R. Kaya, *Radyo Televizyonda Yeni Düzen: Dünya Deneyi ve Türkiye'deki Arayışlar* (Ankara: TOBB Yayınları, 1993).

Aziz, A., '3984 Sayılı Radyo-Televizyon Yasası', *İLEF Yıllık '93* (Ankara: AÜ İLEF Yayınları, 1994), pp. 25–72.

Batmaz, V., 'RTÜK Neden Kaldırılamaz?', *Radikal İki*, 15 Kasım (1998), 5.

Bennett, T., 'Theories of the Media, Theories of Society', in M. Gurevitch *et al.* (eds) *Culture, Society and the Media* (London: Routledge, 1982) pp. 30–55.

Bennett, T., 'Putting Policy into Cultural Studies', in L. Grossberg *et al.* (eds) *Cultural Studies* (New York and London: Routledge, 1992) pp. 23–37.

Çaplı, B., 'Televizyon Sistemlerinde Yeni Düzenlemeler: Batı Avrupa'da Kamu Tekellerinin Kaldırılması ve Türk Televizyon Sisteminde Dönüşüm Arayışları', an unpublished PhD thesis (İstanbul: İstanbul Üniversitesi Sosyal Bilimler Enstitüsü, 1990).

——, 'Turkey', in J. Mitchell and J. G. Blumler (eds), *Television and the Viewer Interest* (London: The European Institute for the Media and John Libbey, 1994) pp. 135–46.

Çaplı, B. and C. Dündar, '80'den 2000'lere Televizyon', *Yüzyıl Biterken Cumhuriyet Dönemi Türkiye Ansiklopedisi*, Vol. 15 (İstanbul: İletişim Yayınları, 1995) pp. 1376–86.

Çelenk, S., 'Türkiye'de Televizyon Program Üretimi: Bağımsız Prodüksiyon Şirketleri Üzerine Bir İnceleme', an unpublished MA Dissertation (Ankara Üniversitesi Sosyal Bilimler Enstitüsü Radyo Televizyon Sinema Ana Bilim Dalı, 1998).

Eryılmaz, T., '1980 Sonrasında Türk Sineması', *Yüzyıl Biterken Cumhuriyet Dönemi Türkiye Ansiklopedisi*, Vol. 14 (İstanbul: İletişim Yayınları, 1996) pp. 1180–83.

Golding, P. and G. Murdock, 'Culture, Communications, and Political Economy', in J. Curran and M. Gurevitch (eds) *Mass Media and Society* (London: Edward Arnold, 1991) pp. 15–32.

Gülizar, J., 'Türkiye Radyoları', *Cumhuriyet Dönemi Türkiye Ansiklopedisi*, Vol. 10 (İstanbul: İletişim Yayınları, 1985) pp. 2738–47.

Gür, A., 'Sermaye Yapısında Değişim ve Dergiler', *Yüzyıl Biterken Cumhuriyet Dönemi Türkiye Ansiklopedisi*, Vol. 11 (İstanbul: İletişim Yayınları, 1995) pp. 145–9.

Gürsoy, Sökmen M., 'Türkiye'de Yayıncılık Ortamı', *Yüzyıl Biterken Cumhuriyet Dönemi Türkiye Ansiklopedisi*, Vol. 15 (İstanbul: İletişim Yayınları, 1996) pp. 1466–7.

Işığan, A., 'Türkiye'de Film Yapımcılığı', an unpublished MA dissertation (Ankara: Ankara Üniversitesi Sosyal Bilimler Enstitüsü Radyo Televizyon Sinema Ana Bilim Dalı, 1998).

Kabacalı, A., (1990) *Başlangıçtan Günümüze Türkiye'de Basın Sansürü (İstanbul: Gazeteciler Cemiyeti yayını).*

Kabacalı, A., '1980 Sonrası Yayıncılık', *Yüzyıl Biterken Cumhuriyet Dönemi Türkiye Ansiklopedisi*, Vol. 15 (İstanbul: İletişim Yayınları, 1996) pp. 1462–5, 1469–70.

Kaya, A.R., 'A *Fait Accompli*: Transformation of Media Structures in Turkey', *METU Studies in Development*, Vol. 21, No. 3 (1994) 383–404.

Kaynardağ, A., 'Yayın Dünyası', *Cumhuriyet Dönemi Türkiye Ansiklopedisi*, Vol. 10 (İstanbul: İletişim Yayınları, 1985) pp. 2824–36.

Kejanlıoğlu, D.B., 'Türkiye'de Yayıncılık Politikası: Ekonomik ve Siyasal Boyutlarıyla Türkiye'de Radyo Televizyon Yayıncılığı', an unpublished PhD thesis (Ankara: Ankara Üniversitesi Sosyal Bilimler Enstitüsü Radyo Televizyon Sinema Ana Bilim Dalı 1998a).

——, '1980'lerden 1990'lara Türkiye'de Radyo Televizyon Yayıncılığı', *Birikim*, 110, Haziran (1998b) 40–45.

Kocabaşoğlu, U., *Şirket Telsizinden Devlet Radyosuna (TRT Öncesi Dönemde Radyonun Tarihsel Gelişimi ve Türk Siyasal Hayatı İçindeki Yeri)* (Ankara: AÜ SBF Yayınları, No. 442, 1980).

——, 'Radyo', *Cumhuriyet Dönemi Türkiye Ansiklopedisi*, Vol. 10 (İstanbul: İletişim Yayınları, 1985) pp. 2732–7.

Koloğlu, O., *Osmanlı'dan Günümüze Türkiye'de Basın* (İstanbul: İletişim 1992).

——, 'Liberal Ekonomi Düzeninde Basın Rejimi', *Yüzyıl Biterken Cumhuriyet Dönemi Türkiye Ansiklopedisi*, Vol. 11 (İstanbul: İletişim Yayınları, 1995) pp. 134–44.

McLuhan, M., *Understanding Media: the Extensions of Man* (New York: McGraw-Hill, 1964).

MDB Media Information Unit, *Mediascape Türkiye '98* (Ankara: MDB, İLEF Faculty of Communication, Ankara University and Konrad Adenauer Stiftung, 1998).

Münir, M., *Sabah Olayı: Sabah ve Dinç Bilgin'in Öyküsü* (İstanbul: Altın Kitaplar Yayınevi, 1993).
Mutlu, E. and H. Tuncel, 'İletişim', *Yüzyıl Biterken Cumhuriyet Dönemi Türkiye Ansiklopedisi*, Vol. 13 (İstanbul: İletişim Yayınları, 1996) pp. 712–18.
Negrine, R., *Politics and the Mass Media in Britain* (London: Routledge, 1989).
Oktay, A., *Toplumsal Değişme ve Basın: 1960–1986, Türk Basını Üzerine Uygulamalı Bir Çalışma* (İstanbul: BFS, 1987).
Öngören, Mahmut Tali, 'Türkiye'de Televizyonla İlgili Çeşitli Tarihler', *İletişim 1982/4* (Ankara: AİTİA GHİYO Yayınları, 1982).
Oskay, Ü., *Toplumsal Gelişmede Radyo ve Televizyon: Azgelişmişlik Açısından Olanaklar ve Sınırlar*, 2nd edition (Ankara: AÜ SBF Yayınları, 1978).
——, 'Medya Kendi Başına Karar Vermiyor', *İktisat Dergisi*, Year 29, No. 342, Ekim (1993), 55–8.
Özön, N., *Sinema: Uygulayımı-Sanatı-Tarihi* (İstanbul: Hil, 1985).
Pekman, C., 'Avrupa Standartları ve Radyo-Televizyon Kanunu', *Ayna*, Vol. 1, Nos 3–4, Yaz-Güz (1994) 68–73.
Şahin, H., 'Broadcasting Autonomy in Turkey: 1961–1971', an unpublished PhD thesis (Indiana University, USA, 1974).
Şenyapılı, Ö., '1970'lerin Başında Sayılarla Türk Basını', *Amme İdaresi Dergisi*, Vol. 4, No. 4, Aralık (1971) 67–115.
Seymour-Ure, C., 'Media Policy in Britain: Now You See It, Now You Don't', *European Journal of Communication*, Vol. 2, No. 3, September (1987) 269–88.
Topuz, H., *Dünyada ve Türkiye'de Kültür Politikaları* (İstanbul: Adam, 1998).
Tuncel, H., 'Bab-ı Ali'den İkitelli'ye', *Birikim*, 64, Ağustos (1994) 33–8.
Tunstall, J., *The Media in Britain* (London: Constable, 1983).
Williams, R., *Culture and Society 1780–1950* (New York: Harper & Row, 1958).

Other Documents:

- Broadcasting Laws of 1963, 1983 and 1994, and amendment in 1972.
- Circular letters of related ministries.
- Constitutions of 1961 and 1982, and amendment in 1971.
- Issues of newspapers and magazines.
- Issues of Official Gazette.
- Parliamentary Minutes.
- RTÜK's regulations: *3984 sayılı Radyo ve Televizyonların Kuruluş ve Yayınları Hakkında Kanun, Yönetmelikler ve Tebliğler* (Ankara: RTÜK, 1996).

6
Religion and [Religious] Minorities

Osman Taştan

Religion and minorities has always been a major policy area ever since the middle of the nineteenth century when Ottoman Turkey made the decision to adopt a European-orientated modernization of state and society, and the issue underlined the particularly delicate ground of uneasy constitutional developments on the eve of the emergence of Republican Turkey.

In Ottoman Turkey, as Gülnihal Bozkurt puts it, 'minorities were identified on a religious or confessional basis rather than on ethnicity'. Thus, Ottoman peoples were called 'millet' (that is, religious community) of Islam, and others Orthodox Christians, Jews, and so on, instead of being called Turks, Greeks, Arabs, and so forth'[1] The identification of the Ottoman peoples in this way, as also indicated by Bozkurt, is a direct result of the rules concerning public order and society in Islamic law which governed the Ottoman Empire.[2] Non-Muslim subjects of a Muslim country are called Dhimmis in Islamic politico-legal terminology. Islamic law discriminates between Muslims and Dhimmis, not always necessarily against the latter, in terms of rights and responsibilities. Islamic law specialist Hayreddin Karaman puts the major points of discrimination for and against Dhimmis as follow:[3]

1. Dhimmis are exempt from payment of Zakat (alms) which Muslims pay.
2. Dhimmis are exempt from military service.
3. In many cases, Dhimmis' trials proceed on their own legal terms.
4. Dhimmis pay annual poll-tax.

5. Unless there is an emergency situation, Dhimmis are not allowed to enter Mecca.
6. Dhimmis are not allowed to imitate Muslims by wearing the same costume.

Also,

a. Dhimmis' life, honour and property are protected by law.
b. Dhimmis who are in need and helpless are eligible to receive social benefits.
c. A Dhimmi who volunteers for military service can be exempted from the payment of poll-tax.
d. Although high-rank duties remain exclusive to Muslims, Dhimmis can be employed in certain public services.
e. Dhimmis' cemeteries and corpses are respected and protected.
f. As in the opinion of some leading Muslim jurists like Abu Hanifa and Shafi'i, Dhimmis who want to learn the Qur'an, the Hadith (sayings attributed to the Prophet Muhammad) and Islamic law cannot be barred from doing so.
g. Dhimmis who have fallen into captivity are entitled to be rescued by ransom payable by the state for this purpose.

There are, of course, further points of inequality between Muslims and non-Muslims in Islamic law in this regard:[4] Family Law bans a non-Muslim man from marrying a Muslim woman,[5] Procedural Law principally bars non-Muslims from testifying against Muslims,[6] the law of Inheritance denies the right to inherit in cases where the kinsmen belong to different religions and particularly bars a non-Muslim from claiming his share from the legacy of his Muslim kinsman,[7] Criminal Law applies differing and, in certain cases, lighter penalties to non-Muslims as compared to treatment of the Muslim criminal accused of the same crime.[8]

Despite these points of socio-legal disadvantages surrounding the non-Muslims in a Muslim country, Lewis believes that they enjoyed tolerance. Acknowledging that 'Non-Muslims were not the civic and social equals of the dominant faith, but were subject to a number of disabilities', he says that non-Muslims in the Ottoman Empire faced discrimination but not persecution. Thus, they enjoyed tolerance and 'the Ottoman record until the late nineteenth century' in this respect, in Lewis's words, 'is excellent'.[9]

However, in the nineteenth-century Ottoman Empire in decline, 'there was', Lewis says, 'a catastrophic change for the worse in the position of the Ottoman non-Muslims'. Lewis continues:[10]

> The material relationship between Muslim and Christian had changed beyond recognition. Even the theoretical basis of association was gone. The old, mutually accepted relationship between Muslims and Zimmis, conferring a definite and agreed status and rights on the latter, had been undermined and destroyed by new ideas and new ambitions. Liberal principles required the Turks to give the subject peoples full equality of rights in the state; national principles entitled these peoples to rebel against it, and set up independent states of their own; Christian and Imperial principles enabled the powers of Europe to intervene on their behalf, supporting their claims both to citizenship and to secession.

The Ottoman Empire was bound to respond to the aspirations of its non-Muslim subjects combined with echoing demands from Europe for change in policies to improve the socio-legal status of non-Muslim minorities. The basic issue was that non-Muslims were suffering inequalities in a Muslim country. Courbage and Fargues[11] are precise in saying:

> Fifty years after the French Revolution, the idea of equality had followed the path that the idea of democracy would follow at the end of the twentieth century: in order to participate in the concert of nations, it was necessary to reform.

In 1839, the Ottomans declared the famous reform package called Tanzimat (reorganizations or rearrangements) and this was followed by another major supplementary programme called Islahat Fermanı (reform edicts). These packages offered a series of fiscal and civic reforms which underscored a break with the past: the statutes of religious discrimination were abolished. Although no miracle could be expected from these reform packages in terms of proving coherent practical changes that were to be applied to centuries'-old

Islamic tradition, the spirit of the reforms was of crucial significance. This was a new idea of Ottomanism which would consider all subjects of the Empire as equal citizens regardless of their religious affiliations.[12]

In public affairs the reforms resulted in barriers and inequalities between the subjects stemming from differing religious affiliations with the upper hand belonging to the Muslim majority being removed and all subjects being made equal, while in private affairs different religious communities retained their autonomy based on different religious requirements and laws. Unsurprisingly, the reforms caused discontent on all sides: Muslims considered that the government had compromised the principles of Shari'a by removing the superiority of Islam over other faiths[13] while non-Muslim communities competing for greater autonomy were not prepared to face certain disadvantages stemming from gaining the status of equality to Muslims. For example, non-Muslims were not willing to come under the law of conscription and, instead, wanted to retain the concessions of being exempt from the payment of a special tax they had previously agreed to pay.[14]

However, the ideology of Ottomanism continued to dominate in all major legal arrangements such as the texts of the 1864 Nationality Ordinance and the 1876 Constitution on the one hand, while non-Muslims' religious autonomy continued to dominate legal reforms through the First World War years, namely the 1917 Family Law which contains different laws for different religious communities instead of enforcing one and the same law for all subjects in line with the political unity sought in equality through the ideology of Ottomanism.[15] However, the discontent continued on the side of non-Muslims for the new Family Law restricted the powers of the confessional leaders while the supreme judicial powers above the application of the law were assigned to Muslims. The Ottoman Empire while undergoing a series of reforms in search of maintaining the integrity of the Empire was defeated in the First World War by 1918 and the forces of Anatolia under the command of Atatürk continued to fight against Greece on major fronts until 1923 when the recognition of Republican Turkey would be secured at the Lausanne Peace Conference. Amid all the major questions remaining from the defeated Ottoman Empire, that of minority affairs was thoroughly reviewed and the scope of the minority problem was demarcated as 'Non-Muslim Minorities'.[16] As arguments by the Turkish delegation that Muslim minorities could not exist in a Muslim country and that all Muslims shared the same cultural values and civic rights prevailed, they [all Muslims] were considered equals and the demands for the protection of Muslim minorities were made irrelevant and inconclusive. Indeed, the strength of such arguments with the prevalence of Islamic law in the disintegrated Ottoman Empire in the background is hardly surprising.

At the time, the failed ideology of Ottomanism was invented to serve the policy of centralism and integrity of the Ottoman subjects. Though the Empire did not survive, the spirit of centralism as the prescription for integrity was deep-rooted in the Turkish political establishment. In line with this orientation, Islam was the most convenient reference to render support to the notion that Muslims constituted a unitary block and, thus, those suffering inequality, as a part of the Ottoman legacy, were the groups of non-Islamic faiths and the new Republic would negotiate on how to provide them with protection. Eventually, the Lausanne Peace Treaty ensured massive rights and liberties for the non-Muslim nationals of Turkey guaranteed by the League of Nations.[17] The rationale behind the legitimacy of demands for the protection of non-Muslim minorities depended mainly on the policy of Islamic law to serve Islam and Muslims as a superior community *vis-à-vis* the non-Muslim residents of the country. Lausanne hosted relentless debates and negotiations to relieve this question. Ironically, within a few years from the Lausanne Treaty, Turkey abolished the rule of Islamic law altogether and introduced various European legal codes. The enforcement of the Lausanne Treaty in terms of the protection of non-Muslim minorities was, thus, overshadowed and the inequalities stemming from the rule of Islamic law concerning non-Muslims were made irrelevant.[18]

In the later 1920s after the Lausanne Treaty of 1923, agreed exchanges of populations were taking place between Greece and Turkey[19] while, on the other hand, legal reforms were accelerated to ensure equality amongst the adherents of all religious communities by a process of secularization to leave no privilege for one religious faith over another. But, could a society with a centuries'-old Ottoman legacy in the background transform itself into a secular one with the swift renewal of the politico-legal system? Critical analysis by Bernard Lewis sheds light on this question:

> In the Turkish Republic, the constitution and the law accorded complete equality to all citizens. Yet even on the official side, in the structure and policies of the state, there were signs that, despite secularism and nationalism, the older idea that Muslim equals Turk and non-Muslim equals non-Turk persisted.[20]
>
> The cosmopolitan Islamic Empire had assigned a definite place and function to the non-Muslim minorities; the nationalist Republic could offer little to those who either would not or could not join the dominant group. While on the one hand Turkish-speaking Orthodox Christians from Anatolia were classed as Greeks and sent to Greece, the children of Muslim Bosniaks or Albanians, Kurds or Arabs settled in Istanbul were accepted as Turks. Significantly, religion still appeared on identity cards and other official documents, and the designation Turk was in common usage restricted to Muslims; the rest were known as Turkish citizens, but never Turks.[21]

Lewis's words suggest that the role of religion as a radical element of policy-making and a major component of substantiating political identity continued to prevail even after the abolition of Islamic laws for religious orientation in private and public life was inherent in the culture. Indeed, it cannot be realistic to think that the historically rooted rivalries between religions shaping both personal and collective identities would easily leave their place to a fully harmonious society and that the outstanding prejudices among the adherents of competing religious faiths would simply be erased. It is not difficult to discern from Lewis's words that there was ground for both Muslims and non-Muslims to grow discontent even after the introduction of the new politico-legal regime: the secular(ized) system would mean dissatisfaction for the Islamic-orientated community since they were destined to lose the superiority they enjoyed under the Ottoman system and for the non-Muslim minorities as they would lose their special confessional privileges previously available under Islamic law while their identity as de facto religious minorities with certain prejudices attached would remain a persisting liability. Thus, it is not surprising to see that Lewis[22] and Courbage and Fargues[23] acknowledge that non-Muslim minorities enjoyed a more favourable position under Ottoman rule as compared to their situation in the Republican era. Ironically, certain pro-Islamic theoreticians often within the domain of RP (pro-Islamic Welfare Party) widely argued, in the 1990s, in favour of a multi-legal system to be an option to achieve an ideal model of society in modern Turkey.[24]

In the mid-1990s, certain pro-Islamic figures like Bahri Zengin, a senior politician within the ranks of the RP, and Ali Bulaç, a famous writer known as a civil society advocate, proposed an alternative multi-legal system model. While Zengin's deliberations, mostly carried out on live TV panel discussions, focused on the merits of pluralism in a multiplicity of legal systems in a theoretical manner,[25] Bulaç was more specific and he substantiated his discussions with the famous political document of the Prophet Mohammed's era known as 'the Constitution of Medina' which provided ground for coexistence in a religiously plural community. Bulaç distils several principles from this constitution:[26]

1. A project aiming to achieve peace among people who honour the rule of law and stability must be based on a Contract negotiated and agreed among various heterogeneous (be they religious, legal, philosophical, political, etc.) groups comprising the society.[27]
2. Participation and representation should be considered essential as opposed to the idea of domination which signifies totalitarianism.[28]
3. 'Every religious and ethnic group [should] enjoy complete cultural and legal autonomy'.[29]
4. In a plural society, more than one legal system can be in effect.[30]
5. In case of controversies among different groups, the principle of arbitration [should] come into effect.[31]

Bulaç adds that the Constitution of Medina also protects the territorial borders of the political union referred to as *ummah* consisting of Muslims, Jews and Polytheists. The document puts all sides under the rule of law and it entrusts the issues of defence and judicial administration to a central authority while it leaves the issues of legislation, science and culture, economy, education, health, and so on, to civil society.[32]

In line with the spirit of this project, Bulaç says that taking care of legal proceedings for the cases of non-Muslim judiciary or leaving their court cases and laws to themselves has been a practice as a part of laws applicable to Dhimmis ever since the Medinan era right up to the late periods of the Ottoman Empire.[33]

For Bulaç, the idea of a modern nation-state did not bear desirable fruit and resulted in further conflicts and tensions, rather than solutions.[34] The following two questions, in Bulaç's words, need to be addressed:[35]

1. How can a solution be found to the religious and ethnic conflicts which presently continue in the context of a modern nation-state and seem [set] to continue at an increasing rate [in the future as well]?
2. How will people who are different and numerically smaller [communities] live their identities; through which concrete and practical mechanism will democracies overcome the concept of 'minority'?

Bulaç is more specific in the questions that, he thinks, could be addressed by a new project in line with the Constitution of Medina in his following conclusive statement:[36]

> In our region where there are numerous reasons for conflicts and war such as the ongoing Arab–Israeli war dragging on for years, newly surfacing Azeri–Armenian conflicts, the religiously divided structure of Lebanon, the ethnic situation in the Balkans, the Kurdish question, etc., we need shared, agreed on and participated in projects which will enable all religious, ethnic and political groups to coexist.

Bulaç's idealization of the Constitution of Medina, unsurprisingly, caused a fierce reaction from Taha Akyol, a well-known pro-right-wing conservative columnist, that it was neither accurate nor plausible. For Akyol, 'the Contract of Medina' was a political experiment practised by the Prophet in a particular historical context, and it was a temporary project. Moreover, as it did not work, it was soon abandoned and the legal status of *Dhimmi* was introduced to apply to non-Muslims.[37] Akyol puts the following question to challenge Bulaç's project:[38]

> How will Bulaç's 'communities', i.e. Sunnis, Alawis, Turks, Kurds, Islamists, Secularists, establish relationships between each other; which supreme law will be in force?

Akyol argues that the only solution is the law based on 'citizenship' which will allow integration between different sections of society. He puts forward how hard Turkey fought over one and a half centuries to achieve a unitary legal system and sovereignty and that this gain could not be made expendable by dividing the law according to beliefs, sects, philosophies or ethnicities.[39] Akyol is clearer in his statement in defence of the idea of nation-state, which Bulaç diagnosed as the sole source of conflicts:[40]

> An indispensable condition of making a 'nation' is the unity of the judiciary. The nation-state is not the result of a pure theory, nor is it the fiction of a political power, but it is the political institutionalization of a process of sociological development during which walls between tribes, feudalities, communities, were brought down by the intensified commercial and civil relationships.

It is obvious that Bulaç and Akyol have diametrically opposing points of view. By clear inference, the former proposing that a project for peace and solution to conflicts in states and societies on the face of the earth could be forged from the spirit of the Medinan Constitution, holds the monolithic nature of the politico-legal systems responsible for the problems and seeks recipes for the solutions in the recognition of diversities, while the latter thinks such approaches with reference to the historically failed experiment of the Medinan Constitution equals nothing less than regression. Also, while Bulaç proposes a theoretical framework to approach region-wide problems without explicit reference to particular nation-states, Akyol disproves Bulaç's project by defending the modern nation-state with particular reference to the case of Republican Turkey. Underneath their disagreement lies the question of political-Islam versus the idea of the modern nation-state. But what they argue about is rather the characteristics they attribute to Islam and modernity. For Bulaç, the multi-legal system is a merit of Islam, while, for Akyol, the unitary politico-legal system and the concept of citizenship is a merit of the nation-state. Thus, while Bulaç's vision favours a reversion to the recognition of diversity which runs counter to the monolithic structures of modernism, Akyol's response sheds light upon the idealized concept of nation-state and citizenship which homogenizes the diversity in order to achieve unity and equality.

As far as the question of minorities is concerned in relation to the Medinan Constitution, Muslims in Medina at that time were politically the dominant group but numerically a minority of 1500 out of 10 000, of which 4000 were Jews and 4500 were Arab-Polytheists.[41] In the Ottoman Empire, by contrast, non-Muslims were the minorities, while Muslims were both politically and numerically superior. But, in either case, religious communities were given their own options of legal systems, according to Bulaç's interpretation. Then, the Lausanne Treaty was agreed upon to protect the minorities in order for them to survive under the religiously unitary Islamic legal system in force in Turkey with a Muslim majority. However, when the secular legal system replaced Islamic law the new system provoked a twofold response: certain elements of non-Muslim minorities, like Jews, opted for the secular system to obtain equality in the new unitary system, while a certain amount of discontent among Muslims would emerge in time for they would feel that they were denied the rights non-Muslim minorities had secured in the Lausanne Treaty. This point is clearly raised, in the 1990s, by a famous pro-Islamic writer İsmail Kara:[42]

> ... the rights of these [non-Muslim] minorities are guaranteed by articles 37–45 of the Lausanne Treaty. We have to say that, particularly in the years of one-party rule and in certain points still today, Muslims do not have religious rights and freedoms to the extent that non-Muslim minorities residing in their country do.

Despite this sense of dissatisfaction, Kara cannot bear to contemplate the identification of Muslims as minorities and recognizes the shared ground between Islam and the new politico-legal regime: the language of unity and homogeneity for both nation and religion. Kara interprets the new regime in relation to the Muslim majority as follows:[43]

> Despite this negative situation, that the Republican ideology could not consider Muslims to have the status of minority, and,

> further, its having to move toward establishing a state based on even a larger Muslim population, should be seen as an advantage. Equally important is another point that it defined Muslims as an integrated body, regardless of which sect, order or trend they belong to and it did not emphasize the differences.

Another famous pro-Islamic writer İsmet Özel reiterates precisely the same point held by Kara:[44]

> We owe the Islamic homogenization in the ethnic sense of the soils we now live on in Turkey to the Republic of Turkey, i.e. the Republic of Turkey is not an entity that acquired its existence by excluding Islamic foundations. Conversely, its fabric being still Islamic, it has a body that considers further Islamization in an ethnic sense essential.

Indeed, during the Lausanne talks, Muslims *vis-à-vis* non-Muslims were defined as an integrated body homogenized under Islamic culture and law. By inference, it is possible to think that the idea of a homogeneous community under Islamic identity was instrumental in both the politics of Ottoman Turkey and Republican Turkey for this concept serves both the consolidation of the perception of the Islamic *ummah* and the idea of secular nation-building. Thus, the Islamic line as far as shown in the statements of İsmail Kara and İsmet Özel is conciliatory in points where discourses of Islamic and secular systems overlap.

There is a bureaucratic apparatus considered centripetal in this religious homogeneity, that is the Directorate of Religious Affairs. It was established in 1924[45] and is entrusted with the duty of 'executing the religious affairs of Islam concerning creed, worship and morals; enlightening the society with regard to religion, and administering places of worship'.[46] It employs over 80 000 personnel with a giant government-allocated budget under the office of the Prime Minister. This institution is an asset in the connection of state, religion and politics. The following statements of Hamdi Mert, a former Deputy President of the Directorate, are remarkable:

> While defining the place of the Directorate of Religious Affairs in the spiritual life of Turkey we need to see how necessary

> 'Religion' is with regard to our national unity and togetherness.[47] In Turkey where unity of religion that makes nation and nationhood has reached about 99 per cent, the simplest way to secure national integrity is this [becoming united in the vast tolerance and integrating character of Islam]. It must be a rational manner to benefit from the integrating [character of] 'Religion' in preventing the exploitation of the claims of differences [on the basis] of 'Region', 'Wealth' and 'Ethnicity'.[48]

However, in the 1990s, this institution has been a focus of controversies which attracted certain interesting debates among intellectuals. Speaking in defence of laicism, Mehmet Ali Kılıçbay, a famous academic, says:

> I want to answer the following question: How can a society be laic? For a society to be laic, the state needs to have no religious function. More specifically, the Directorate of Religious Affairs, all religious education under the authority of the state, all religious cadres, should be abandoned. There are 72 000 mosques, 80 000 personnel under the supervision of the Directorate of Religious Affairs. The figure allocated from the General Budget is 100 trillion Turkish Lira.[49] Let alone laicism, this is not an acceptable situation when considered on the basis of the equality of the citizens either. You can never encounter something like this anywhere else in the world. Allocation of a resource of taxes collected from the entire society to a particular interpretation of a particular sect [madhhab] is not something that is acceptable. Also, mosques should be transferred to *cemaat*s (religious communities). Those mosques which have an historical and architectural speciality should be kept within the public sphere as our cultural legacy. All other places of worship should be transferred to *cemaat*s, that is, no religious function of the state should be retained. The state cannot have [a] religion. This is the first principle of laicism. The [laic] state is at equal distance from all religions, it cannot support any religion, nor can it impede any religion ... ... The state, today, with a Directorate of Religious Affairs organized according to the Hanafi branch of the Sunni sect, is favouring a state religion. This is a theocratic structuring.[50]

In line with Kılıçbay, Sami Selçuk, the President of the Court of Appeal, is equally critical of the official status of the Directorate of

Religious Affairs[51] and argues that its status as a department of State should be annulled and that religions and beliefs should be entrusted to the relevant communities.[52] Selçuk also believes that 'the Republic of Turkey is, in a sense, theocratic as far as the organization of the state is concerned'.[53]

The suggestions of Kılıçbay and Selçuk with regard to the status of the Directorate of Religious Affairs were already known discussions in the 1990s and were noticed by certain pro-Islamic writers.[54] Saying that different sections of the community, including the pro-Islamic, may demand that the Directorate be transferred to *cemaat*s with different intentions being for or against Islam, İsmail Kara urges cautious thought into the suggestions from pro-Islamic people who demand that ... 'the Directorate cease to be a state-run office, and that its functions be undertaken by the Muslim *cemaat*s or that the Directorate be transferred to these *cemaat*s.[55]

Kara continues:

> The issue I wanted to draw attention to, in this essay, is the question of *cemaat*. In Turkey, there are no Muslim *cemaat*s which have a legal status, whose rights and duties are specified or known to the society and who have opportunities. In this sense, [the term] *cemaat* is used only for reference to non-Muslims: Armenian community, Greek (Orthodox) community, Jewish community, etc. Indeed, the existence of these *cemaat*s as well as their rights are specified, recognized and guaranteed by both regulations of Turkish law and international legal conventions and agreements. The second point which needs to be stressed here is that these *cemaat*s are, also, *minorities*.[56]

Thus, in Kara's view, the idea of transferring the Directorate to *cemaat*s cannot be substantiated. Hasan Hüsrev Hatemi is more direct in revealing his fear of *cemaat*s connoting disunity in Islam and his confidence in state supervision of religion to secure homogeneity. In concert with Kara, Hatemi says 'If the [Directorate of] Religious Affairs is taken from the state and transferred to the people a homogeneous organization will have been replaced by many *cemaat*s.[57]

It is clear that the Islamist discourse as in Kara's and Hatemi's views puts the idealized identity of Islam as an integrated whole, ideally *ummah*, albeit limited to the borders or by the reality of nation-state, before the sociological reality of the Muslims as one consisting of many different interpretations or trends. Thus, pluralism within

Islam is not easily recognized. On the contrary, an idealized homogeneity is the target and the Directorate of Religious Affairs is favoured to the extent of its instrumentality in proving unity in Islam. The identity of *cemaat* is considered exclusive to non-Muslims and bound to be dissociated with Muslims as it connotes the identity of a minority.

Apart from the few civil society advocates within the Islamist trends like Ali Bulaç, Bahri Zengin *et al.*, and certain profound laicists, like Mehmet Ali Kılıçbay, who favour the recognition of diversity corresponding to societal realities as opposed to the prevalence of the idealized perceptions of unity, there has been a persistently dominant common line of policy across the Ottoman Islamic system, the discourse employed at the Lausanne talks by the emerging Republican regime and the current Islamist or Turkish-Islamist trends, that resorts to the perceived ground of homogeneity associated with Islam.

In 1924, the year in which the Directorate of Religious Affairs was established, a law for the unification of education was also introduced to secure that all educational institutions, apart from the non-Muslim schooling issue as protected by the Lausanne Treaty, be connected to the authority of the Ministry of National Education. The crucial point here would be that Muslim religious education would come under centralized state control. Since then, according to a specialist report, the following practice has been the case: the course on religion was taught in middle schools (ages 12 to 15) until 1928, in primary schools (ages 7 to 12) until 1933, in the countryside primary schools (age 7 to 12) until 1939 on equal terms with other courses. From 1939–48, the course on religion was removed from the curriculum altogether, while, in 1948 it was reintroduced but, this time, it was made optional.[58] Following the 1980 coup d'état, a policy toward making religious education compulsory began to emerge as was clearly stated by the coup leader General Kenan Evren in his speech in Erzurum on 24 July 1981:

> ... I am saying to the parents who do not send their children to the state schools and, instead, give them to the care of ignorant people who open clandestine Qur'anic recitation courses. 'You do not have the right to do this. ... Now, by a new decision we took,

> [a] compulsory course of Teaching Religion will be put in primary and middle schools, [and] high schools [ages 15 to 18]. ... I had mentioned on various occasions that laicism does not mean atheism. ... Also, Atatürk had said that religion should be taken from the hands of ignorance and given to the authority with the expertise and issued the law for the unification of education (Tevhid-i Tedrisat Kanunu).[59]

In 1982, during the reign of the military, the course on religion was renamed as the Knowledge of Religious Culture and Morals (Din Kültürü ve Ahlak Bilgisi) and made compulsory in the primary and secondary schools.[60] With Article 24 of the 1982 Constitution, made during the military regime of 12 September presided over by General Kenan Evren, the new practice was sanctioned. The relevant section of Article 24 reads:

> Training and Teaching of Religion and Morals take place under the control and supervision of the state. Teaching of Religious Culture and Morals takes place among the compulsory courses taught in the primary and secondary teaching institutions. Further training and teaching of religion can take place only on the individual's own will or by demand of the legal representatives of the young.

The general aim and objective of Teaching of Religion and Morals was specified in the Ministry of National Education's *Tebliğler Dergisi* (announcements journal) of 29 March 1982 as follows:

> To have [the student] gain sufficient basic knowledge concerning religion, the religion of Islam and Knowledge of Morals in primary education and secondary level teaching, in line with the Turkish National Education Policy, consistent with the aims and principles of Turkish National Education and with Atatürk's principle of laicism; thus, to secure the improvement of Atatürkism, national unity and togetherness, human loving, in religious and moral respects and to raise human beings with good [sense of] morals and virtue.[61]

In a study, entitled *Din Eğitimi Raporu,* sponsored by the Foundation of the Students and Graduates of Ankara Merkez İmam-

Hatip High Schools, the background conditions leading to the idea of making the Teaching of Religion compulsory is put as follows:

> At the top of the factors leading to the Teaching of Religion becoming compulsory with the 1982 Constitution come lessons taken from the Republican experience nearing 60 years. It has been thought that an anti-religious, laicist Atatürkism, could not but lead to the raising of youths who are Marxist-Leninist, enemies of homeland and state, leading actors in the terror events of pre-1980. The belief that religious Atatürkist generations would protect the principles of Atatürk better resulted in making these courses compulsory.[62]

The relevance of these statements poses immensely significant implications proving the instrumental value of religion in addressing the perceived grounds of problems home and abroad. The prescription for domestic peace and stability is sought in religious Atatürkism while this would also serve to combat left-wing ideologies along the global Cold War divisions [providing ground in favour of the right-wing ideology rendering support to the US-led Western Bloc as opposed to the Soviet-led Eastern one]. Thus, religion would have to be considered indispensable in serving a dual purpose. This approach provides nothing less than a plausible ground for the discussions of the concept of Turkish-Islamic synthesis, which Poulton depicts as semi-official.[63] From the very same point of view, further remarks are made in respect of religious education through the same source:

> While, in the West, missionary activities are being carried out by the support of huge educational and research institutions our citizens are becoming the unequipped addressees of these activities. Both the training of men of religion up to the standards of the religious missionary men in the West and the equipping of our citizens encountering such activities is a task for religious education with priority. The most widely shared value of the people coming from different ethnic origins [but] as individual[s] of the Turkish Nation is Islam. Our national culture fostered by Islam has taught to treat individuals, not according to their ethnic

> origin but, according to the religion they belong to. At a time when ethnic nationalisms encompass the world and at a time when it [ethnic nationalism] turns into a bleeding wound for us in our region of South East Anatolia, religion is the unique power to unify us. This unifying power can [only] come into existence by religious education which condemns separatist attitudes.[64]

Here, again, religion is considered as the basis of national unity and driven to a dual-fronted battle to circumvent the ethnic nationalism at home and to repel the perceived threat of Western religious missionaries abroad. In another work, called *Türk Eğitim Sistemi: Alternatif Perspektif*, sponsored by Türkiye Diyanet Vakfı, the same approach is articulately proven:

> The family ties that keep the society standing; values like loyalty to homeland, nation and state, are accepted as religious value[s] in Turkish society. 'Love for homeland comes from [religious] belief.' Obedience to the State is a religious duty. Fighting for homeland and nation is a religious duty. To die for the sake of homeland elevates the person to the religiously highest attainable level, martyrdom. Without the belief of martyrdom, it would not be so easily possible to drive our people to war[ing]. Not to ignore this point should be a duty for the state.[65]

In these statements, a shared ground between state and religion is established and the indispensable need of the state for religion is emphasized; furthermore, the service of religion to the military is underlined in the concept of martyrdom. Accordingly, religion plays the pivotal role in achieving and maintaining the integrity and unity of the community which the state badly needs. But, what if religion itself, the indispensable recipe for the integration of state and society, proves to bring about disunity in varying forms of interpretations and confessions? This question is carefully addressed by the same source as follows:

> ... [while] in the tradition the Turkish society has, turning religion into an institution within the body of the state has taken place as a necessity in order to establish social peace. In order not

> to allow different religious interpretation and the controversies stemming from them to lead the society into turmoil, there is need for a religious interpretation approved by the state and for an official institution to do [provide] this interpretation. The reason why the Republic incorporated the Directorate of Religious Affairs and state-monopolized religious education into [its] official understanding of laicism is this historical tradition it inherited.[66]

If there is a state-sponsored interpretation of religion in a country where 99 per cent of its population is often quoted to be Muslims and all of its citizens are identified as 'Turk[ish]' by the Constitution,[67] could the reality still prove religious pluralism or conflicting identities? Nuray Mert, a young sociologist, has the following to say in this regard:

> Turkey does not have a society which has reached a monolithic culture and lifestyle to the aspired level ... On the other hand, Turkey, rising from the territories where various civilizations lived, undoubtedly as their inheritor, does not harbour the difference in an equal manner to the extent it is thought or desired. More specifically, not every kind of difference equally affects the sociological process. There are Lazs, Georgians and similar ethnic groups, but the cultural difference of none affects the social life as the ethnic-cultural difference of the Kurds. There are Christians and Jews, but their social existence is not the same thing as that of Islam. Thus, it is not sensible to speak of Islam simply as one of these religions and beliefs. Similarly, there are certainly people who follow different Islamic sects and beliefs, but the differences between the Sunni Muslims and the Alawis have [a particular] social significance ...[68]

A true democratic approach, in Mert's view, would neither consider certain regional and numerically very small religious groups equal to Muslims, nor would it employ the discourse of defining Turkey as a '99 per cent Muslim [populated] country' for such a discourse is not only 'anti-democratic by definition' but also 'problematic' in terms of defining Islam from a monolithic viewpoint.[69]

Notes

1 Gülnihal Bozkurt, 'Türk Hukuk Tarihinde Azınlıklar', *Ankara Üniversitesi Hukuk Fakültesi Dergisi*, vol. 43 (1993), Nos. 1–4, p. 50.
2 Gülnihal Bozkurt, 'Türk Hukuk Tarihinde Azınlıklar', p. 50.
3 Hayreddin Karaman, *Anahatkarıyla İslam Hukuku*, Ensar Neşriyat, Istanbul, 1984, vol. I, pp. 264–5.
4 See Gülnihal Bozkurt, 'Türk Hukuk Tarihinde Azınlıklar', p. 51.
5 Hayreddin Karaman, *Anahatlarıyla İslam Hukuku*, vol. II, p. 85.
6 Abdülaziz Bayındır, *İslam Muhakeme Hukuku: Osmanlı Devri Uygulaması*, İslami İlimler Araştırma Vakfı, Istanbul, 1986, pp. 159–60.
7 Hayreddin Karaman, *Anahatlarıyla İslam Hukuku*, vol. II, p. 170.
8 Ahmed Özel, *İslam Hukukunda Milletlerarası Münasebetler ve Ülke Kavramı*, Marifet Yayınları, Istanbul, 1982, pp. 217–23.
9 Bernard Lewis, *The Emergence of Modern Turkey*, Oxford University Press, London, 1961, p. 349.
10 Ibid., pp. 349–50.
11 Youssef Courbage and Philippe Fargues, *Christians and Jews under Islam*, tr. Judy Mabro, I.B. Tauris Publishers, London and New York, 1997, p. 104.
12 See Bernard Lewis, *The Emergence of Modern Turkey*, pp. 104–5 ff.; Youssef Courbage and Philippe Fargues, *Christians and Jews under Islam*, pp. 104 ff.; Azmi Özcan, *Pan-Islamism: Indian Muslims, the Ottomans and Britain* (1877–1924), Brill, Leiden, 1997, pp. 31 ff.; Gülnihal Bozkurt, 'Türk Hukuk Tarihinde Azınlıklar', pp. 52–3.
13 Azmi Özcan, *Pan-Islamism. Indian Muslims, the Ottomans and Britain (1877–1924)*, p. 32.
14 Youssef Courbage and Philippe Fargues, *Christians and Jews under Islam*, p. 104.
15 See Gülnihal Bozkurt, 'Türk Hukuk Tarihinde Azınlıklar', pp. 52–5.
16 See Bilal N. Şimşir, 'Lozan ve Çağdaş Türkiye'nin Doğuşu', *70. Yılında Lozan Barış Antlaşması Uluslararası Semineri* (25–26 October 1993, the Marmara Hotel, İstanbul), İnönü Vakfı (Ankara), pp. 32–4.
17 See *Lausanne Conference on Near Eastern Affairs 1922–1923: Records of Proceedings and Draft Terms of Peace*, H.M. Stationery Office, London, 1923, pp. 698–702 (articles 36–44).
18 See Bilal N. Şimşir, 'Lozan ve Çağdaş Türkiye'nin Doğuşu', pp. 41–2.
19 For the details of this issue, see Bernard Lewis, *The Emergence of Modern Turkey*, p. 348; Youssef Courbage and Philippe Fargues, *Christians and Jews under Islam*, pp. 112 ff.
20 Bernard Lewis, *The Emergence of Modern Turkey*, p. 350.
21 Ibid., p. 351.
22 Ibid.
23 See Youssef Courbage and Philippe Fargues, *Christians and Jews under Islam*, pp. 91ff.
24 Taha Akyol, *Medine'den Lozan'a*, Milliyet Yayınları, sixth edition, Istanbul 1998, pp. 181ff.

25 For one instance, see Taha Akyol, *Medine'den Lozan'a*, 181.
26 See Ali Bulaç, 'Asr-ı Saadet'te Bir Arada Yaşama Projesi: Medine Vesikası' in Vecdi Akyüz (ed.) *Bütün Yönleriyle Asr-ı Saadet'te İslam*, Beyan Yayınları, Istanbul, 1994, vol. II, pp. 186–95.
27 See Ali Bulaç, 'Asr-ı Saadet'te Bir Arada Yaşama Projesi', p. 187.
28 Ibid., p. 188.
29 Ibid., p. 190.
30 Ibid., p. 191.
31 Ibid., pp. 190–1.
32 Ibid., pp. 192–3.
33 Ibid., p. 191.
34 See Ali Bulaç, 'Bir Arada Yaşamanın Mümkün Projesi: Medine Vesikası', *Bilgi ve Hikmet*, 5 (1994), pp. 3–15.
35 Ali Bulaç, 'Bir Arada Yaşamanın Mümkün Projesi', p. 5.
36 Ali Bulaç, 'Asr-ı Saadet'te Bir Arada Yaşama Projesi', p. 194.
37 *See* Taha Akyol, *Medine'den Lozan'a*, p. 183.
38 Ibid., p. 184.
39 Ibid., pp. 184 and 187.
40 Ibid., p. 190.
41 Ali Bulaç, 'Asr-ı Saadet'te Bir Arada Yaşama Projesi', p. 178.
42 İsmail Kara, Şeyhefendinin Rüyasındaki Türkiye, Kitabevi, Istanbul, 1998, p. 48.
43 Ibid., pp. 48–9.
44 See İsmet Özel, 'İsmet Özel: Benim Kuşağımdan Olup da Çektiklerime Benzer Şeyler Çekmiş Olan İnsanların Müslüman Olmayışlarına Şaşarım' (an interview) in *Yeni Dergi*, April–May 1994, p. 9; see also the quotation by Hasan Husrev Hatemi, 'Diyanet İşleri Başkanlığı ve Diyanet İşleri Teşkilatının Önemi'. Türkiye Günlüğü, July–August 1994, p. 88.
45 Hamdi Mert, 'Diyanet İşleri Başkanlığının Türkiye'nin Manevi Hayatındaki Yeri Resmi Statü ve Fonksiyonu', *Din Öğretimi ve Din Hizmetleri Semineri (8–10 Nisan 1998)*, Diyanet İşleri Başkanlığı Yayınları, Ankara, 1991, p. 415.
46 Hamdi Mert, 'Diyanet İşleri', p. 413.
47 Ibid., p. 421.
48 Ibid., p. 419.
49 The Directorate of Religious Affairs' budget for 1998 (the year Kılıçbay refers) totalled 119.7 trillion TL (or about $459.9 million at the average TL/$US exchange rate), representing 0.82 per cent of the government's total spending. Its allocated budget for 1999 is 172.6 million TL (about $413.3 million at an expected average TL/$US exchange rate), representing 0.63 per cent [*source*: Ministry of Finance]. The actual year-end figures may come out higher as the budget will possibly post a higher deficit.
50 Mehmet Ali Kılıçbay, ('Dünyada ve Türkiye'de Laiklik'), in Mehmet Gündem (ed.), *Gazeteciler ve Yazarlar Vakfı Abant Toplantıları 1: İslam ve Laiklik*, Gazeteciler ve Yazarlar Vakfı, Istanbul, 1998, p. 133.

51 See Sami Selçuk, *Adli Yıl Açış Konuşması* (1999–2000), Yargıtay Başkanlığı (6 September, Ankara) 1999, p. 43; idem, ('Dünyada ve Türkiye'de Laiklik') in Mehmet Gündem (ed.), *Gazeteciler ve Yazarlar Vakfı Abant Toplantıları 1: İslam ve Laiklik*, Gazeteciler ve Yazarlar Vakfı, Istanbul, 1998, p. 174.
52 Sami Selçuk ('Dünyada ve Türkiye'de Laiklik'), p. 174.
53 *Adli Yıl Açiş Konuşması (1999–2000)*, p. 44.
54 For example, *see* Hasan Husrev Hatemi, 'Diyanet İşleri Başkanlığı ve Diyanet İşleri Teşkilatının Önemi', Türkiye Günlüğü, July–August 1994, pp. 86–8; İsmail Kara, *Şeyhefendinin Rüyasındaki Türkiye*, pp. 79–88.
55 Ismail Kara, *Şeyhefendinin Rüyasındaki Türkiye*, pp. 86–7.
56 Ibid., p. 87.
57 Hasan Husrev Hatemi, 'Diyanet İşleri Başkanlığı', p. 87.
58 See Beyza Bilgin, *Eğitim Bilimi ve Din Eğitimi*, Yeni Çizgi, Ankara (1995), pp. 97–8.
59 Ibid., p. 97.
60 See Beyza Bilgin and Mualla Selçuk, *Din Öğretimi: Özel Öğretim Yöntemleri*, Gün Yayıncılık, Ankara, 1995, p. 65.
61 Ibid.
62 Süleyman Hayri Bolay and Mümtaz'er Türköne, *Din Eğitimi Raporu*, Ankara Merkez İmam-Hatip Lisesi Öğrencileri ve Mezunları Vakfı, Ankara, 1995, p. 109.
63 Hugh Poulton, *The Top Hat, the Grey Wolf, and the Crescent: Turkish Nationalism and the Turkish Republic*, Hurst, London, 1997, p. 238.
64 Süleyman Hayri Bolay and Mümtaz'er Türköne, *Din Eğitimi Raporu*, p. 7.
65 Süleyman Hayri Bolay *et al.*, *Türk Eğitim Sistemi: Alternatif Perspektif*, Türkiye Diyanet Vakfı, Ankara, 1996, pp. 126–7.
66 Süleyman Hayri Bolay *et al.*, *Türk Eğitim Sistemi*, p. 115.
67 Article 66 of the present Turkish constitution reads: 'Everyone connected to the Republic of Turkey with the connection of citizenship is Turk(ish).'
68 Nuray Mert, *İslam ve Demokrasi: Bir Kurt Masalı*, İz Yayıncılık, Istanbul, 1998, p. 32. I have restructured the last sentence of this quotation while translating it from its Turkish original to secure an exact translation into English with the verbal consent of the author who authorized me to do so during a telephone conversation in October 1999. The comment is left open-ended as it was in the original.
69 Nuray Mert, *İslam ve Demokrasi: Bir Kurt Masalı*, pp. 32–3.

References

1995 Değişiklikleriyle TC Anayasası (Istanbul: Alfa, 1997).

Akyol, Taha, *Medine'den Lozan'a*, sixth edition (Istanbul: Milliyet Yayınları, 1998).

Bayındır, Abdülaziz, *İslam Muhakeme Hukuku: Osmanlı Devri Uygulaması* (Istanbul: İslami İlimler Araştırma Vakfı, 1986).
Bilgin, Beyza and Mualla Selçuk, *Din Öğretimi: Özel Öğretim Yöntemleri*, (Ankara: Gün Yayıncılık, 1995).
Bilgin, Beyza, *Eğitim Bilimi ve Din Eğitimi* (Ankara: Yeni Çizgi, 1995).
Bolay, Süleyman Hayri and Mümtaz'er Türköne, *Din Eğitimi Raporu* (Ankara: Ankara Merkez İmam-Hatip Lisesi Öğrencileri ve Mezunları Vakfı, 1995).
Bolay, Süleyman Hayri, *et al.*, *Türk Eğitim Sistemi: Alternatif Perspektif* (Ankara: Türkiye Diyanet Vakfı, 1996).
Bozkurt, Gülnihal, 'Türk Hukuk Tarihinde Azınlıklar', *Ankara Üniversitesi Hukuk Fakültesi Dergisi*, Vol. 43 (1993), Nos. 1–4. pp. 49–59.
Bulaç, Ali, 'Asr-ı Saadet'te Bir Arada Yaşama Projesi: Medine Vesikası' in Vecdi Akyüz (ed.), *Bütün Yönleriyle Asr-ı Saadet'te İslam*, Vol. II (Istanbul: Beyan Yayınları, 1994), pp. 167–95.
Bulaç, Ali, 'Bir Arada Yaşamanın Mümkün Projesi: Medine Vesikası', *Bilgi ve Hikmet*, 5 (1994), pp. 3–15.
Courbage, Youssef and Philippe Fargues, *Christians and Jews under Islam*, tr. Judy Mabro (London and New York: I.B. Tauris, 1997).
Hatemi, Hasan Husrev, 'Diyanet İşleri Başkanlığı ve Diyanet İşleri Teşkilatının Önemi', *Türkiye Günlüğü*, July–August 1994, pp. 86–8.
Kara, İsmail, *Şeyhefendinin Rüyasındaki Türkiye* (Istanbul: Kitabevi, 1998).
Karaman, Hayreddin, *Anahatkarıyla İslam Hukuku* (Istanbul: Ensar Neşriyat, 1984), 3 vols.
Kılıçbay, Mehmet Ali, *et al.*, '(Dünyada ve Türkiye'de Laiklik)' in Mehmet Gündem (ed.), *Gazeteciler ve Yazarlar Vakfı Abant Toplantıları 1: İslam ve Laiklik* (Istanbul: Gazeteciler ve Yazarlar Vakfı, 1998), pp. 123–89.
Lausanne Conference on Near Eastern Affairs 1922–1923: Records of Proceedings and Draft Terms of Peace (London: H.M. Stationery Office, 1923).
Lewis, Bernard, *The Emergence of Modern Turkey* (London: Oxford University Press, 1961).
Mert, Hamdi, 'Diyanet İşleri Başkanlığının Türkiye'nin Manevi Hayatındaki Yeri Resmi Statü ve Fonksiyonu', Din Öğretimi ve Din Hizmetleri Semineri (8–10 Nisan 1998) (Ankara: Diyanet Işleri Başkanlığı Yayınları, 1991), pp. 413–21.
Mert, Nuray, *İslam ve Demokrasi: Bir Kurt Masalı* (Istanbul: İz Yayıncılık, 1998).
Özcan, Azmi, *Pan-Islamism: Indian Muslims, the Ottomans and Britain (1877–1924)* (Leiden: Brill, 1997).
Özel, Ahmed, *İslam Hukukunda Milletlerarası Münasebetler ve Ülke Kavramı* (Istanbul: Marifet Yayınları, 1982).
Özel, İsmet, 'İsmet Özel: Benim Kuşağımdan Olup da Çektiklerime Benzer Şeyler Çekmiş Olan İnsanların Müslüman Olmayışlarına Şaşarım' (an interview), *Yeni Dergi*, April–May (1994), pp. 6–14.
Poulton, Hugh, *The Top Hat, the Grey Wolf, and the Crescent*: Turkish Nationalism and the Turkish Republic (London: Hurst, 1997).

Selçuk, Sami, *et al.*, '(Dünyada ve Türkiye'de Laiklik)', in Mehmet Gündem (ed.), *Gazeteciler ve Yazarlar Vakfı Abant Toplantıları 1: İslam ve Laiklik* (Istanbul: Gazeteciler ve Yazarlar Vakfı, 1998), pp. 123–89.

Selçuk, Sami, Adli Yıl Açış Konuşması (1999–2000), Yargıtay Başkanlığı, 6 September, Ankara (1999) 55 pp.

Şimşir, Bilal N., 'Lozan ve Çağdaş Türkiye'nin Doğuşu', 70. *Yılında Lozan Barış Antlaşması Uluslararası Semineri* (25–26 October 1993, the Marmara Hotel, Istanbul), İnönü Vakfı, (Ankara), pp. 25–43.

7
Aspects of the Kurdish Problem in Turkey

Doğu Ergil

Introduction

This article examines the Kurdish problem in its Turkish context. It focuses on those factors which have contributed to it and which may equally apply to other groups who feel excluded from and unrepresented by the political process of the regimes to which they belong. There is an in-depth section about HADEP (Peoples' Democratic Party) and the final section is the *Document of Mutual Understanding* which points to possible paths to be taken towards a satisfactory resolution.

Overview of the Kurdish problem in Turkey

A nation is a collectivity of citizens whose rights and responsibilities are registered and guaranteed by a constitution. Citizenship is a legal-political quality acquired by being a member of a nation organized under the roof of a state regardless of ethnic, cultural and religious affiliation. So nationhood is a legal-political construct based on the will of the people who desire to live together. However, the concept of nation-state is founded on the premise that the nation is a homogeneous entity both culturally and racially/ethnically. The term 'melting pot' is suitably created to define or to achieve this 'undifferentiated' entity.

Turks and Kurds, Greeks, Armenians, Albanians, Bosnians, Arabs and so on, among other ethnic and religious groups, are the heirs of the multiethnic and multicultural Ottoman Empire that was dismantled following the First World War. The Republic of Turkey was one of the nation-states that emerged out of the debris of the Ottoman Empire. When it was established in 1923 it started off with a pluralistic vision of its cultural heritage. The state was not named after its founding majority, the Turks, but rather after the political geography it was based on: (Republic of) Turkey. Most of her problems today, including the 'Kurdish problem', really emerged after the dissolution of the loose administration of the imperial rule that allowed autonomy at the local level. Here are some typical contributory factors or problem areas that led to the formation of the Kurdish Problem:

- Nation-building that started in a multicultural environment took a decisive turn towards the Turkification of the population after the Kurdish rebellions shook the republican regime as early as 1925.
- The vision of multiculturalism or 'cultural federalism' was abandoned early in the nation-building process in search of unity. A heavy dose of centralism and a hastened modernization programme, implemented from above, marked the character of the republican regime: 'progressive centralism'.
- In the absence of a progressive bourgeoisie who would pick up the banner of nationalism in its mission of nation-building or a working class who would struggle for social justice and equitable distribution of wealth and power, the Turkish bureaucracy took on the mission of creating a modern nation-state.

Turkey is experiencing serious difficulties in overcoming her systemic problems due to the bureaucratic nature of the political institutions that have been shaped since the creation of the Republic in 1923. As a result of these conditions, she is increasingly unable to keep up with the pace of change, manage her complex social structure and satisfy multiplying popular needs and demands.

In addition, the state-centred structure of the polity has become too centralized, restrictive, and authoritarian. Hence, neither individual, nor group expectations and demands (including cultural freedoms) are fully understood or met by the central authority (the state). The detachment of the political 'centre' has led to the estrangement of society from the state. As a result, this has had an adverse effect on the political unity and social solidarity of the country.

In fact, bureaucratic state structures have several seminal shortcomings which are also evident in the Turkish case:

- They are authoritarian and maintain a hierarchy in which the bureaucracy preserves its critical or strategic place/role.
- The central/bureaucratic or simply the ruling élite see themselves not only as the saviours of the nation but also as its vanguards and guides. This attitude gives them the sense of a historical mission to shape and lead the nation the way they see fit.

In the Turkish context, although not unique, the way they want(ed) to see the nation is/was as:

a) devoid of a history that could hinder planned reforms and could legitimize an alternative leadership;
b) devoid of cultural/ethnic diversity that could be the source of political instability;
c) an obedient and solidaristic body politic (nation) that would follow the new national leadership without serious objection or resistance.

From the very beginning, then, the seeds of alienation and an unequal relationship between the state and society were sown. The insistent lust of the state to control the nation stifled the growth and maturing of civil society resulting in a lack of capacity to solve conflicts within that has retained a heavy dose of violence at all levels of social relationships. Violence as a form of social control as well as problem-solving has dwarfed the rule of law and hampered feelings of justice and equity within society.

Failure to acknowledge the multicultural nature of society ended up in the rather restrictive definition of 'nation': Turkishness became the criterion for citizenship and Turkish nationalism became the driving force behind nation-building. This restrictive definition of nationhood created a sense of exclusion and marginalization among the non-Turkish citizens of Turkey, a fact which has never been realized by the Turkish élite. Thus the 'Kurdish question' is more than anything else a Turkish question. Kurds are the largest ethnic group – an estimated 10–12 million, although some estimates put the figure at 20 million, or roughly a quarter of Turkey's population of 63 million.

This sense of exclusion or not properly being represented was exacerbated by poverty, unemployment, repression, a low level of education, and so on, factors which in turn led to massive discontinuation among non-Turks – especially the Kurds as the largest minority – as well as Turks who expressed their disagreement with the system in religious terms. However, the bureaucratic élite of Turkey felt more threatened by this 'fundamentalist' streak than the Kurdish unrest.

Furthermore, there is an established belief that 'Whatever the state does, gives, or decides is good; neither its motive nor the consequences of its deeds can be questioned.' The state is sacred (this statement was in the preamble of the Turkish constitution until a few years ago). Its actions cannot be criticized. Its mistakes cannot be questioned and corrected. The perception of any popular demand or objection to government policies represents an unjustified rebellion, undeserved quest or outright subversion. The centralist system looks upon the emergence of new social power centres or alternative policy proposals as extraordinary, subversive, and even deviant. As a result, popular demands are addressed inadequately, tardily, or are simply suppressed. One recent example (autumn 1998) of this phenomenon was the pre-emptive initiative of YÖK (Council of Higher Education) which stipulated that any academic personnel will be stripped of her/his (professional) titles if they do not behave the way the Council expects them to. Similarly, some students who protested against the cost of university education (1997) were suppressed and some were dismissed.

The fact that social expectations are met callously or simply suppressed causes violence in the society. The social fabric is seriously damaged when both the official method of problem-solving and the method of conveying popular demands to the central authority are violent. Violence 'from above' and 'from below' reinforce and legitimize one another. 'Violence from above' is official violence employed by state/official agencies. Its aim is twofold: social control and problem-solving. Official violence which aims at social control is not only geared to the suppression of demands but also new inclinations for (eventually) structural change. Hence, official reliance on state violence is in fact a reflex of the establishment to hang on to the status quo. 'Violence from below' is a violent response of the populace to the insensitivity of the establishment or administration in meeting popular demands. It is in inverse relationship to the capacity of the administration/state to meet the needs and expectations of the people. Lack of representation and expression of positions and expectations is another reason for violence from below which cannot find any other channel and form of formulating itself.

At the root of Turkish society's problems lies the process of nation-building which progressed not from the nation towards the creation of the state, but rather evolved as a process of building a nation within the initiative of the existing state apparatus and bureaucracy. In the Turkish example, therefore, the state preceded the nation. This is not a criticism, but a historic fact. The Ottoman State was not a nation-state. It was a cosmopolitan political union of diverse nationalities, ethnic and religious groups. The Republic of Turkey was founded as a nation-state. However, the already existing state and powerful bureaucracy took on the mission of creating a new concept of nationhood that was forged and shaped by the state. This may have been a historical necessity then, but the state's role as the creator rather than the coordinator still persists. This phenomenon renders the state omnipotent and omnipresent *vis-à-vis* society.

After the population exchanges with Greece in 1924, and a major Kurdish rebellion in south-eastern Turkey in 1925, official inclination towards pluralism was abandoned and the ideological tool of nation-building became Turkish nationalism. Members of other ethnicities would accept the Turkishness declared by the administration to be a political construct, or be assimilated – either peacefully or forcefully. Among the ethnic groups accepted or assimilated were most urban Kurds. However, in a country which was 80 per cent rural/agrarian in the 1920s, approximately 90 per cent of the Kurds were living in the countryside divided along tribal lines and as clients of powerful Kurdish landlords. Tribal cleavages were further aggravated by keen competition over meagre resources. Violent clashes over water, pastures and cultivable land prevented the development of political solidarity, if not a cultural identity.

Peace and order could have prevailed in the Kurdish provinces of south-eastern Turkey if the republican administration had not started to force local communities to obey the new national leadership which was intent on modernization and control of all vestiges of life. The republican government began to thereby undermine the power of local traditional authorities – tribal chieftains, big landlords and religious sheikhs. Used to exercising their authority over their people, the Kurdish rulers were very upset by this encroachment into their turf. Successive rebellions from 1925 to 1937 left south-eastern Turkey under a state of siege.

A deal was struck with the Kurdish rulers in return for public order but that agreement left the area undeveloped, out of touch with the rest of society, and a punishment posting for unruly civil servants. The government invested little in the area, not trusting it because of its rebellious character. In short, the poverty and detachment, together with the traditional nature of the south-east, rendered the area the least integrated part of Turkey. This has hampered Turkey's development as well as its integration with the rest of the world.

So, while a culturally rich and diverse society grew both in size and complexity, the authoritarian state structure that was created to meet the needs of the early 1920s remained to a great extent loyal to its policy of uniformity (liquidating cultural differences) over unity (respecting and reconciling differences) which resulted in an increasingly incompatible relationship between the state and society. Tension and conflict, which arises between the tutelary central authority and the populace, can be likened to the immature son (the populace) of the house (the state) in which the latter induced the former to be rebellious by its harshness and insensitivity. Further problems arise from the perception that the 'son' – who is neither satisfied nor free in his father's home – wishes to leave. Moreover, the Republic of Turkey has several children, some of whom believe that they are treated like stepchildren! Although Turkey officially (or constitutionally) does not accept the fact that there are minorities in the country, other than the non-Muslims, a part of the Kurds feel that they are not registered under their own name as the legitimate son. Some of the Kurds go further than protesting this negligence and want to leave home, but with their dowry. It is this radical group which is organized as the PKK

(Kurdistan Workers' Party) and employs violent ways to achieve its ends an independent or autonomous political entity carved out of Turkey. (The aim changed from being an independent Kurdistan after 1992.)

One of Turkey's major political problems emanates from a dramatic shift in the notion of nationhood. At the time of the declaration of the Republic, the republican elite accepted the pluralistic nature of the population and the multicultural richness of the society inherited from the Ottoman Empire. At the onset the 'nation' was deemed to be the political union of all groups living in Turkey. This understanding could have created a pluralistic political structure out of a plural demography in which the nascent pluralist political organization would inevitably be democratic. However, creating a nation based on pluralist principles out of a poor, backward, uneducated and cosmopolitan populace was not realized by the political elite of the time.

The urgent need to create a common political culture as the basis of the envisaged nation prompted the ruling élite to adopt the policy of uniformity rather than unity. This preference led the republican elite to the acculturation of the 'nation' with the qualities of the majority, namely Turkishness and Sunni, even Hanefi branch of Islam. While the republican élite laid down this blueprint, it made a special effort to keep the visibility of religion out of the public domain.

Based on the decision to standardize the population, the political élite or the central authority took on the task of defining 'Turkishness' and 'Islam' as well as the qualities of a 'Turk' and 'Muslim', the latter as a supportive (and historically inevitable) quality of Turkishness. Once these qualities were determined, they became the arsenals of nationalist and secularist standardization. This intense effort of the last seventy odd years has been partly successful. However, it is becoming clearer that this process is flawed because it emanates from a fictive reality rather than the existing realities of the country/society.

Whatever the reasons behind it, economic backwardness has hampered eastern Turkey's integration into the rest of the country and the world. This impoverished and least integrated part of the country has to be upgraded and brought to par with the rest of society while Turkey's overall economic performance has to be improved, simply because there can be no popular satisfaction, and, for that matter, democracy, with an annual average per capita income of $3000 which is much less in the poorer areas of Turkey, especially in eastern and central Anatolia.

Failure to eliminate imbalances in lifestyles due to the differential development of the regions (especially eastern Anatolia, which still suffers from the yoke of tribalism and feudal landownership); the widening of inequalities amongst social strata; the perception and treatment of cultural differences as deviant (this policy exhibits itself as an exclusionist attitude towards non-ethnic Turks, non-Muslims, and non-Sunnis among the Muslims), combined with underdevelopment, unemployment, and the insensitivity and inefficiency of the state thereby give rise to criticism of the system. After 1960 Kurdish students started to create modern political groups, all leftist, and many in cooperation with Turkish leftist groups and youth movements marking a significant development for Kurds and Turks alike. However, this development created a huge difference between Kurdish groups on different sides of the country, and especially between groups in neighbouring countries. Successive military interventions, the first of which was staged in 1960, and authoritarian laws could not halt increasing opposition, which from time to time took on a violent character. Violence, on the other hand, served as a dirty shawl concealing corruption and moral decadence.

It was not until the early 1970s though that a strong Kurdish movement appeared on the political scene. Although some Kurds took part in the Turkish leftist movement which accommodated them, in the wake of two military coups (1971 and 1980) the more militant Kurds disassociated themselves from the Turkish left, which had been crushed by the army. So the more intellectual, urban and élite ingredients in the Kurdish movement were drained off, leaving behind a younger, inexperienced, rural and adventurist cadre which opted for armed struggle. This group had been socialized in a culture of conflict – infatuated with firearms but also influenced by the heavy-handedness of security forces against the expression of Kurdishness. This is not well known to the great majority of the Turkish people. The souring of Kurdish sentiments and trust in the administration has led to widespread discontent and armed rebellion by the most radical factions.

After the 1980 coup the Kurdish language was banned by the military administration, and names of Kurdish towns and villages were changed. Kurdish families were forced to give Turkish names to their children. Fortunately this ban and the prohibition of Kurdish publications (which sometimes also included recorded Kurdish music) were removed in 1991. However the scar of humiliation has remained in the Kurdish psyche till this day, exacerbated by the rejection of other demands like education and broadcasting in the Kurdish language.

The PKK was conceived in this atmosphere of frustration. It was founded in 1978 by a university drop-out (from the Faculty of Political Science of Ankara University where the author of this article teaches) from the rural south-east. His name: Abdullah Öcalan. After years of preaching along Marxist-Leninist and Kurdish nationalist lines (although they may seem contradictory) and recruiting militants, the PKK staged its first terrorist act, in 1984, killing more than a dozen people.

Although the organization was home-grown and was recruiting in Turkey, Öcalan and his close associates had taken refuge in Syria after the 1980 military coup. Damascus sheltered, trained and equipped this runaway Kurdish group, which grew like a snowball. One reason the PKK gained in influence is that the Turkish government shut down all rival democratic Kurdish organizations and repressed all forms of expression of Kurdishness. The Kurdish political scene was as dry as the desert and the PKK was seen as the only visible and available oasis. Moreover, the PKK was ready to make the sacrifices required by armed struggle on mountain tops.

Thus, dependence on tradition and subjugation to traditional leaders has in recent years shifted to allegiance to the PKK. This shift is understandable for the PKK tries to build ties across tribal divisions and cultural norms besides providing an exalted cause for the Kurdish youth in search of a dignified identity, self-respect and a brighter future who feel they have none of these.

The PKK offers a relatively modern political-paramilitary organization with regional and international links. It represents the only organizational structure for 'impatient' Kurds to join and struggle for a common end. The risks involved, the violence in its methods and the high price to pay are only secondary considerations to some of the Kurdish youth in their choice of a meaningful life no matter how short it is. Before death or arrest, the rural Kurdish youth male and female alike – can find spiritual and political elevation in the activities of the PKK although they are just wasted as peons in a warfare behind which the military-strategic interests of larger regional powers loom. The guerrilla group had to confront a stronger regular army, but at first it seriously hurt the ill-prepared troops who had no knowledge of guerrilla combat, nor were equipped for the purpose. In the 1980s, the superiority of the PKK was clear – it staged hit-and-run attacks and escaped into mountainous territory. It was only in the 1990s that the Turkish army trained commando troops and special police forces and outfitted them with new equipment, including helicopters, which Kurdish guerrillas dreaded most of all. With these reinforcements the Turkish armed forces got the upper hand first in the cities, then in the rural areas. But the pressure exerted on both the urban and rural civilian populations in the south-east led to widespread migration.

The PKK's efforts to gain a footing or acquire a broker's position in northern Iraq was aborted by frequent Turkish operations into Iraq which were facilitated by US consent and eased by the reinforcement since 1991 of the 'no fly zone' over northern Iraq. Ankara also received cooperation from Masood Barzani's Democratic Party of Kurdistan, a rival Kurdish group which wanted the PKK out of its territory. However, Öcalan's entrenchment in Syria and that country's continuing support of the PKK made it impossible to eradicate the group completely. For Damascus, the PKK was a lethal instrument to pressure Turkey into a firm commitment to share the headwaters of the Euphrates and Tigris, which are vital for both Syria and Iraq.

In 1998, the Turkish army top brass lost its patience with Hafez al-Assad's Syrian administration (as well as its hope in Turkish politicians) and threatened to attack Syria if Öcalan was not squeezed out. The recent strategic military agreement between Turkey and Israel left little choice for President Assad, who by then had already made his point through his effective use of the PKK. Öcalan started his career as a 'global wanderer' in the autumn of 1998 and ended up in a Turkish jail in February 1999. Barring Italy's blunders and Germany's reluctance to prosecute Öcalan, Europe demonstrated sufficient determination not to give support to terrorism by shutting its doors to the guerrilla commander. But it fell short of trying him on its territory as the European convention against terrorism requires. Only Greece and Greek Cypriots fell prey to the 'my enemy's-enemy-is-my-friend' trap.

The PKK may be truncated and beheaded, but what about the grievances and cultural demands of Kurds born out of economic deprivation and socio-political exclusion? The Kurd sense of victimization has been looked upon by Turkish administrations as a sign of subversion or treason. Will these problems be addressed now? When? These two questions await answers.

Turkish officialdom says there's no Kurdish problem; only a terrorism problem. This position has led to the awkward inference that 'the Kurds have a Turkish problem'. Indeed the unresponsiveness of the Turkish establishment to the Kurds' grievances has added to the artificial ignorance for which Turkey is paying a heavy toll – with its sons' lives, its valuable economic resources, social solidarity and international reputation.

Kurds in Turkey so far have demonstrated an incapacity to develop independent leadership and a peaceful political movement to divert Kurdish politics away from the violent ways of the PKK. There are two basic reasons for this failure:

Firstly, official repression of anything associated with ethnic identity in Turkey, for example, Kurdishness. (Speaking any of the Kurdish languages/dialects and calling oneself a Kurd were all banned until 1988.) Hence the most violent and risk-taking organization remained on the stage dominating Kurdish politics. This situation bears a contradictory outcome: the heavier the official Turkish repression of Kurdishness, the more representative the PKK becomes for there is no alternative on the political stage. In eliminating representative peaceful political organ(ization)s both the Turkish government and the PKK demonstrate their monopolistic and authoritarian characters.

Secondly, most Kurds in Turkey (and Iraq for that matter) express their wish for a peaceful and democratic solution. But,

i) they do not agree among themselves;
ii) they have not yet taken effective steps to put an end to violence and repression among themselves and against each other.

Furthermore, the bloody struggle going on for years has long ago become more than a mere conflict between two armed groups. It causes strife between the Turkish and Kurdish citizens of the country and damages social solidarity. Ongoing internal strife has sharpened both Turkish and Kurdish nationalism alike. It is no wonder that HADEP, a diverse Kurdish political party (in the fashion of Sinn Fein of the IRA and Herri Batasuna of ETA) has increased its popular support as the tide of the monolithic MHP (Nationalist Action Party), that represents ultra-Turkish nationalism has risen concomitantly.[1] The provocation that emanates from nationalist centres on both sides is further exacerbated at funeral ceremonies of Turkish youth (soldiers) and PKK militia. Yet, this provocation has not affected the spirit of the people to the extent of making them enemies of each other. Whilst there is sporadic tension and isolated acts of violence, there is no sign of sustained hostilities outside the eastern provinces under Martial Law mostly populated by Kurds where the two nationalisms feed off and sharpen each other up.

Meanwhile, the issue of the PKK, which cannot be, or rather, is not being solved domestically, has become a regional (Middle Eastern), and even international, phenomenon which creates opportunities for outside intervention. This very fact makes the need to find a solution even more urgent, something easier said than done when the perception of one side by the other is so at odds with their view of themselves.

So much for the problem, what about a solution?

Because the problem is seen merely as a security issue and not as a 'social conflict', the people of Turkey are suffering from an unnamed war fought on their own lands, amongst themselves, in which citizens kill each other. Should this war not be controlled, the enmity that it leads to especially in the countryside and the eastern provinces where armed struggle persists could last for generations. However, the common sense of the people elsewhere has not allowed differences to turn into conflict. Yet this extraordinary common sense or collective wisdom has not been rewarded by the system which is based more on nationalism than citizenship.

The Turkish administration or top level administrative officials have been saying that the Kurdish nationalist phenomenon is merely a matter of security that Turkey has been struggling with for years, therefore the historical, political, economic and psychological dimensions of the problem have been neglected and the solution as well as all decisions regarding security in the region have been left to the security forces. In other words, the problem has been pushed out of the political realm.

If a complex social problem is looked at as a matter of security, one party to the dispute must be treated as an 'enemy.' As this 'internal enemy' cannot benefit from the opportunities of institutional solutions, it faces all the negativities of illegality. The manifestations of this negativity are also expressed as extra-judicial killings, evacuations and destruction of villages, leaving the villagers to their fate after forced evacuations and creating an Emergency Rule Region (and law) that is different from the rest of the country, while at the same time claiming that Turkey is faced with the threat of division. None of these facts has been opened to popular or even legislative discussion.

While the problem was bubbling along for years and being extended into the international arena, Turkey, with no self-questioning, wanted to join the European Union (EU), a body that operates with a different approach to politics, different legal standards and with a much higher level of wealth. Turkey has chosen to find easy excuses as to why it has had so many problems in the drawn-out application process, ranging from differences in religion and the West's prejudices against Turks, to a supposed belief that the West is still smarting at the overturning of the 1920 Treaty of Sèvres.

What Turkey has not realized is that it has violated many fundamental rights and freedoms while fighting the PKK. While complaining about separatism, it has not seen that it was implementing a different legal and administrative method in the region and restricting democratic rights using the excuse that there were internal and external 'threats'. It did not want to see. ... It did not understand that rather than reconciling with Europe the relationship was actually deteriorating. Now, when she is reminded of the distance between Europe and herself, Turkey displays anger towards the West and to the Kurds, whom it believes are responsible for the rift.

When the PKK and its leader were in Syria, it could not demand democracy, human rights or recognition of a Kurdish ethnic identity. Neither could it succeed in its armed struggle, simply because it demanded political rights, against the far superior Turkish Armed Forces. Terrorism is not a sufficient means to establish a broad political transformation, but it is an effective way to attract the public's attention to a political problem, to an extensive social demand or a complaint. Turkey's administrations have never understood this fact.

With Apo's (Kurdish for 'uncle', as Abdullah Öcalan is known) expulsion from Syria in late 1998, his position as commander of a paramilitary organization was terminated. Because of the manner of his leadership and his own personality, Apo has prevented the finding of a democratic way out both in the Kurdish political realm and inside the PKK – for the PKK had become an extension of the war-machines of the authoritarian regimes of the Middle East that helped and sheltered it. Despite this stark reality, Turkey has referred to the PKK as the equivalent of the Kurdish problem and has therefore not allowed expressions of Kurdish cultural identity through normal ways and institutions, ways that could 'normalize' the political situation.

Together with masses of Turkish people who have been unable to find a proper status, representation or satisfactory standard of living for themselves in Turkey, multitudes of Kurds have also departed for abroad and have explained to the West their feelings of uprootedness and exclusion from Turkey. Indeed some of the difficulties they face or have faced are not known by ordinary Turks. In their contacts with non-governmental organizations, political parties and parliaments, they have been much more impressive in arguing their case than Turkey has been in the arguments she has attempted to put forward through official channels. Therefore, the West faces a block of insensitivity, in the form of Turkey, both in regard to the Kurdish problem and Turkey's problems with Europe.

A part of this insensitivity originates from the average Turk's lack of knowledge about Europe from a cultural and legal point of view. In Turkey, where everything is politicized and where politics is reduced to the dimension of 'security', politics – which even influences the process of the judiciary – is not leading, and will not lead, to popularly desired outcomes in regard to Europe.

If Turkey doesn't want to be isolated from the world she has to adopt the world's progressive legal and political standards. Otherwise, in terms of her methods in fighting terrorism, she will continue to face the humiliating treatment of being put into the same category as Öcalan, a man whom she rightly judges.

The so-called 'Apo crisis' that began when the PKK leader fled from Syria, turned up in Rome after a brief sojourn in Russia, ended in early 1999 after several tense weeks when the Turkish special forces snatched him en route to the airport in Nairobi, Kenya, where he had been sheltered by the Greek embassy.

The whole snatch and imprisonment affair did nothing to enhance Turkey's international standing, and only served to open the floodgates to a tidal wave of further condemnation. Stunned and baffled by this response to the arrest of a wanted terrorist, she seemed unable to adequately respond, with the result that she inadvertently further distanced herself from the West.

For Turkey, what is significant is not the eradication of Apo, but of the Kurdish problem. The way for that is not to sit at the table with this or that terrorist organization or leader but with citizens of Kurdish origin in the Republic of Turkey and meet their 'reasonable' demands without the complex of disintegration.

The capture of Ocalan is a golden opportunity for Turkey to solve this home-grown problem domestically. The much-lamented 'foreign intervention' – in the sinister form of aid to terrorists, or the innocent admonishment regarding more cultural rights or the state of the country's legal standards – will ease to a great extent. If not, whatever remains of the PKK will serve as a mercenary force to the highest bidder in the Middle East with unsettled scores with Turkey. On the other hand, the unsettled 'Kurdish question', which is now internationalized, may find a new leader who is more suitable to the new circumstances. Öcalan is not fit for the leadership role of a peaceful political organization that extends from the Middle East to the Caucasus, all the way to Europe and the US. His extreme authoritarian and cruel character leaves no place for conciliation. His leadership style, forged as a guerrilla commander, has served its purpose. Now he is history. One hopes the Turkish authorities, under sentimental public pressure, do not turn a criminal into a martyr or at best, a victim by ridiculing him.

The problem is multifold. Besides economic, cultural and psychological dimensions, there is the political aspect. However, whenever 'politics' is mentioned, everybody is immediately annoyed, as if politics can only mean the granting of land and a flag to an insurgent group. But, politics means establishing the conditions of common coexistence and creating the feeling that the state is indeed a state of and for all of its citizens.

If the Kurdish problem is to be solved, the Kurds must be believers and practisers of democracy and peaceful methods of conflict resolution. This is yet to be seen. So far, they have waited in the hope that the government might change and abandon its harsh methods.

They must not be satisfied with merely ethnic politics/rights or concessions that will start and end with ethnic recognition – that is not enough. The Kurds must contribute and think of contributing to the development and globalization of those countries of which they are citizens. They must struggle to democratize Iran, Iraq and Syria and work together to bring Turkey closer to EU membership whose standards will be beneficial to all citizens, Turk, Kurd and others alike.

Today, as always, approximately one-fifth of the Grand National Assembly (Parliament) of Turkey comprises members of Kurdish origin. A quarter of the top business people of Turkey are Kurdish. These figures point out the fact that there is no discrimination at the individual or civil societal level. The problem is in the public domain that does not allow the expression of different group (ethnic, cultural, religious and/or ideological) identities other than the designated and approved official identities. Hence, this restriction is not a handicap for Kurds only. In chronological order, Leftism, Liberalism, Kurdishness and Muslimness are all barred from public visibility and subjected to legal prosecution.

The majority of the Kurdish population of Turkey manifest their desire to live in peace and harmony. But just like their Turkish brethren (who are proud to be Turkish) they want to be respected for what they are (Kurdish) and be included in the mainstream society. Otherwise, their support for the violent PKK could have turned every city of Turkey with Kurdish enclaves into a war zone. Considering that Kurds constitute a quarter of Istanbul's ten million population and that HADEP received only a small percentage of the Kurdish votes in this metropolis in the 1995 national elections, Kurds seem to be inclined to integration rather than separation.[2] This fact must be fairly considered by the authorities and unnecessary suspicions must cease in order to devise more constructive policies that will normalize politics in Turkey.

Moving on, let us assume for one moment that a new Kurdish leader appears on the political stage which was controlled by the PKK and the Turkish armed forces until now. This leader may wear a bow tie or a silk dress and speak several Western languages and never advocate violence. Is the Turkish government ready to confront and meet all the reasonable Kurdish demands voiced by this man or woman? Especially if the whole world likes this person and supports him or her? Now it is time to respect cultural differences and protect them legally while affording no special privilege to any ethnic or religious group.

This is no time to show off, with one foot on the hunted criminal. It is time to prove that Turkey is a country where the rule of law reigns. Let us put an end to capital punishment and release incarcerated Kurdish members of parliament who were arrested on charges of being accessories to a terrorist organization. Their prison terms are coming to an end anyway. Let us not allow adventurous prosecutors or judges with an eye on future political careers or the State Security Court to hijack this opportunity. Let us allow political parties and actors to appear on the stage and compete with each other, no matter who they are, provided they do not condone violence. It is time to reward Turkey's Turkish and Kurdish citizens for not becoming each other's enemy despite the provocation of chauvinists on both sides.

Even developed societies may have their share of fanatics who choose violence as a means of political expression. As long as these people use violence to achieve their goals, there will be a need for effective police measures to deter them. However, when violence becomes a widespread method of protest involving thousands of armed peoples supported implicitly or explicitly by hundreds of thousands, then such a phenomenon is of a social character. Therefore, the social dimension of the conflict needs to be taken into consideration and its roots need to be examined. Primarily and most importantly, the parties to the conflict should meet independently of the official institutions which are the creators of the conflict. These parties should work together to define the problem and formulate solutions. Their common assessment must be translated into policy proposals and presented to the public, the real bearer of the problem(s).

All of these shortcomings have to be understood, tackled and resolved before any major socio-political conflict can be solved in Turkey. This means democratization, strengthening civil society, establishing the rule of law, human rights and accepting conflict resolution techniques to ease tensions between communities.

This presents an enormous challenge to all involved and calls for exceptional leadership. From Turkey's point of view, many a vociferous European has been all too ready to condemn Turkey, yet has not been able to suggest measures that would assist her in the search for a solution. All Turkey's citizens, at home and abroad, would benefit from a dose of international understanding and assistance at this critical juncture.

The Peoples' Democratic Party: HADEP

HADEP is the latest of the Kurdish political parties that emerged on the Turkish political scene at the onset of the 1990s and through which Kurdish nationalism is expressed. HEP, or the Peoples' Labour Party was founded in 1990 and its candidates ran in the 1991 national elections among the ranks of the Social Democratic Peoples' Party (SHP) because of the 10 per cent national electoral threshold needed to enter parliament. HEP distanced itself from the SHP and became an independent party in 1993. However, it was banned on 14 July the same year. In expectation of such a development, members of HEP joined the Democracy Party (DEP) which they had founded on 7 May 1993 while the court case against HEP was underway. Unfortunately, this new Kurdish party survived for only a year. Dwelling on their previous experience, members of DEP founded HADEP on 11 May 1994.

Three dramatic events mark DEP's short political life:

Firstly, the nation-wide row that started with Leyla Zana's oath sworn at the opening session of the Parliament in Kurdish instead of Turkish. The only female Kurdish Member of Parliament, Ms Zana was a popular figure and a role model. So her 'unusual' act was blown out of proportion and deemed to be subversive.

Secondly, Mr Mehmet Sincar, a HEP parliamentarian was assassinated at point-blank range in daylight on 2 September 1993 as he walked in Batman's crowded shopping district. It seemed that the 'establishment' used its triggerman with no fear of public retort in order to intimidate the Party and its supporters

And thirdly, Mr Hatip Dicle, the leader of DEP, and most of its other representatives, were tried and sentenced to 15 years each because of an inflammatory speech he delivered following the bombing of a train station (by PKK militants) in Istanbul (12 February 1994). Mr Dicle said that the casualties – six cadets of the Infantry Reserve Officer School – were only normal in a state of war. Following this speech a spree of violence directed against DEP buildings and members started. On 18 February 1994, the DEP headquarters was bombed. The act was attributed to covert government personnel. Heavy repression of the Party led Mr Dicle to declare that the DEP would not run in the 1995 elections because of 'unbearable pressure'.

In the meantime DEP was prosecuted with the indictment of subversion. The charges pressed against HEP emphasized its intention as trying to 'change the basic characteristics of the Republic' and 'trying to create a minority called Kurds'. Separatism was not among the justifications that banned HEP and DEP. Accusations were based on harmful propaganda. Hence the relations between these political parties and the state have never been legal but rather political.

The state also accused these parties of harbouring people affiliated to the PKK. The Party lawyers said: 'It was only normal because both the PKK and the Party (HEP–DEP) drew their membership from the same political grassroots. This is also true for HADEP. On the other hand, this fact provided prosecutors with sufficient excuse to harass the Party at all times.

Indeed, all the Kurdish political parties were accused of promoting the cause of the 'terrorist organization', meaning the PKK. This official conviction became the raison d'être of the continuing harassment and prosecution of the members of the Party, its affiliated press organs and sympathetic associations. The result was cruel: in 1992, 17 people died and eight disappeared in custody while 594 people were tortured. In 1993, 29 people died during interrogation, 13 disappeared in custody, and 872 people were tortured. In 1994, 34 people died in custody or in prison, 49 disappeared in custody and 1128 people were tortured. In 1995, 19 people died in custody or in prison, nine people died due to neglect following torture, 43 people disappeared in custody and 1232 people were tortured. These verified cases mostly involved Kurds and in particular DEP, HEP and lately HADEP members, supporters and sympathizers.

Neither DEP nor HEP could dissociate themselves from the influence of the PKK and offer independent insights for a peaceful solution to the 'Kurdish problem'. This flaw was conveniently used by the government. Failures by the Kurdish parties to denounce violence were interpreted by the state as defiance of its authority and triggered violence 'from above'. Under the influence of pro-government media the majority of the Turkish people predominantly accepted such a rationale. Violence bred violence.

It would be a mistake to think that only the Kurds or any expression of Kurdishness at the political level is officially demonized. It was the Liberals and Communists that were repressed in the 1930s and the 1940s. Socialists followed suit in the 1960s and 1970s. Kurds and Islamists have been the targets of oppression and ostracism since the inception of the Republic, which increased to unbearable degrees in the 1980s. So what Turkey suffers from is state repression of cultural diversity and political pluralism. Authoritarian politics has left no room for the public visibility of group identities. This phenomenon has dwarfed Turkish legal standards and restricted politics to state control of civic life. Basic freedoms have been seen not as rights for everyone but privileges for the loyal citizens who seldom use them.

The PKK is even more authoritarian because it is a paramilitary organization living under *force majeure* conditions. The unbreakable hierarchy in the organization stifles diversity of opinion as well as innovation. HEP, DEP and HADEP were all kept under harness by the organization so they could never diverge from Öcalan's orders and contribute to the development of democracy in Turkey. Being a college dropout (Faculty of Political Science, Ankara University) and a peasant, Öcalan's anti-intellectual, anti-urban stance has greatly influenced all of the Kurdish parties and this combination of authoritarianism and anti-intellectualism deprived HADEP of receiving the votes of millions of urban, middle and upper-class Kurds especially those living outside the conflict-ridden south-eastern provinces.

Today members of HADEP do not have any projects that could satisfy the dire needs of the Kurdish people of Turkey. This party derives its strength mainly from opposition to Turkish nationalism imposed on the predominantly Kurdish provinces of south-east Turkey by the security forces whose powers are virtually limitless due to Martial Law that has been in effect there for a decade and a half.

Just like HADEP, the Turkish government has no viable plan to solve the 'Kurdish problem' in particular and the democratization problem of Turkey in general. So HADEP – among other 'suspicious' organizations such as the Islamists or Leftists – are under close scrutiny. From time to time the security forces create public disorders and blame these organizations in order to sustain and legitimize their grip over civil society.

One of the most dramatic official acts of this kind was the bombing of the HADEP headquarters in Ankara on 12 February 1994. This aggression was also directed against *Özgür Ülke*, a Kurdish newspaper known for its closeness to both HADEP and the PKK. *Özgür Ülke* began publication in April 1994 and was banned from circulation in February 1995. Its predecessor, *Özgür Gündem* started its life in May 1992 and was banned in April 1994. During the two years of its publication 'unidentified assassins' murdered seven of its authors and reporters, including the renowned Kurdish sage, Mr Musa Anter alongside 13 of the paper's distributors. According to official figures 1538 Kurdish intellectuals and/or activists were assassinated by unidentified murderers between 1989–96.

Given this unpleasant background, the national elections that took place in April 1999 have revealed that the majority of the Kurds of Turkey have not opted for radical or ethnic politics but rather sought the solution of the so-called 'Kurdish problem' through conventional wisdom. Deemed to be the voice of the radical wing of Kurdish politics, HADEP received a fraction of the votes of Kurds living in towns other than the south-east (traditional Kurdish areas). That is why the government just about tolerates HADEP but with distaste.

There is a wide-scale belief that HADEP was to run in the April 1999 elections in order to break the power of the Islamist Virtue Party at the national level. Another argument is that it would have been unwise to ban HADEP during the trial of Öcalan. The party may serve as a safety valve to stave off Kurdish resentment as well as Western intervention on behalf of the Kurds. Yet many people believe that not forbidding HADEP from competing in the last elections was a democratic move.

Moderation and conciliation may help the Kurds to better integrate into the wider society. In fact, the basic factor behind Kurdish protest against the system is its exclusionist character which does not only fail to satisfy the material exigencies of the majority but also refuses to recognize cultural diversities/identities. A partial or regional electoral victory for HADEP, be it restricted to only the eastern provinces, provides a chance for the local populations to identify further with the system which so far they have felt to be alien or unresponsive to them.

The outcome of the April 1999 national and local elections on the whole is interpreted as a victory for nationalism. The most favoured parties are characterized as being 'nationalist'; but so is HADEP. The important question is whether these (Turkish and Kurdish) ethnic nationalisms will confront each other in the political sphere as they do on the battleground?

The nationalist character of the new government can only limit the pressures toward structural reform that emanate from within and without the system. It can not halt it altogether. What may shorten the time frame for the realization of the much-needed democratic reforms is the moderation of the radical Kurds, which will eventually evoke a positive response from the 'establishment'. This means abandoning the violent methods which they rely on in exerting their cultural identity and voicing their dissatisfaction with the system.

Mutual problems can only be solved with the involvement of the existing sides. So far the Turkish government has regarded the 'Kurdish problem' as one of mere terrorism and tried to solve it through repression and liquidation. The PKK in turn acted only as an armed group devoid of the capacity to be a political organization proposing solutions other than violence. Trapped in violence, both the Turkish and Kurdish citizens of Turkey have suffered and still suffer equally. This is a conflict which they have not created but have been pushed into and then systematically denied the opportunity to develop a consensual solution.

The *Document of Mutual Understanding*

The following is the *Document of Mutual Understanding*, a proposal for further democratization and solving the Kurdish problem in Turkey. It is the product of a group of citizens of the Republic of Turkey who deeply feel the responsibility for ending the ongoing fratricide that negatively affects almost everything in their country. An equal number of Turks and Kurds representing different social cohorts met throughout 1995 and 1996 in neutral locations at home and abroad detached from all forms of political or other influence and discussed their mutual problems.

They speculated about why they have different perceptions of their common problem and contemplated possible solutions. At the end of this discussion they recorded all the points on which they agreed and called it the *Document of Mutual Understanding*. They agreed to create an institution with the aim of promoting the views and suggestions contained in this document that would work to lay a new constitutional foundation for Turkish democracy based on multiculturalism, political pluralism and the rule of law. The Foundation for the Research of Societal Problems (TOSAV), which was formally founded on 13 February 1997, is the product of this collective decision. Following a series of comprehensive regional meetings at home and (one) abroad throughout 1997 and 1998 whereby Turkish and Kurdish local opinion leaders were brought together, the *Document of Mutual Understanding* was thoroughly discussed and improved. Seeing that the *Document* reflected a high degree of consensus among the citizens of Turkey regarding the further democratization of the system and solution of the Kurdish problem, the Founding Board of TOSAV has decided to submit the *Document* to the public.

Document of Mutual Understanding

A proposal for further democratization and solution to the Kurdish problem in Turkey

One of Turkey's major political problems emanates from what we attribute to the notion of nationhood,[3] a fundamental concept in our political culture. At the time of the declaration of the Republic, the republican elite accepted the pluralistic nature of the population and the multicultural richness of the society inherited from the Ottoman Empire. Disregarding their ethnic, cultural, religious, and linguistic heritage, the 'nation' was deemed to be the political union of all groups living in Turkey. This understanding could have created a pluralistic political structure out of a plural demography in which the nascent pluralist political organization would inevitably be democratic. However, this could not be realized. The policy of 'uniformity', or eliminating differences was preferred to forging 'unity' out of differences. Hence, creating a nation based on pluralist principles out of a poor, backward, uneducated and cosmopolitan populace was not realized by the political élite of the time.

Had the armed struggle been a conflict between security forces and a group of bandits on remote mountain tops, then the society would not have been much affected by it, and the matter would not be regarded as a national security issue. But we are confronted with a widespread economic disaster that impoverishes the nation, minimizes investments, and aggravates inflation.

Even developed societies may have their share of fanatics who choose violence as a means of political expression. As long as these people use violence to achieve their goals, there will be a need for effective police measures to deter them. However, when violence becomes a widespread method of protest involving thousands of armed peoples supported implicitly or explicitly by hundreds of thousands, then such a phenomenon is of a social character. Therefore, the social dimension of the conflict needs to be taken into consideration and the roots of the conflict need to be examined.

Primarily and most importantly, the parties to the conflict should meet independently of the official institutions which are the creators of the conflict. These parties should work together to define the problem and formulate solutions. Their common assessment must be translated into policy proposals and presented to the public, the real bearer of the problem(s).

It is with this vision and aim that we, the citizens of Turkish and Kurdish origin of the Republic of Turkey, got together motivated by the belief that watching the enfeeblement of our society, like a patient with internal bleeding, is equivalent to partaking in the historical irresponsibility. We discussed our mutual problem(s) at length in environments clear of external political influences. As a result of long and heated discussions free of prejudices and ready political menus, we agreed that:

Politics and philosophy of public administration

1. Turks and Kurds of Turkey are not the citizens of two inimical states. They are members of the same state. The root cause of the existing conflict is not the two parties/communities, but the official institutions, practices, and ideology.
   1.a) The official (political) institutions have lost their effectiveness. They have become unresponsive to local characteristics and exigencies of the people because of their ultra-centralized and hierarchic structures.

1.b) Official practices so far have reflected an unresponsive attitude to the existence of Kurdish and other cultural realities.

1.c) The official ideology adopted as the driving force of nation-building, i.e. (Turkish) nationalism has turned out to be perceived as exclusive rather than inclusive for non-ethnic Turkish citizens of the state contrary to the intention of the founders of the Republican regime. Indeed, citizenship has been based on ethnic Turkishness.

1.d) In the geographic areas with a Kurdish majority, the official ideology, with the approval of some of the Kurdish sovereigns, has frozen backward feudal economic and social relationships and prevented them from changing.

The Republican regime has restored sovereignty to the people. However, due to inadequate democratization of the regime, the impact of people over decisions concerning their own welfare has been minimal. The most important reason behind the bottleneck in the system is that the state has never really transferred power to the people. Despite official doubts, democratization of the regime is possible through the creation of a pluralist political structure without hampering the unitary nature of the state.[4] However, neither individual politicians nor political parties take responsibility for realizing this outcome. Social conflict continues because of their opportunistic and irresponsible attitude and as a result politics acquire a confrontational character.

The people of Turkey would have been able to solve their internal problems much more easily, we believe, if the political parties had not supported political factionalism and resisted change. The people wish to live together and have the common sense to produce practical solutions to achieve this end through mutual consensus. Quarrels, lack of understanding, insensitivity, and resistance to popular demands stem more from existing political structures and authoritarian mentality. This leads our society to live in constant fear of division despite the official emphasis on unity and integrity. The Kurds do not want to carve a second state out of Turkey. Division of the country is neither a political requirement nor a necessary result of current circumstances. The Kurds only want legal and concrete steps that would make them feel that this is their state too. Despite many events and policies that could create a rift between the Kurds and Turks, the fact that neither community feels any enmity towards the other is a great achievement. However, this society has not yet been rewarded for the common sense it has hitherto demonstrated. This reward can be delivered only by ending the practices and conditioning that lead to ethnic and cultural discrimination and animosity.

The presence of Kurds in Turkey, that is, 'The Kurdish reality', was unfortunately discovered after considerable bloodshed. Nevertheless, recognition of the Kurdish reality represents an achievement in itself. What does the recognition of Kurdish reality mean? It implies the acknowledgement of the existence of a cultural group (people), which includes several million persons. The Kurds have been and are one of the main elements of the Republican and the Ottoman states. They lay claim to unique cultural characteristics and are sensitive about conserving them.

Such acknowledgement of cultural distinctiveness is based not only on scientific observation, but also on political realities. The Kurds want official/legal acknowledgement of their existence as a unique cultural group (a people). They would like this acknowledgement to extend beyond oral commitments to include legal warranties that would have an effect on daily life, such as being counted in censuses and having the freedom to exercise their cultural identity.

The Kurds do not want these rights in order to distance themselves from the state or to divide Turkey. Neither do they want to alter the basic qualities of the state. Rather, they want to be able to preserve their cultural heritage and still live in safety as equal and respected citizens of Turkey in spite of the fact that they are not from the majority ethnic group.

In summary, Kurds are one of the original peoples of this country and a large majority of them favour living in peace and prosperity with their Turkish brethren within the boundaries of the Republic of Turkey. Unlike in democratic and civilized countries, Kurds feel rejected and victimized as the state and political institutions resist their needs. These feelings of victimization and ensuing wounded self-perception (identity) are the basis of many societal problems.

2. It is impossible to establish stability and solidarity in a society that includes a major group of people who feel politically excluded or victimized, even if such people are of the same race

or religion as the majority. The two pillars of stability are justice and equality. Social peace and stability can be achieved only through a democratic state organization and constitutionally based rule of law, which guarantees equality of all social groups. Poverty and underdevelopment, while aggravating the situation, are not the primary causes of the problem.

3. Citizenship and ethnic, religious, and cultural identity should not be confused. Citizenship is a legal phenomenon that includes existing diversities in the society. Cultural identity (belonging), on the other hand, is a personal and/or group phenomenon involving the private domain and civil society. Official authorities should not intervene in these domains because any intervention would make the state a proponent of one side as it already has. This harms social solidarity.

   The role of the State in this matter must be limited to preventing one cultural group from dominating another.

Culture and education

4. Freeing the private or cultural domain from intervention by the political domain/institutions is presumed in democratic society, which preserves political equality. These conditions must be met if the feeling of 'pluralist nationhood' is to be cultivated. Reductionist nationalism based on the ethnic identity and religious creed of the majority or a privileged minority can not ensure stability. It carries, in itself, the seeds of exclusion and segregation.

   Then, what is to be done is obvious:

   Institutionalizing respect for all ethnic and religious values and strengthening democratic institutions, which safeguard cultural diversities and political freedoms, are necessary steps. We see these as effective measures to prevent further politicizing ethnic and religious differences. We propose the expeditious implementation of the following legal and institutional infrastructure:

5. To extend constitutional guarantees of the country's cultural richness including the rights of other cultural groups[5] to safeguard their traditional values. To this end:

5.a) The authorities should recognize and support the Kurds' efforts[6] to teach their mother tongue besides Turkish, the official language of the country, and to convey their traditional cultural values to the community's younger generations, and;

5.b) Extend these rights to other cultural groups as a necessary prerequisite of democracy and civic equality, and;

5.c) To restructure our educational system so that it will exalt universal human values and civic virtues rather than ethnic and religious affiliation. Stripped of religion and ideology, these principles of education can serve in the building of democracy.

Law

6. 6.a) To put into practice the requirements of all international agreements on human rights and basic freedoms signed by (successive) government(s).

   6.b) To ensure that laws relied on in the struggle against political violence are in harmony with universal legal principles based on human rights; to ensure that the personnel employed in the fight against terrorism comply with universal legal principles.

   6.c) To abandon all arbitrary habits and policies that lead to dual legal and administrative structures and practices. To end in the shortest time possible institutions and practices such as State Security Courts, the state of siege, temporary village guards, the evacuation of villages, and illegal executions.

7. To rapidly adopt more liberal laws concerning the election system, political parties, and freedom of expression and assembly, in order to widen the base of democracy and to open the way for popular will to influence the decision-making mechanisms. To prepare a new constitution safeguarding such laws based on the principles of multiculturalism,[7] political pluralism, and participatory democracy. To remove all laws that are autocratic or clash with this constitution and the principles of human rights and participatory democracy; to purify all other laws to achieve congruency.

8. To implement the principle of separation of powers in the central government; to render the judiciary autonomous of other powers; to upgrade the total quality of the judiciary's

procedures, personnel, and practices by making the judiciary independent of the other organs/powers of the national state. To create systems for government accountability including the establishment of an Ombudsman to oversee whether administrations at all levels work in accordance with the law and are harmonized with their designated responsibilities.

9. To create an Assembly of Provinces under the umbrella of the Grand National Assembly of Turkey (the Parliament) in addition to the Assembly of Representatives. To enable the election of two representatives with or without party membership from each province – regardless of the size of the province – as long as they are respected by the members of the province and have high popular support. To reduce the already high number of seats in the existing one-chamber Parliament.
10. To make the concept of local government a reality and to try to solve local and regional problems which the central government cannot solve with the will and initiative of the local people. To equip and empower local governments with the organs of democratic administration and financial resources. To create elected councils, which can make decisions at the local–regional level without contradicting national laws and principles.
11. To establish regional development administrations in which local representatives elected by regional councils and a body of experts carefully selected by the central government will work together. To ensure the fruitful coordination of these groups without excessive bureaucratic red tape.
12. To have all official and civilian actors refrain from considering, using or praising violence as a problem-solving method; to be cautious of provoking people against each other for the sake of fighting against terrorism; to adopt the habit of solving problems in ways other than violence as a necessary condition of democratic ethics.
13. To provide security through the legal personnel and institutions of government, according to the rule of law.
14. To bring together the parties of this ongoing 'social conflict' in order to build a 'common ground' of understanding; to organize and encourage the silent majority, which does not

believe in violence and is ready for a conciliation.[8] To build a constituency for peace.

15. Work should be done to provide legality to all political parties that in their views and programmes claim to practise non-violent politics and adhere to the democratic principles of non-violence and respect for different views.

Economy

16. With regard to the individuals who had to leave their villages voluntarily or involuntarily;
    16.a. To equip those who want to return with new productive skills and initial capital so that they can produce for the market and not be condemned to poverty and backwardness once again.
    16.b. Cognizant of the fact that urbanization is a variable of social development, to provide adequate housing and vocational training for those who want to remain in urban settings where they have recently settled.
    16.c. To take the constitutional requirement of 'welfare state' as a guiding principle to build the incomplete physical infrastructure of Eastern and South-eastern Turkey and to provide special funds to encourage economic entrepreneurship by declaring the region a 'disaster area'. To coordinate the efforts of the central and local administrations in this respect.
17. Starting with eastern Turkey, to prepare master plans and related projects that will be put into effect in the short, medium, and long terms in order to reduce the level of poverty and unemployment which act as the incubators of many social ills.
18. With regard to industrialization;
    18.a. To encourage industrial growth in less developed regions, especially Eastern and South-eastern Anatolia through special incentives.
    18.b. To set up industries which can use the local natural resources of the region.
    18.c. Foreseeing future exports to the Middle East, to design a system of discounts, rebates or other incentives for

the buyers of goods and services produced in the region.

19. To plan and organize the livestock sector and related industries which are so vital for the economy of the region with an eye to the national and Middle Eastern markets. To increase the grasslands and pastures available for grazing in line with the economic necessities of the region rather than security concerns, thus ending one of the region's most important problems.
20. To institutionalize vocational training in order to educate a qualified workforce which will increasingly be needed as industry grows.

Every individual and every group who is a citizen of the Republic of Turkey should question how much they contribute to democracy while they demand democracy from the State. Every citizen and group in this country must be called upon to defend the rights of others while they demand rights for themselves. The rights of all citizens will be elevated to the level of those in democratic countries and will be protected internationally as Turkey develops and integrates with the global system. The basic aim of every individual and group that demand democracy should be to contribute to the efforts of putting Turkey in the league of 'civilized nations'.

Solving social conflict in a democracy depends on the parties' understanding the nature of the problem and their agreement on possible solutions. However, to reach a durable solution, the parties must first discuss the problem internally and, later amongst themselves freely and openly. This atmosphere of freedom can be created by both the State and the parties if they can approach differing views with tolerance. Doing this is everyone's responsibility.

Having agreed on these points, we, a diverse group of citizens of the Republic of Turkey, who want to see their country stronger, more peaceful and more stable than ever appeal to the society with this *Document* which represents a wide-ranging consensus. No country that is not at peace with itself can maintain stability and prosperity. As we look toward the democratic Turkey of the future, we invite all our fellow citizens to support our initiative, which aims to base our national unity on the principles of pluralism, the rule of law and multiculturalism. We also pledge to support similar initiatives.

Board of Founders
TOSAV
March, 1999

Notes

1 The April 1999 elections saw the MHP win enough votes to see them not only in parliament for the first time but also forming part of the coalition government.

2 A contributory factor behind the low votes is sometimes blamed on voters' records being held in their place of origin rather than their present place of settlement and as distances are so great many lose their right to vote by not being able to reach their designated polling station.

3 A *nation* is a political union of social groups and communities with differing ethnic, religious, cultural roots and special histories. A nation is a solidarity group that has forged a political union regardless of these differences. The nation-state is the organized, institutionalized form of the consensual political union achieved by the nation.

4 a) The Unitary State symbolizes the administrative-political organization of the nation intent on self-rule. The central authority or political-administrative centre created out of the solidarity of communities that comprise the nation may be pluralistic and participatory or authoritarian and monopolistic, depending on the level of development of the society. The central authority may be democratic if and to the degree it relies on a constitution which is built on universal human rights and on the principle of pluralism.

While a democratic and pluralistic unitary state attributes the highest value to indivisibility or unity of the society, it does not reject proliferation of the form of political participation and formation of local governments.

b) Alludes to a central authority, which makes the final decisions on issues that concern the unity of the country such as defence, finance, foreign relations and education. While modern democratic centralism leaves all other decisions and policy implementations to local administrations, it facilitates local participation in the decision-making process at the centre. The central government also foresees the equal, just and efficient distribution of services and investments throughout the country. A central government, which can not realize these goals, can neither provide social stability nor the political unity it seeks to establish.

5 Anthropologically, a Cultural Group may be called a 'people'. 'Society' is culturally a neutral collective concept. Each society consists of diverse cultural groups and religious communities. What keep them together are the political culture, contractual legal system, division of labour, and their free collective will to live together as a nation.

6 For example, a factor that is common to the education models in Uzbekistan, Ireland and the Basque Country, can be implemented here: when students belonging to different cultural groups reach a certain number, if the parents so desire, classes are created for these students to be educated in their own languages. By removing the prohibitions on the language issue, a similar process can be developed in Turkey. In the initial stage, having Kurdish classes upon demand within existing schools can satisfy the need for education in the mother tongue.

7 Multiculturalism is; a) the provision of legal equality between cultures and allowing their presence or visibility in public life; b) a pluralistic policy of representing all existing cultures or cultural groups within the official identity of the 'nation'; c) the effort of forging social peace by eliminating prejudice, improving communication and by ending hierarchy between different cultural groups in the society.

8 Meetings must be organized by local administrations and NGOs by which individuals belonging to different ethnicities, creeds and political convictions may be brought into contact in order to build confidence and understanding among them.

Suggestions for further reading

Barkey, Henri J. *et al.*, *Turkey's Kurdish Question* (Lanham, MD: Rowman and Littlefield, 1998)

Bruinessen, Martin van, *Agha, Shaikh and State: the Social and Political Structures of Kurdistan* (London, Atlantic Highlands, NJ: Zed Books, 1992).

MacDowall, David, *A Modern History of the Kurds* (London: I.B. Tauris, 1997).

Macdowall, David, *The Kurds. A Nation Denied* (London: Minority Rights Group, 1992).

TOSAV's web-site: www.tosav.org.tr

8
International Relations: from Europe to Central Asia

Canan Balkır

Introduction

Since its establishment in 1923, the Republic of Turkey has pursued a foreign policy aimed at international peace based on the principle of 'Peace at home and peace in the world', as laid down by its founder Mustafa Kemal Atatürk. Respect for the independence, sovereignty and territorial integrity of the neighbouring countries has been the main pillar of Turkish foreign policy.

Turkey is located where Europe and Asia meet and is, therefore, often regarded as a bridge between the East and the West. Such a unique geographical position gives the country European, Balkan, Middle Eastern, Caucasian, Mediterranean, and Black Sea identities, explaining the multidimensional foreign policy which Turkey pursues.

Central Asia became of particular renewed interest with the collapse of the Soviet Union, since, despite the reality of a sense of common roots, pan-Turkic movements at the beginning of the twentieth century had been short-lived.

However, Turkey's relationship with Europe has been long-lasting in terms of diplomacy, military cooperation and trade. The new republic leaned towards the West and became a member of the United Nations (UN) in 1945, and of the North Atlantic Treaty Organization (NATO) in 1952. The Truman Doctrine of 1947 marked the beginning of a new era in Turkey's relations with the US and close working relations were developed between Turkey and the US in the political, military, economic, technical and cultural fields.

Turkey took part in the Korean War and applied to the European Economic Community (EEC) in 1959. During all these years, she became a genuine military-strategic partner of the Western Alliance. And in the 1980s relations with Europe developed as Turkey's economic liberalization process gained momentum.

This chapter will aim to direct the reader to Turkey's international concerns as seen and heard from within the country. And as is to be expected from such a viewpoint, in most of these relations politics and economics intertwine uneasily. Relations with Europe will be the main concern of the chapter, as this reflects the economic and political core reality of Turkey's international relations.

Turkey–Europe Relations

Since the beginning of the new republic in 1923, Turkey has adopted European legal, social and political norms and participated in most European institutions; she became a member of the Council of Europe in 1949, took an active part in the military organization of NATO, and was one of the founding members of the Organization for European Economic Cooperation (OEEC) which later became the Organization for Economic Cooperation and Development (OECD). Turkish policy-makers wanted to be included in almost all the institutions of the Western Alliance and her ties with the West were believed to be a key to prosperity and stability.

However, it was at the end of the 1950s, when domestic economic and political difficulties began to be experienced, that the Turkish government looked for policy alternatives abroad and applied to the EEC in July 1959. Having already signed a treaty of association with Greece, being careful to balance its relations between the two countries, and not underestimating the role of Turkey for security concerns, the Community welcomed this application. Turkey gained the status of associate membership by signing the Association Treaty, namely the Ankara Agreement, on 12 September 1963.

The objective of the Ankara Agreement[1] was to promote a constant and well-balanced intensification of trade and economic relations between the contracting parties with the aim of establishing a customs union. Article 28 of the Agreement went even further and foresaw the possibility of eventual full membership for Turkey if and when she was able to meet the necessary obligations.

The Ankara Agreement envisaged the economic association developing in three stages, namely the preparatory, the transitional, and the final. The first stage was completed in five years and the second stage, which aimed at setting the timetable towards the establishment of a customs union between the parties, commenced right afterwards. Hence the customs union between the EU and Turkey represents a process that started in 1964 with the signing of the Ankara Agreement and was reaffirmed in 1973 with the entry into force of the Additional Protocol[2] to that Agreement which laid down the conditions and timetables for the progressive setting-up of the customs union over a period of 22 years.

In the trade of manufactures during the transitional stage, the obligations imposed directly by the Additional Protocol included the elimination of all customs duties and quantitative restrictions, alignment by Turkey on the Common Customs Tariff (CCT), elimination of protective measures between the parties, and the treatment of matters such as workers' rights. By 1973, the European Community (EC)[3] had abolished all customs duties and quotas for Turkish manufactured products, with the exception of certain sensitive products such as cotton yarns and textiles, and machine-woven carpets. Petroleum products were subject to tariff reductions within quota limits.

Contrary to the stipulations of the Additional Protocol, textiles and ready-made garments were later treated under the so-called voluntary export restraint agreements concluded between the EC authorities and Turkish private-sector textile exporters. The Association Council was the governing body to oversee the timely implementation of the other complementary measures too.

Turkey was given a longer period of adjustment to make reductions to the customs tariff for manufactured imports from the EC within the framework of two separate lists with different time-spans, a 12-year list and a 22-year list, taking into consideration the competitiveness of the industries concerned.

As for agricultural imports from Turkey, they were subject to the Common Customs Tariff, although the Community granted tariff concessions from the beginning since it protects its agricultural sector with the sophisticated non-tariff barriers of the Common Agricultural Policy (CAP). The gradual elimination of duties by January 1987 on primary agricultural products having a regulated market in the EC was granted, while for processed products, there are variable levies and additional duties.

On the free movement of persons and services, Article 36 of the Additional Protocol stipulates that 'freedom of movement for workers between Member States of the Community and Turkey shall be secured by progressive stages in accordance with the principles set out in Article 12 of the Association Agreement between the end of the twelfth and the twenty-second year after the entry into force of that Agreement.' Thus the free movement of workers, one of the main pillars of the Association, was expected to be established by 1 December 1986, and the Association Council was to decide on the rules necessary to that end. However, the free circulation was not even considered then.

The oil crisis of 1973 that damaged the economic growth of Turkey as well as Europe, and the military intervention of Turkey in Cyprus in 1974 adversely affected relations between them. This delicate relation was further complicated by the privileges granted by the EC to third countries under the General System of Preferences, the Lomé Convention, and the Global Mediterranean Policy. The preferences granted to Turkey under the Association Agreement were eroded substantially by all these privileges. Along with this, the failure of the EC to fulfil its obligations regarding the free movement of persons, the freezing of the Fourth Financial Protocol and the imposition of quotas on Turkish textile exports were the main factors which strained the relationship.

Financial aid was especially important to Turkey which had entered into a foreign exchange crisis in the second half of the 1970s and needed aid desperately to help ease the negative repercussions of the tariff reductions on the economy. However, not only was the Fourth Financial Protocol blocked by the Greek veto, but the financial aid already received under the previous three protocols was frustrating enough since it only amounted to a total of ECU 827 million, a negligible amount compared to what other non-member Mediterranean countries were receiving as financial aid from the EC. The same comparison would also be valid for Eastern European countries in the 1990s.

Concerning the tariff reductions, Turkey reduced tariffs only twice, in 1973 and 1976, and delayed further tariff reductions on EC-manufactured products due to the economic problems she faced at home in the second half of the seventies, namely inflation and a foreign exchange shortage, along with political unrest. As regards the CCT, Turkey could not even commence the adjustment, as was the case with the agricultural sector, where the necessary steps to close the structural gap were not taken.[4]

Therefore, being in great economic difficulties and frustrated by the EC's lack of response to her financial demands, in 1978 Turkey took the step leading to the freezing of the terms of the Association Agreement under Article 60 of the Additional Protocol which allowed either of the two parties to take requisite measures in the case of regional or general economic disruption. After this point Turkey's relations with the Community came to a standstill which was further aggravated by the military intervention in 1980. This intervention came at a time when the EC was placing the utmost emphasis on democracy and human rights issues. Thus, in January 1982, the Turkey–EC Joint Parliamentary Committee was suspended by the European Parliament.

The structural adjustment programme introduced on 24 January 1980 targeted the liberalization of the economy, commencing with the foreign trade sector and later moving on to capital movements. Under this new export-oriented industrialization policy, Turkey's trade relations with Middle Eastern and North African Muslim countries increased considerably, while the volume of trade between Turkey and the EC declined. There was also the emergence of diverging views on political issues. The issues of human rights and democracy were gaining priority on the Community agenda, while Turkey continued to perceive the Community as an economic entity and interpreted the EC's insistence on democracy and the promotion of human rights as interference in her internal affairs.

At the same time, the export-oriented industrialization policy of the 1980s brought on a major transformation in the economy, increasing the competitiveness of industry. Foreign trade was liberalized to a large extent and considering the importance of the EC as a trading partner, proceeding with the Association Agreement looked like the most indisputable outcome. This idea was voiced by the business community, frustrated by the declining trade alternative of the Muslim countries in the Middle East and North Africa due to the reduction in oil prices, and concerned about the impact of the second and third enlargements of the Community on Turkish manufactured exports. Intellectual circles seeing full membership as a guarantee for the recently gained civilian democracy, also welcomed the idea.

On 14 April 1987 Turkey applied for full membership. This application did not meet with the approval of the EC due to reasons stemming from both sides, such as the fact that the Turkish economy was still insufficiently developed to compete within the EC's emerging single market, along with other factors such as the Greek veto over the Cyprus issue, and Turkey's record on democracy and human rights. The report also pointed out the concern about any new membership at that particular time when the EC was already engaged in a deepening process.

Although not approving Turkey's full membership, the Commission proposed the reactivation of the Ankara Agreement, presented as the 'Matutes Package', which was also rejected by the EC Council due to the Greek veto. After this frustration, a customs union seemed the only feasible option left to rescue the floundering relations, and in 1988 a new timetable for tariff reductions and adoption of the CCT by Turkey was agreed upon. The Common Steering Committee was set up to prepare for the completion of the customs union by reactivating the implementation of the provisions laid down in the Association Agreement.

However, as Rittenberg points out:

> Throughout this period, Turkey has officially clung to the idea of eventual full membership, while Europe has moved away from linking the customs union to this issue. Thus the creation of the customs union with the EC did not relieve the tension between the parties, the divergence of opinion continues.[5]

Turkey was the first country to conclude a customs union with the EC without being a full member, which meant in practice doing without the aid and support mechanisms. In addition, the establishment of a customs union was more than the abolition of customs duties and taxes having equivalent effect between the two sides and the implementation of the CCT on third countries by Turkey, as was stipulated in the Ankara Agreement and the Additional Protocol. Due to the evolution of the *acquis communautaire*[6] and the changes in the rules of the global economy, such as the stipulations of the Uruguay Round, the General System of Preferences, the concept of 'customs union' had undergone vital changes. Thus the agreement on the current form of the customs union also meant the abolition of all non-tariff barriers such as import levies, acceptance of all the preferential trade agreements concluded by the EC with third countries, and adaptation of trade agreements to the respective EC position, granting trade preferences to a number of developing countries.

The customs union also required Turkey to implement rules of competition compatible with those of the EC, and to eliminate state aid and incentives that were incompatible with the proper functioning of the Customs Union.

With third countries, for limited product groups, Turkey can retain customs duties higher than the CCT until January 2001.

Therefore, the customs union was binding Turkey in a unique way to the European Community: it has no access to decision-making activities yet accepts the EC's *acquis communautaire* with respect to the free movement of industrial products and common rules of competition and trade.

This was not as easy as it seemed, since certain highly protected sectors such as automotive and pharmaceuticals needed a transition period. In addition, Turkey was to bring its legislation in line with that of the Community concerning the regulatory framework of competition, such as state subsidies, anti-trust law, and the law concerning industrial and intellectual property rights.

The trade in agricultural products was excluded from the customs union, although the Association Council reaffirmed its intention concerning the move towards the free movement of agricultural products, conditional upon Turkey's adoption of CAP measures. Concerning processed agricultural products, Turkey was allowed to apply tariffs on imports from third countries for listed goods with agricultural components.

The EC, on the other hand, had to end the quotas on textile and clothing imports from Turkey by abolishing the voluntary export restraint arrangements, conditional upon Turkey's adoption of the EC's textile policy, both with regard to commercial policy, including the agreements and arrangements on trade in textiles and clothing and state aid granted to this sector.

The Council expressed its wish to conclude the negotiations for the free movement of European Coal and Steel Community (ECSC) products in 1995.

But all the economic measures expected to be taken by Turkey were not enough to commence the customs union since for the EC there was also a political side to the issue. The significance of this was already illustrated by the 1991 political conditionality clause, which placed the protection of human rights as one of the main objectives of the EC's external relations. The large-scale military operations in the south-eastern region of Turkey against the separatist Kurdistan Workers' Party (PKK) affected relations adversely, and Turkey's legitimate fight against terrorism has sometimes been viewed as a violation of human rights. Turkey was expected to take steps towards enhancing her democratization process.

Turkey showed sincere concern over these criticisms and took some steps such as the amendment of Article 8 of the anti-terrorism law. Prisoners held under this article were released. The Community welcomed these reform measures as steps towards the improvement of the democratic situation.

Finally, the 36th Turkey–EC Association Council on 6 March 1995 approved the legal framework agreement which set the coverage and implementation schedule of the customs union and which was to enter into force on 31 December 1995.

The Association Council also agreed on two more documents, the first being the Resolution of the EC–Turkey Association Council on the development of the Association. It is a type of action plan calling for cooperation in economic matters and for political and institutional dialogue. The second document is the Community Declaration Concerning Financial Cooperation, which stated the funds Turkey is to receive between the years 1996 to 2001 and the related sources. The overall aid over a five-year period is expected to be around ECU 1.5 billion.[7]

The Association Council meeting of 30 October 1995 confirmed that Turkey had met the conditions set out in the decision of 6 March by adapting its laws and taking steps to bolster democracy and the rule of law. Therefore the customs union became not only an economic issue but also a political link for Turkey to the market-based, liberal democracy of Europe.

The European Parliament's (EP) decision for the implementation of the final phase of the customs union was a political decision. As Pauline Green, the leader of the Socialist Group in the EP voiced it, they wanted to encourage democratic evolution in Turkey 'in favour of individual and minority rights'. Many both in Europe and in Turkey saw it as an assurance against ultra-nationalistic and religious political developments. It was also promoted as a process which would contribute to the improvement of relations with Greece, and to a solution to the Cyprus question.

On 1 January 1996 the Customs Union commenced.[8] What concerned Turkey most was the economic impact of the Customs Union (CU) on her economy. The CU gave rise to an expectation of an increase in the total two-way trade. The trade gap for Turkey was expected to widen in the short run since it is Turkey, not the Community, which is dismantling barriers to trade, as the Community had abolished all tariff and non-tariff barriers in 1973, with few exceptions.

Therefore imports from the EC were expected to increase first, and this is exactly what happened. After the CU, Turkey became the EC's eighth trading partner in the world, with the EC in return accounting for more than a 50 per cent share of Turkey's external trade, with a trade deficit of around US$12 billion.

A large percentage of Turkey's imports are raw materials and investment goods needed for increasing manufacturing capacity. These imports were oriented towards the EC resulting in a trade diversion effect in favour of the EU and increasing the foreign trade deficit. The tariff reduction to third countries due to the application of the CCT is expected to reduce the trade diversion costs of the CU in the future.

Trade is just one part of the picture. There is also the fact that over two million Turkish workers are employed in the member countries of the EU and their remittances are an important source of foreign exchange.

The advantages to Turkish industry included the removal of the remaining restrictions on the export of manufactured goods to the EU, simplification of border procedures, improved access to third-country markets with which the EU has preferential trade agreements, and lower prices on imported inputs.

The benefits to Turkey are expected to be more noticeable in the medium and long term, when the economy adjusts to the economic standards of the EC and gains international competitiveness. According to World Bank estimates (Harrison *et al.*, 1996),[9] the impact on Turkey's GDP was calculated to be between 1.1–1.5 per cent of its

Table 8.1 Turkey's Exports to and Imports from the European Union

	Exports (fob) to EU		*Imports (fob) from EU*	
	US$ billions	*% of total*	*US$ billions*	*% of total*
1967–80 (average)	0.7	48.5	1.3	46.6
1980–84 (average)	1.9	36.3	2.7	29.8
1985–89 (average)	4.4	44.5	5.2	37.0
1990	6.9	53.3	9.4	41.9
1991	7.1	51.8	9.2	43.8
1992	7.6	51.7	10.0	43.9
1993	7.3	47.5	13.0	44.0
1994	8.3	47.7	10.3	47.0
1995	11.1	51.2	16.8	47.2
1996	11.5	49.7	23.1	53.0
1997	12.2	46.6	24.9	51.2
1998	13.4	50.0	24.1	51.5

Source: Undersecretary of Foreign Trade, Turkey.

GDP per year, depending on the adoption of the complementary policies.

As for Turkey's obligations arising from her membership of other integration schemes, such as the Economic Cooperation Organization (ECO) and the Black Sea Economic Cooperation (BSEC) project, they will be subject to consultations with the Association Council, since Article 52 of the Decision stipulates the waiver of sovereignty into areas which are of direct significance to the functioning of the CU.

Relations with Greece and the Cyprus question

Relations with Greece constitute one of the most important aspects of Turkish foreign policy, since there are a number of long-standing problems between the two countries, although they share some of the same geography and are both NATO allies, associates in the EU and the Western European Union (WEU).

The fundamental source of tension between the two countries can be cited as the problems related to the Aegean sea,[10] the Cyprus issue, the Turkish minority in Western Thrace and Greece's support to the PKK. And it was not until July 1999 that the relations between the two countries relaxed, resulting in a meeting in which they finally agreed to take up issues of common concern, namely tourism, environment, culture, terrorism, organized crime, drug trafficking and illegal migration and to hold further bilateral meetings on these issues.

As for the status of the Turkish minority in Western Thrace, it is defined by the Lausanne Peace Treaty of 1923. The main problems are the practices aimed at restricting freedom of worship of the Turkish Muslim minority, stripping the Turkish Muslim minority of their citizenship under the former Article 19 of the Greek Nationality Law which enabled authorities to pursue administrative discrimination against those of 'non-Greek ethnic origin', and restricting the Turkish minority from establishing or operating its own educational establishments.

Finally, the Cyprus issue is not only between Turkey and Greece but concerns all the countries involved in the peace in and security of the eastern Mediterranean. Greece's insistence on linkage between the Cyprus issue and the customs union made sure that this issue was on the table throughout the customs union negotiations. When the European Council promised to undertake accession negotiations with Cyprus six months after the conclusion of the Intergovernmental Conference, Greece withheld its veto concerning the finalization of the customs union. However, Turkey reserved her right to achieve a similar integration with the Turkish Republic of Northern Cyprus[11] if the EU opened accession negotiations with Cyprus before an island-wide negotiated settlement was reached, since under existing international agreements Cyprus's membership of international organizations of which both Turkey and Greece are not also members is barred.

Other countries in the Balkans figure on Turkey's foreign policy agenda. They had been part of the Ottoman Empire for centuries and had always been Anatolia's gateway to Europe. Being concerned in the affairs of the Balkans, Turkey established working relations with all the states of the former Yugoslavia, including Serbia, and developed close ties with Muslim Albania and with Macedonia, to the initial annoyance of Greece. Over the human tragedy in Bosnia and Herzegovina and later in Kosovo, she contributed to the international peace-keeping efforts in this region. Along with security interests, she is also investing in increasing economic and cultural ties with the Balkan countries.

Relations after the Customs Union

Turkey's relations with Europe after the Customs Union did not go smoothly: there was a loss of public revenues, the trade deficit with Europe grew, contrary to expectations foreign investments declined, financial aid has been blocked, and it soon became evident that the Customs Union did not increase the chances of full membership.

Domestically, the debate continues in Turkey between the defenders of the CU who believe that it will yield positive results in the long term, and the opponents who argue that it will harm Turkey's interests. The latter often say that Turkey, as a Muslim country, will never be accepted as a full member in a Christian club, therefore the economic sacrifices concerning the Customs Union are forgone. Irrespective of the political stance, there has been criticism concerning Europe's attitude towards Turkey, in particular for not honouring its obligations, including the free circulation of labour and the implementation of financial cooperation, especially when the EP, citing human rights violations and the failure of Turkey to fulfil pre-Customs Union democratization pledges, froze its financial obligations once more on 19 December 1995 after a decision on 16 December 1995 by the European Court of Human Rights ruling that Turkey should pay compensation to a group of villagers whose villages had been burnt.

Other events which strained relations are those in the Aegean involving the islands of Kardak/Imia in 1996, where the EP remained impartial at the beginning, later supporting the Greek argument, and also the events following the escape of Abdullah Öcalan, leader of the PKK in 1998. Even the efforts suppressing the Islamist movement in order to maintain the secular nature of the Turkish regime aroused criticism from the West, particularly with regard to the influence of the army in domestic politics.[12]

The collapse of the Soviet Union presented new opportunities and challenges not only for Turkey but maybe more so for the EC. Feeling that it cannot afford to exclude the central and eastern European countries in the reshaping of Europe, the Community concluded agreements with them with the possibility of eventual full membership. Finally, at the Luxembourg Summit of 12–13 December 1997, it became apparent that Turkey was not being given a place in the accession queue that included the central and eastern European countries, as well as Cyprus. Turkey, reacting strongly to the outcome of this Summit, declared that although she would maintain the existing association relations with the EU, the further enrichment of these relations would depend on the EU's fulfilment of its commitments. The relatively positive development at the Cardiff and Vienna Summits in 1998 and the Cologne Summit in June 1999, did not present a clear political message for Turkey.

During all this time, however, one sees that Turkey has never changed her objective of full accession to the EU. She also became an associate member of WEU in 1992, a formula enabling non-EU members to be in the security arrangement. Relations with the EU have been the driving force in mobilizing society in favour of democratic as well as economic reforms. However, the state of Turkish politics and the unstable macroeconomic performance of the economy, high public sector debt, persistent inflation, human rights record, the Kurdish issue, as well as the continuing friction with Greece, have all served to undermine her standing in Europe.

New horizons: multi-tiered diplomacy

When one visualizes the geographical location of Turkey, a portion of which rests in Europe, but the bulk of which rests in Asia Minor, south of the Bosphorus and Dardanelles, one may regard it as a European, Balkan, Mediterranean, Middle Eastern, Caucasian, Asian, and Black Sea power.

Due to this geographical location, therefore, it is naive to consider issues arising in any of these areas without reference to Turkey. She is one of the major players in the political and economic affairs of Eurasia which has been going through a total transformation since the end of the Cold War.

The collapse of the Soviet Union and the emergence of the independent states led to a restructuring of the regional balance of power and put Turkey's geostrategic status in a new light. The geostrategic importance of Turkey, which seemed to have been eroded until the beginning of this new era, changed later on as the Gulf crisis, the conflicts in the Balkans and the Transcaucasus, put Turkey once more on the security agenda.

Pax Turkica

After the Soviet collapse at the beginning of the 1990s, new areas opened up for Turkey in the Caucasus and Central Asia promising connection with other Turkic peoples. The rediscovery of ethnic and linguistic brothers was greeted with great enthusiasm, and raised hopes of producing a Turkic-speaking block.[13]

Transportation and communication links were quickly established between these states and Turkey, as well as the creation of a number of institutions to promote and coordinate closer relations, such as the Turkish Cooperation and Development Agency (TİKA) operating under the auspices of the Ministry of Foreign Affairs, and the Foreign Economic Relations Board (DEİK), an association of bilateral business councils. Turkey served as a role model for many of these countries in the process of trade liberalization and restructuring their economies along the lines of a market economy, as a country which had already dealt with these changes. It also has certain characteristics such as a secular state and a democratic system which appealed to these societies. The Central Asian republics were not interested in Islamic formulas proposed by countries like Saudi Arabia and Iran.

Turkey also assumed a guidance role in promoting the participation of the Central Asian republics in international forums such as the Conference on Security and Cooperation in Europe (CSCE) and the United Nations. Turkey's efforts were fundamental in getting the five Turkic states to join (Kazakhstan as an observer) the Economic Cooperation Organization (ECO), which was originally established in 1992 to promote economic, cultural, and technological cooperation between Turkey, Iran and Pakistan.

Turkey developed economic relations with these countries through economic cooperation, namely the successfully realized examples are BSEC and ECO. Turkey became the initiator of the BSEC, which is a loose regional economic integration with the objective of the progressive elimination of obstacles to trade in a region with a population of more than 400 million. It does not specifically refer to a free trade arrangement but refers to the free movement of business people. The economic value of BSEC was promoted by basing the discussion on the complementary structure of the economies, as Turkey exports consumer goods and construction services needed by the ex-Soviet countries, which in return have abundant raw materials and energy resources that Turkey needs.

The BSEC is composed of 11 participating states: Albania, Armenia, Azerbaijan, Bulgaria, Georgia, Greece, Moldova, Romania, Russia, Turkey and Ukraine, and seven states as observers: Poland, Slovakia, Italy, Austria, Tunisia, Egypt, Israel. Therefore BSEC has Balkan, Mediterranean, Caspian, EU, Middle Eastern, and North African dimensions.

The BSEC was formally launched in Istanbul in 1992.[14] It was not perceived simply as a regional economic cooperation, but also as an arrangement which could contribute to the maintenance of peace and stability in the region. Although it can be argued that it has not been capable of preventing the rise of conflicts between its members such as the Armenian–Azeri conflict – the development of closer economic ties and shared interests is expected to contribute to peace and security in the region.

The BSEC has already established a trade and development bank. And the fact that the signatory countries have approved a declaration of intent which envisages the formation of a free-trade area in the long term indicates that the road is open to making encouraging progress.

Turkey has signed numerous agreements with the Central Asian republics and Azerbaijan in economic, cultural, educational, communications, transportation, technical assistance, and training fields. The Turkish private sector is very active in the region and is involved in a wide range of investment projects in Central Asia and Azerbaijan.

While the predominant role of Turkey within the region was expected to increase her bargaining power and strengthen her position *vis-à-vis* the EU, none of these integration schemes was considered as an alternative to the EU, but rather represented complementary initiatives reinforcing the process of rapprochement with European countries. For example, the possibility of establishing a free-trade agreement between the EU and BSEC or having the three Mediterranean members of BSEC serve as a link between BSEC and the Euro-Mediterranean partnership were some of the schemes envisioned.

The weakening of Russian power, and the Western world's desire to isolate Iran have created a historic chance for Turkey to reassert herself as a leading player in the reshaping of the region. However, the initial euphoria was later replaced by a more pragmatic outlook, as soon as she became aware of Russian security concerns. From that point onwards, she kept a certain distance from getting involved in the political and security affairs of the Transcaucasus, while being deeply involved with the region's economic growth as well as developing cultural links with the Central Asian republics.

There have been important shortcomings in Turkey's foreign policy also. Lack of know-how and experience in such a complex situation, coupled with Russian proximity, and balance of power politics including Iran, conflicts of interest among the Turkic states and the inclination of these states to diversify their foreign relations, rather than depending only on Turkey can be cited as the main limitations.

Unresolved political and ethnic conflicts in the region make it harder to step in. Even for a country like Azerbaijan, with which the linguistic and cultural ties are close, there have been some problems when the strongly pro-Turkish Elçibey government was forced out, clearing the way for Heydar Aliyev to take office. Relations took a favourable turn again when President Aliyev managed to reassure the Turkish government that he enthusiastically supports the construction of a pipeline from Azerbaijan (Baku) to the Mediterranean Turkish port of Ceyhan.

Turkish–Armenian relations have been intensely strained by the unresolved Karabakh conflict, the border issue and the heavy burden of history. They have been placed under further strain by the coming to power in Armenia of Robert Kocharyan, a veteran of the Karabakh wars. Azerbaijan's greatest hope is that Turkey will continue to seal its border with Armenia, although this involves considerable economic sacrifice on the part of Turkey. The damage to trade from the border closure has been so great that local Turkish politicians have seen fit to ask for the gates to be reopened.

Eurasian oil issue

A role for Turkey in the production and transportation of Eurasian oil was considered to be one of the main opportunities presented in the post Cold-War era. The economic benefits considered were a decrease in the dependence on Middle Eastern oil and Russian gas, the royalties and transportation fees that would accrue if a pipeline passed through Turkey, the benefits to Turkish construction firms that would construct the pipeline, and the related employment opportunities. On the political side, the marketing of Eurasian oil was expected to bring prosperity to some of these newly independent states, consequently decreasing Russian influence in the region.

The Russian proposal aimed to bring the oil to the terminal at Novorossiysk, a Russian port on the Black Sea coast, and then carry it by tanker via the Turkish straits, while Turkey's proposal for the pipeline was the Baku–Ceyhan route. Turkey argued that the Russian proposal would put a strain on the already overloaded straits' traffic, create further environmental problems and present greater risk to inhabitants in Istanbul. Russia on the other hand argued that the Turkish proposal is more costly and the route is not safe due to terrorism in south-eastern Turkey.

Later, due to the possible effects of large amounts of oil flooding into the world market, the oil-producing countries became more concerned with the project. Nevertheless, as the Eurasian oil producers were in need of cash, the compromise was to transport only the early oil and the Baku–Ceyhan route was not considered viable as the route for this relatively small quantity of oil.

Given the complexity of interests, it is hard to predict the outcome. But the role of the USA, which promotes multiple pipelines thereby decreasing dependence on one route, will be one of the decisive factors.[15] The post-Cold War developments have clearly shown that Turkey and the US continue to share a set of common strategic and security concerns, leading to Turkish–US cooperation in the field of energy and on regional issues. Therefore there is strong conviction in the country that the US will use its power in favour of the Turkish route.

Although the pipeline issue has been a source of rivalry between Turkey and Russia, bilateral trade relations have grown intensely due to the complementary economic structure of both countries. Turkey imports military equipment and fuel from Russia, and exports consumer products and services in return. There is also an important suitcase trade between individuals and small businesses which is not officially recorded. Other areas of cooperation are natural gas, tourism, transportation and construction.

The competition for influence over Eurasia is increasing not only because of it being an important source for oil, gas and other commodities and the related negotiations on the energy and pipeline routes but also because of the growing significance of the interdependence of this region within the global system. This increases the geopolitical importance of Turkey not only for the stability of the region but also in terms of linking Eurasia to the international system.

Turkey as part of the Middle East

Turkey always advocated a peaceful solution to the Arab–Israeli conflict and the Palestinian issue which lie at the core of the tension in the Middle East. She was among the first states to recognize the Palestine National Council's 'Declaration of Independence for Palestine'. At the same time, being also one of the first states to recognize Israel, she clearly shared interests with that country.[16]

In 1996, three major agreements were approved that powerfully support bilateral ties with Israel: a military training and cooperation agreement, which allows each side to train in the other's air space; a defence industrial cooperation agreement; and a free-trade agreement. The economic component of Israeli–Turkish relations has also developed considerable importance. Turkish exports to Israel have increased from $30 million in 1989 to $390 million in 1997. Overall trade volume has grown sevenfold during this period. It is expected to increase more, due to the free-trade agreement which came into effect in 1997.[17] The Arab world and Iran have been increasingly critical of Turkish–Israeli relations.

Turkey took part in the US-led coalition against Saddam Hussein in Iraq in 1991. The solidarity shown to the Western Alliance, despite the frustrations of Arab states, ended with absolute disappointment on the part of Turkey as her economic losses were never compensated for by the coalition countries.

Turkey also ascribes great importance to furthering her relations in all fields with the Muslim countries. She plays an active role in the Organization of the Islamic Conference (OIC).

Turkey with Iran and Pakistan in 1964 established a trilateral economic organization namely, the Regional Cooperation for Development (RCD) which in 1985 was restructured as the Economic

Cooperation Organization (ECO). The Muslim-majority states of the former Soviet Union were added later. Through BSEC and ECO, Turkey is involved in a regional multilateral relationship with six of its eight bordering neighbours, the exceptions being Iraq and Syria.

Another significant topic which affects Turkey's relations with its Middle Eastern neighbours is her involvement in a US$32 billion project referred to as the Southeastern Anatolian Project (GAP).[18] The waters of the Euphrates and Tigris rivers are being used to create one of the greatest irrigation projects in the world covering about one-tenth of the country's territory. This could accelerate a multi-faceted and multisectoral development in this poorest region of Turkey. The project aims at a final annual production of a total of 27 billion kWh of power and hundreds of miles of tunnels and canals to irrigate 1.7 million hectares of land annually. Turkey shares this potential with its southern neighbours, but this cooperation does not soften their concern as they are uneasy about Turkey's control of this vital source of water.

Conclusion

With the spread of globalism the EU, the North American Free Trade Area (NAFTA) and the Asia Pacific region became the new centres of attraction. Liberalization required the emergence of large single markets within the boundaries of each one of these regions. In short, trade is liberalized within the individual blocs but not so much among them. As for the investment flows, the credit worthiness of countries is much higher when they are within these large trading blocs than otherwise.

Turkey needed to anchor herself firmly within one of these trading blocs. The EU, a bloc whose trade volume with Turkey has already reached some US$40 billion making it the major trading partner of Turkey, was a logical choice.

Although the changing international climate in the post-Cold War period increased Turkey's strategic importance, her relationship with the European Union has become more problematic, while that with the United States has progressed. Turkey's role in enhancing regional stability in Eurasia as well as her efforts in integrating the region into the international system has been affected by her strained relations with Europe.

However, when one considers the growing interrelationship between events in Europe, the Middle East and Eurasia, one can easily see that it would be difficult for Europe to maintain a stable economic and political system with instability reigning in her adjacent areas. Turkey is a key player in the promotion of this stability. Consequently, the Customs Union between Turkey and the EU which already goes beyond a classical customs union, should aim at going even further and incorporate political and security considerations, more specifically considering a crucial role for Turkey in the linkage between NATO and the emerging European security system.

Turkey is well aware that the European link would make her stronger in regional orientations. However the development of the EU's relationship with Turkey is tied to a broader agenda which includes the process of enlargement with 13 applications on the table, the pressures from all other near neighbours for special arrangements, efforts to reorient the relationships of EU Mediterranean countries with the eastern and southern non-EU Mediterranean countries with a European free-trade area.

The question then arises what should be done to enhance a properly functioning relationship between Turkey and the EU? A quick recipe would be for both sides to work on improving the operation of the Customs Union and the development of complementary areas of cooperation that would simultaneously address mutual interests.

Although Turkey's modern identity involves a desire for further integration with the Western world, the merits of constructive multilateralism should never be undermined. This requires Turkey to develop her portfolio of policies in which the partnership with the EU is one, but a significant one, of several components. This would save Turkey from having a marginal identity on the periphery of Europe and, instead, give her one at the centre of Eurasia.

Notes

1 For the text of the Ankara Agreement see the Official Journal of the EC (December 1964).

2 For the text of the Additional Protocol, see the Official Journal of the EC (December 1972).

3 This chapter will mainly refer to the European Community and not to the European Union, primarily because in the customs union relationship between Turkey and the Community, the EC is the main institutional mechanism in the legal text.
4 For detailed assessment of trade relations see Balkır (1993: 100–39).
5 Rittenberg, 1998:6.
6 The set of rules governing the EC.
7 Turkey is also to be a beneficiary of the budgetary component of the EC's cooperation policy with Mediterranean countries (MEDA funds) and the EIB loans component. The financial assistance under this budget was the subject of an Indicative Programme agreed between the Community and Turkey and included a number of cooperation projects, whose aim is to facilitate the implementation of the customs union and to help Turkish small enterprises to face European competition.
8 For discussions before and after Customs Union, see Balkır 'Beyond Customs Union' in Rittenberg, 1998.
9 Harrison *et al.*, 1996.
10 The main problems related to the Aegean Sea are:

- the delimitation of the continental shelf, breadth of territorial shelf,
- airspace-related problems,
- militarization of eastern Aegean Islands by Greece contrary to the provisions of international agreements,
- islets and rocks in the Aegean which were not ceded to Greece by international agreements.

11 During the second half of the 1960s, differences between the Greek-Cypriot administration and Greece developed and in 1974, backed by the Greek troops stationed in Cyprus, the regime of Archbishop Makarios was overthrown. The Turkish-Cypriot community was spread all over the island, with very limited self-defence capability, and Turkey, after a few unsuccessful attempts to find a peaceful solution to the issue, intervened militarily, basing it on her rights as a guarantor power. After the inter-communal talks concerning a new form of partnership had failed, the Turkish-Cypriot administration renamed itself the Turkish Republic of Northern Cyprus.
12 See Balkyır in Rittenberg (eds).
13 Despite common cultural roots, historically, Turkey's relations with the Turkic regions of Central Asia have been limited. The ruling élite of the Ottoman Empire did not see themselves as being Turkish, a term reserved for the Anatolian peasants. From the early days of the republic, pan-Turkic movements were generally suppressed. In the late 1960s, a pan-Turkic political party was established which gained representation in the parliament. In spite of this, relations with the Turkic Republics were instituted through Moscow, and were mainly of a cultural scope.
14 For detailed analysis see Balkır, 1993b.
15 Altunısık in Rittenberg (eds).

16 The two countries have historical roots dating from 1492 when the Ottoman Empire embraced the Sephardic Jews banished from Spain. Turkey also opened her doors to thousands of Jewish people during the Second World War.
17 Free Trade Agreement, see Official Gazette 18.7.1997 No. 23053 mukerrer and 1.8.1997 No. 23067 mukerrer.
18 Referred to by its Turkish acronym GAP

References

Ad-Hoc Commission on Turkey–BSEC Relations, *Türkiye-Karadeniz Ekonomik İşbirliği İlişkileri* (Turkey–BSEC Economic Relations), (Ankara: Turkish State Planning Organization (SPO), 1995).

Akder, H., 'Constant Market Share Analysis of Changes in Turkey's Exports to the EC (1981–1985)', *Yapı Kredi Economic Review*, 1, (2) (1987) pp. 33–42.

Balkır, C., 'Trade Strategy in the 80s', in A. Eralp, M. Tünay, B. Yeşilda (eds), *Socioeconomic Transformation of Turkey in the 1980s* (New York: Praeger, 1988) pp. 135–69.

Balkır, C., 'Turkey and the European Community: Foreign Trade and Direct Foreign Investment in the 1980s', in Canan Balkır and Allan M. Williams (eds), *Turkey and Europe* (London: Pinter, 1993a) 100–40.

——, *Karadeniz Ekonomik İşbirliği (KEİB) – Ekonomik bir Değerlendirme* (Istanbul: TÜSİAD, 1993b).

Balkır, C. and Allan M. Williams (eds), *Turkey and Europe* (London: Pinter, 1993).

Barkey, Henri J., 'Iran and Turkey: Confrontation across an Ideological Divide', in Alvin Rubinstein and Oles M. Smolansky (eds), *Regional Power Rivalries in the New Eurasia: Russia, Turkey and Iran* (New York: M.E. Sharpe, 1995).

Baysan, T. and C. Blitzer, 'Turkey's Trade Liberalization in the 1980s and Prospects for its Sustainability', in T. Aricanli and D. Rodrik (eds), *The Political Economy of Turkey* (London: Macmillan Press, 1990). pp. 9–36.

Celasun, M. and D. Rodrik, 'Debt, Adjustment, and Growth: Turkey' in J.D. Sachs and M.S. Collins (eds), *Developing Country Debt and Economic Performance* (Chicago and London: University of Chicago Press, 1989) pp. 617–820.

Central Bank, Bulletins.

Conway, P., 'The Record on Private Investment in Turkey' in T. Aricanli and D. Rodrik (eds), *The Political Economy of Turkey* (London: Macmillan Press, 1988) pp. 78–97.

Dervis, K., and S. Robinson, *The Foreign Exchange Gap, Growth and Industrial Strategy in Turkey, 1973–83*, World Bank Staff Working paper No. 306 (1978), Washington DC.

Eralp, A., 'The Second Enlargement Process of the European Community and its Possible Effects on Turkey's External Relations', *Yapı Kredi Economic Review* 11 (1988) Nos 2–3, pp. 3–24.

Erdilek, A., 'Turkey's New Open-door Policy for Direct Foreign Investment: a Critical Analysis of Problems and Prospects', *METU Studies in Development*, 13 (1986), (1/2): 171–91, Ankara.

Ersel H. and A. Temel, 'Turkiye'nin Dissatim Basarisinin Degerlendirilmesi', *Toplum ve Bilim*, No. 27 (1984), Ankara.

Fuller, Graham E., 'Conclusions: the Growing Role of Turkey in the World', in Graham E. Fuller and Ian O. Lesser (eds), *Turkey's New Geopolitics*, (Boulder, CO: Westview, 1993).

Goble, Paul A., 'The 50 Million Muslim Misunderstanding: the West and Central Asia Today', in Anoushiravan Ehteshami (ed.), *From the Gulf to Central Asia: Players in the Game* (Exeter: University of Exeter Press, 1994).

Gültekin, N.B., and A. Mumcu, 'Black Sea Economic Cooperation', in Vojtech Mastny and R.C. Nation (eds), *Turkey between East and West: New Challenges for a Rising Regional Power* (Boulder, CO: Westview, 1995).

Güran, N., *Turkiye-Avrupa Topluluğu İlişkileri*, SPO Publication No. 2230-AET b: 23 (1990), Ankara.

Hale, William, 'Turkey, the Black Sea and Transcaucasia', in Richard Schofield, John F. Wright and Suzanne Goldenberg (eds), *Transcaucasian Boundaries* (New York: St. Martin's, 1996).

Harrison, Glenn W., Thomas F. Rutherford, and David G. Tarr, 'Economic Implications for Turkey of a Customs Union with the European Union', Working Paper 1599 (World Bank, Washington, DC, 1996).

Ibrahimhakkioğlu, N., *Planli Donemde Ihracat Tesvik Politikasi* (Ankara: IGEME Yayini, 1986).

Kazgan, G., *Prospects for Turkey's Accession to the Community* (Istanbul, mimeo, 1987).

——, *Summary Report of the Manufacturing Survey with Special Reference to Turkey's Integration with the EC* (mimeo, 1988).

——, *Studies in Economic Development* (Istanbul: Middle East Business and Banking Publication, 1991).

Kramer, Heinz., 'EC–Turkish Relations: Unfinished Forever?' in Peter Ludlow (ed.), *Europe and the Mediterranean* (London: Brassey's, 1994).

——, 'Turkey and the European Union: a Multi-Dimensional Relationship with Hazy Perspectives', in Vojtech Mastny and R.C. Nation (eds), *Turkey between East and West: New Challenges for a Rising Regional Power* (Boulder, CO: Westview, 1995).

Krueger, A.O., *Foreign Trade Regimes and Economic Development: Turkey* (New York: Columbia University Press for the NBER, 1974).

Lasonde, P. and H. Kozanoğlu, *A Review of Turkish Eximbank's Exports Credit Strategies* (Ankara, mimeo, 1989).

Milanovic, B., *Export Incentives and Turkish Manufactured Exports, 1980–1984* (World Bank Staff Paper No. 768, Washington DC, 1986).

Robins, P., 'Between Sentiment and Self Interest: Turkey's Policy toward Azerbaijan and the Central Asian States', *Middle East Journal* 47, No. 4 (1993) pp. 593–610.

Rubinstein, A. and Oles M. Smolansky (eds), *Regional Power Rivalries in the New Eurasia: Russia, Turkey and Iran* (New York: M.E. Sharpe, 1995).

SPO, *1980'den 1990'a Makroekonomik Politikalar-Türkiye Ekonomisindeki Gelişmelerin Analizi ve Bazy Değerlendirmeler* (Ankara: SPO Publication, 1990).

SPO, *Turk Sanayiinin AT Sanayii Karsısında Rekabet Imkanları*, ÖIK, Raporu, pub. No. 2, 141, Ankara, 1988.

Senses, F., 'An Assessment of Turkey's Liberalization Attempts since 1980 against the Background of her Stabilization Program', *METU Studies in Development*, 10 (3), (1983) pp. 271–321.

Tekeli, İlhan, and Selim İlkin, *Türkiye ve Avrupa Topluluğu* (*Turkey and the European Union*), 2 cols (Ankara: Ümit Yayıncık, 1991).

Togan, S., H. Olgun and H. Akder, *Report on Development in External Economic Relations of Turkey* (Istanbul: Turktrade, 1987).

World Bank, *Turkey: Industrialization and Trade Strategy* (Washington DC, 1982).

——, *Turkey – Country Economic Memorandum towards Sustainable Growth*, Report N. 7378-Tu (1988), Washington DC.

——, *Country Report: Turkey 1988* (Washington DC, 1989).

Yagci, F., *Protection and Incentives in Turkish Manufacturing*, World Bank Staff Working Paper No. 660 (1984), Washington DC.

Yased (Association for the Coordination of Foreign Capital), *Selected Opinions on Foreign Capital* (Istanbul, 1983).

Zviagelskaya, Irina., 'Central Asia and Transcaucasia: New Geopolitics', in Vitaly Naumkin (ed), *Central Asia and Transcaucasia: Ethnicity and Conflict* (Westport, CT: Greenwood, 1994).

Index